P O W E R
Communication

← →

Plan • Organize • Write • Edit • Revise

Thomas D. Clark
Xavier University

COLLEGE DIVISION South-Western Publishing Co.

Cincinnati Ohio

Acquisitions Editor: Jeanne R. Busemeyer
Production Editor: Thomas E. Shaffer
Production House: Shepherd, Inc.
Cover Designer: Lotus Wittkopf
Cover Photographer: © J. Miles Wolf, Photography
Internal Designer: The Book Company
Marketing Manager: Scott D. Person

EH60AA
Copyright © 1994
By SOUTH-WESTERN PUBLISHING CO.
Cincinnati, Ohio

Library of Congress Cataloging-in-Publication Data

Clark, Thomas D.,
    Power communication : plan, organize, write, edit, revise / Thomas D. Clark.
        p.   cm.
    Includes index.
    ISBN 0-538-82299-6
    1. Business communication. 2. Business writing. I. Title.
HF5718.C57 1993
658.4'5—dc20   93–32163
                                                                          CIP

1 2 3 4 5 6 7 MA 9 8 7 6 5 4 3
Printed in the United States of America

International Thomson Publishing

South-Western Publishing Co. is an ITP Company. The ITP trademark is used under license.

CONTENTS

INTRODUCTION

Surveys of the importance of effective written and oral communications in organizations reveal what most managers already know: they are crucial to success. And in this Age of Information and Globalization, the amount and importance of written and oral communications continues to grow dramatically.

As business contributors, many of us face the dilemma of knowing the importance of communicating effectively while lacking the knowledge or confidence to succeed. Most communicators face two key problems: (1) the difficulty of the task itself: developing an argument that key decision makers regard as clear and persuasive, and (2) finding sufficient time to plan, organize, compose, edit, and revise messages.

POWER Communication teaches you how to work on messages in the small, discreet units of time available to you during your busy workdays. With each step, Planning and Organizing; Writing; and Editing and Revising, you will be continually improving both the logic and the persuasiveness of your messages. Specifically, you will improve your ability to demonstrate clear alignments between data, company goals and indicated actions, and to position your message sensitively to the needs of readers and listeners.

How the POWER Communication System Can Help You

By following the guidelines in this book, you will learn to write and deliver well-reasoned and well-written memos, letters, reports, and presentations quickly and confidently—just like hundreds of management, administrative, and technical workers who have taken POWER Communication workshops. You will also learn techniques for editing, revising, and delivering these messages efficiently and comprehensively.

The POWER Communication system works because it treats the composing process as a series of ongoing and interrelated steps which describe what successful writers and speakers do when they tackle a communications assignment. The **previewing** steps include analyzing the situation and the audience, generating information, drawing inferences, and creating a design for the message. The **writing** steps cover composing a rough draft and visual aids. The **revising** steps include editing to improve audience adaptation and revising to make sure that the message is concise, inviting to read, clearly organized, well-argued, persuasively presented and free of errors.

When writers disregard this process and focus exclusively on writing a first draft or speaking entirely extemporaneously—skipping the previewing and revising steps—the result is typically a piece of work far below their potential, a message less well-argued and adapted to readers and listeners than one generated by following the process approach.

By contrast, workshop participants who have followed the steps of the POWER Communication process have found that it provides them with consistent control by moving through communication assignments in a series of logical and manageable steps. As a result, they immediately improved their ability to compose messages which were clear, correct, concise, well-organized, and responsive to both situation and audience.

The POWER Communication System

The system is organized around the acronynm POWER, which stands for Planning, Organizing, Writing, Editing, and Revising. Its guidelines are easy to learn and to implement. They work in brief letters, memos, and presentations as well as in longer, complex messages.

A section devoted to annotated model documents reinforces the POWER Communication guidelines. Modelling, when used in conjunction with an understanding of writing principles, is an efficient way to help business managers produce excellent documents. In fact, I suggest to workshop participants that they keep the best documents they have written and received in "good books," so that new employees can see how others in the company successfully completed written assignments similar to the ones they are required to write. You can use the examples in this book as models for your own documents.

These step-by-step methods also work because they are responsive to the reality of how readers and listeners actually read and listen to messages, the questions they want answered in them, and how they want them answered.

For example, the principles of document design outlined in this book will show you how to write documents that enable readers to readily understand your meaning, immediately retrieve key information without having to read the entire document, and clearly understand the significance of information in tables and graphs.

And you will learn how to write documents that readers can easily scan, so they get an extremely clear and accurate understanding of the memo from reading only the subject line, opening paragraph, headings, highlighted information, and action steps.

In addition, this book also shows you how to construct a sound argument, one that uses excellent evidence and demonstrates clear, logical, consistent, and convincing relationships among Objectives, Evaluations, Reasons, Data, and Actions.

Two chapters on oral communications discuss how to prepare and deliver effective presentations.

POWER Communication also offers useful advice on graphics, style, and revising. Guidelines are provided to help you learn to write sensitively to the diversity of people in the workplace, to avoid antitrust and other legal liabilities, and to shape positive images of you, your department, and your company.

And simple steps are described for editing for effective style, as well as for revising your own work and that of your coworkers.

How This Book Is Organized

The acronym POWER is a mneumonic device for remembering the order of steps in the writing process: Planning and Organizing, Chapters 1–5; Writing, Chapters 6–7; Edition and Reviewing, Chapters 8–11. Additional chapters are devoted to Speaking with POWER, Chapters 12–13 and Model Documents, Chapter 14.

The Appendix includes a compact guide to usage, punctuation, spelling, capitalization, and diction, as well as insight into letter formats; composing telephone messages; writing and reading computer-generated messages; team writing, and writing for another's signature.

How To Use This Book

Initially, read the chapters in order, because each assumes an understanding of the one which went before it. After you are comfortable writing and speaking with the POWER Communication system, simply turn to the chapters where a quick review is needed.

Acknowledgements

I have many people to thank. I am particularly grateful to a number of managers at The Procter & Gamble Company, "the writing academy of the business world." Bob McDonald, Rob Matteuchi, Bob Wurzelbacher, Carol Tuthill, Kathy Fitzgerald, Gibby Carey, Jim Troppman, Dick Glover, Jess Tyler, Bob Braun, Paul Franz, and

John Dupuy, over the past ten years, have allowed me to interview them. They helped show me how to reveal one's best thinking on paper, while simultaneously being sensitive to the needs of readers. They also showed me that the best way to organize a presentation was to view it as an "oral memo," a concept which revolutionized my approach to teaching presentational speaking.

I am also grateful to other business managers I interviewed including Steve Battalia and Ilene Reinfleisch of Nestle; Mary Ann Fernandez, Dick McPherson, and Larry James of Lenscrafters; Steve Scheurer of Coopers & Lybrand; Bill Bagley of Deloite Touche; Buzz Boughard of Griffith Laboratories; Bonnie Carlson of Comart; Marybeth Mapstone of On Target Media; and Sara Paxton of Drackett. Each gave me valuable feedback which helped me better understand the communication needs of business managers.

I thank Xavier University for granting me a sabbatical leave to pursue this project. My students and participants of CommuniSkills workshops also helped, serving as "editors" for this book while it was in draft form. The editorial suggestions made by the following reviewers also contributed significantly to clarifying ideas in this volume:

Laurence Barton
University of Nevada, Las Vegas

Robert E. Brown
Bentley College

John P. Leland
Purdue University

John D. Stegman
The Ohio State University

I am grateful to Richard Zaunbrecher, Arthur Shriberg, Robert Friedenberg, Diana Hamann, and Diane Senseman, who have taught CommuniSkills courses and offered valuable suggestions for improving them.

My greatest thanks go to my wife, a thoughtful and tactful editor *par excellence,* for her support and many helpful comments.

Thomas Clark, Ph. D.
President, CommuniSkills,

and

Professor of Management
Xavier University

Cincinnati, Ohio
November 1993

PART I

PLAN AND ORGANIZE YOUR MESSAGE

CHAPTER 1

Plan a Message Strategy

Have you ever felt overwhelmed by the complexity of writing a report or a speech? Has the difficulty of these tasks convinced you that writing well is beyond your mastery? Consider the case of Charlie Virtue and see if you have experienced some of the same thoughts and emotions when confronted with a challenging writing assignment.

Charlie sits at his desk looking at the blank screen of his word processor. He glances at the notes that he has recorded on a legal pad. He keeps reminding himself that he has to finish this report by the end of the day. He has run out of excuses for not writing. He has sharpened all his pencils, refilled his coffee cup, and returned all his calls.

Yet he does not know where or how to begin preparing it. He wishes he had spent the time he had available to him more productively. As his deadline approaches, he still is unsure of his readers' expectations for content and treatment. And he knows there must be better ways of gathering and interpreting the information he needs to document his report.

Almost all of us have felt like Charlie, intimidated by a writing assignment in which there is a great deal of information to analyze and interpret and an uncertainty about exactly how to meet our readers' expectations. We experience "writer's block" because we are pressed for time and we do not know where to start.

The purpose of this book is to teach you a step-by-step process for composing messages that will help you become a confident and skillful writer. The first step is "strategic planning." In fact, one of the best antidotes to writer's block is to develop a plan for meeting your communication objectives either as soon as you decide you need to write or speak, or as soon as others in the organization ask you to prepare a memo, report, or oral presentation.

Just as you would not begin a cross-country vacation without a map and an itinerary, neither should you begin writing without taking time to plan an overall message strategy. Many experts consider planning and organizing to be the most important steps that writers take in preparing a message. In fact, a survey of professional writers found that most spent about 50% of their time planning and organizing, 20% on writing, and 30% on editing and revising.

This chapter discusses the two initial steps you should take when planning a message strategy: (1) assessing the communication situation by filling out a planning sheet, and (2) developing a plan and schedule of execution.

FILL OUT A PLANNING SHEET

Often the best way to get started is to develop a preliminary message strategy. Start by jotting down a plan which takes into account your objectives, your audience, and the time available to communicate. Fill out a planning sheet, such as the following one, for each message you prepare. Do not worry if you cannot fill in all the blanks precisely the first time you fill out the form; your omissions will help direct your efforts toward finding the information you need to compose an effective and well-received message.

PLANNING SHEET

Purpose

1. What do I want to happen as a result of this message?

   When do I want a response?

Strategic Alignment with Organizational and Reader Goals

2. Who are the key message receivers?

3. What information should I provide?

4. How does this information relate to a key company objective? How does it relate to departmental or personal objectives of readers and listeners?

Information	Company Objectives	Reader/Listener Objectives	My Objectives

5. What questions or objections do I anticipate from readers and listeners? How can these be addressed?

Execution

6. Is this a good time to send this message?

7. When should I have this document ready to meet reader and listener needs? What other responsibilities do I have during this time period?

8. Would it be best to present this information in oral or written form, or both? How can I best transmit this information? Fax? Phone? Face-to-face? U.S. Mail? Express Mail?

Let's look at each question in order:

Purpose   Define the What and the When of your message, a decision about what you want to have happen and when you want it to happen. Defining a clear purpose gives direction to your writing efforts, as it helps you decide what information to include and what to omit. In addition, it helps you clarify for readers exactly what you want them to do in response to your message.

You will find yourself continually refining this portion of your message. For example, you may start off defining your purpose as simply requesting information for a report that you are writing. As you develop your message, you may revise your thesis to communicate how vitally important it is that this information be timely and accurate given the crucial nature of the decisions it will help the company make.

Strategic Alignment   To assure strategic alignment, visualize your readers. Then think strategically. Given what you want to accomplish and your knowledge of your audience, what information should you provide and how can you relate it to your own objectives as well as to those of your company and key decision makers? What questions and objections do you anticipate? How do you believe you should respond to them? How much information should you provide? How can you make this information and its implications clear to this audience? How can you make it persuasive, given audience knowledge and biases? Will audience members differ in their reactions to this document? If so, how can you adapt it to these multiple responses?

Execution   Ask yourself key questions about execution. Is this a good time for readers to receive this message? If not, when would be a good time? What kind of constraints is my own schedule likely to put upon the time I have available to prepare this message? Should I prepare an oral or written message? By what means should I deliver this message: fax, hand delivery, U.S. mail, small group, or formal presentation? An example of a completed planning sheet follows.

Note how the completed planning sheet allows its author, an engineer at a telecommunications company, to gain a clearer understanding of what he needs to do to achieve his objectives, including defining his purpose, analyzing the goals of readers and listeners, determining the data needed to prove his points, anticipating questions, and planning a sequence of oral and written messages in support of his objectives.

PLANNING SHEET

Purpose
1. What do I want to happen as a result of this message?

For management to know the costs of maintaining and retaining unused equipment. For management, as follow up, to request that I propose a plan that addresses this issue.

When do I want a response?

By October 1, the end of the third quarter, when management is likely to be most open to cost savings after seeing that we are over budget year-to-date.

Strategic Alignment with Organizational and Reader Goals
2. Who are the key message receivers?

J. Smith, Director of Operations; L. Myers, Manufacturing Manager; C. Rogers, Quality Director.

3. What information should I provide?

Detailed records demonstrating the nonuse and limited use of equipment. Costs of maintaining and calibrating unused equipment; amount of space this equipment takes up.

4. How does this information relate to a key company objective? How does it relate to departmental or personal objectives of readers and listeners?

Information	Company Objectives	Reader/Listener Objectives	My Objectives
records of nonuse	*efficiency*	*meet budget*	*recognition for*
maintenance costs	*current expense*	*maintain quality*	*initiative;*
calibration costs	*avoidance*	*maintain work*	*achieve cost*
space taken up	*capital avoidance*	*teams*	*savings, a key*
			objective of
			my job

5. What questions or objections do I anticipate from readers and listeners?

How can these be addressed?

a. *How do I know your figures are accurate?*

Show sources, calculations, others who agree with figures.

b. *Will sales of little used equipment compromise flexibility and versatility?*

Volunteer to investigate this issue in a follow-up study.

c. *Will these efficiencies lead to layoffs?*

Volunteer to investigate this issue in a follow-up study.

Execution

6. Is this a good time to send this message?

Yes, my division is searching for cost savings to meet annual budget goals.

7. When should I have this ready to meet reader and listener needs?

By September 15, when they are preparing third-quarter results and will be sensitive to budget shortfalls. Will need to begin the report immediately.

What other responsibilities do I have during this time period?

Trip to Dallas plant September 5-9; monthly report; performance evaluations for new hires.

8. Would it be best to present this information in oral or written form, or both?

Initial results will be reported in writing, with action steps suggesting a meeting to discuss the implications of the numbers and to gain commitment to further study.

DEVELOP A PLAN AND A TIMETABLE FOR COMMUNICATION

Once you've assessed the situation by filling out a planning sheet, devise a plan and timetable for execution. In his studies of business executives, psychologist Charles Garfield found that the most successful business executives practiced both visualization and mental rehearsal, a process in which they simultaneously visualized everything they had to do to achieve their objectives while also predicting the response of their audience to their behavior during each step.

In preparing either written or oral messages, one of the most productive ways to apply the skills of mental rehearsal and visualization is to fix a final deadline and then determine what you have to do between then and now to effectively achieve your communication objectives.

First, given what you want to accomplish and the time you have to accomplish it, determine what types of information would best be gathered and communicated through oral means and which in writing.

For most complex messages, you will normally use a combination of both. The following chart shows the advantages and disadvantages of each. Use written communication when you have time available, when the issue is significant, when precise communication is important, when a permanent record is necessary, when readers need time to think before responding, and when the audience is geographically distant.

Use oral communication when time is limited, when you are not ready to make a permanent record of the information, and when receiving nonverbal feedback is important. Be aware that in many organizations when you choose oral communication, you will still be expected to write a file memo summarizing the meeting!

For example, if you are working on a proposal, you might test the waters orally with key decision makers as a way of finding out what ideas, data, and reasons would best address your readers' perception of the issues.

Plan your time realistically, separating each of the steps, even if only by a brief period. Putting time between steps gives you distance from your work, allowing you to gain the benefits of perspective. In short, plan and organize before you write, write before you edit and revise.

This process is essential to sound message planning because most poorly received communications are the result of attempting to cram all three steps into a single step. By contrast, planning a timetable encourages you to practice each of the three steps in POWER Communications, leading to clearer, better documented, and more audience-appropriate messages.

Key Differences Between Written and Oral Communications

	Written	Oral
Time	Takes longer for writer to prepare Takes less time of reader	Takes less time to prepare Takes more time of listener
Precision	Higher level of precision to argument Higher level of detail May be edited many times	Lower level of precision Lower level of detail
Argument	Better for clarifying "logic flows" in arguments, especially complex discussions	More difficult to clarify logic of argument
Record	Serves as permanent record	May go unrecorded
Response	Allows reader more time for reflection and response	Allows less time for reflection and response; permits immediate feedback
Visibility of sender and receiver	Writer cannot see reader Reader cannot see writer Writer may not know all who will be reading the document	Speaker can see audience Listeners can see speaker Speaker sees who is listening
Vocabulary	May not be tailored to all readers	May be designed to fit listeners
Rate of reception	Controlled by reader	Controlled by speaker
Timeliness	Material "ages" after distribution	Material can be up to the moment
Correctability	Difficult to correct, once distributed	Usually can be corrected immediately

The following case study shows how a sales manager planned his time in developing a communication schedule for gaining approval for a proposal.

Case Study A sales manager for a computer software firm that leads the nation in accounting applications observes that sales have been flat for the past six months after five years of double-digit growth. He has anecdotal knowledge that competitors are taking away some of his company's business. Thus, his objective is to convince management to authorize a $15,000 increment to the sales budget to purchase empirical information about competitors' products and services as a step in assessing an appropriate response to the changing marketplace. His goal is to begin using the information service within a month.

Communication Plan

Objective: Authorization to purchase, within the next 45 days, information about the competitive environment for accounting software applications.

Communication Plan: I will immediately call a meeting of the sales staff to collect information verifying the need for this data and to agree on the consulting firm that can best provide it. I will discuss this information with my supervisor, one-on-one, to get her buy-in and to add any suggestions she may propose. After clearing both an outline and a draft of my proposal with her, I will write a memo to the Budget Committee highlighting the three strongest reasons justifying the purchase of this information.

Timetable: I will complete my data gathering by June 28 and summarize this information on a talksheet. By July 3, I will have spoken with the sales staff in a group meeting and subsequently will speak to my supervisor and revise my talk sheet to incorporate their suggestions.

I will show my supervisor a one-page outline of my proposal by July 5. I will write a first draft on Monday, July 8 and revise it by Wednesday. After forwarding the draft to my supervisor for comment and approval, I will write a final draft by Monday, July 15, proofread the draft by July 16, and submit it to the Budget Committee on July 17, asking for approval to hire a consultant by August 1.

Timetable for Completion

	Schedule	Activities
Delivery deadline	July 17	Hand deliver proposal to Budget Committee; add note offering to answer questions in person
Typing/Rehearsal deadline	July 16	Proofread proposal
Final draft deadline	July 15	Revise final draft; have it typed; send copy to supervisor, sales reps.
Editing deadline	July 10	Edit for logic, clarity, and style
First draft deadline	July 8	Complete first draft
Planning, organizing, and information-gathering deadline proposal	June 28-July 5	Do library research; meet with sales reps. Complete outline for review with supervisor.

SUMMARY

Filling out a planning sheet and determining a timetable for completion are crucial steps in planning a message. They allow you to see the "big picture" including the interaction between your message objectives, your audience, and your company's situation. And they help you plan your time wisely—so your finished product represents your best work.

Once you've outlined a plan of action, move on to the next step, developing an outline of your argument.

On Your Own   Determine a communication plan for the following case study or develop a timetable for an actual project you need to complete.

1. Determine a plan of oral and written communication.

2. Write out a timetable for completion.

Case   You have received permission to attend a convention during the first week of September and will be required to write a trip report within a week of your return.

You want to make sure your trip report impresses your supervisors, making it clear that the company will benefit because of your attendance. Describe the oral and written communication you will do before, during, and after the convention to achieve this objective.

Communication Plan

Objectives

Plan

Timetable for Completion

	Schedule	Activities
Delivery deadline		
Typing/Rehearsal deadline		
Final draft deadline		
Editing deadline		
First draft deadline		
Planning, organizing, and information-gathering deadline		

CHAPTER 2

Outline Your Message

Global competition, workforce reductions, and increasing reporting requirements have added substantial paperwork burdens to contemporary work environments. Business readers are pressed for time, and they want to receive concise messages which they can immediately understand. As they read a document from beginning to end, readers first need to be oriented to the topic and purpose of the document. Once oriented, they are ready to comprehend details and analysis, preferably composed so they are clearly aligned with stated objectives. At the end of a message, they want an answer to the "therefore what should we do next?" question, with an action section that shows "who should do what and when."

OUTLINE YOUR MESSAGE INTO PURPOSE, ANALYSIS/DATA, AND ACTION SECTIONS

To help meet these needs and expectations, organize the initial outline of your message into purpose, analysis/data, and action steps sections. This will allow you to highlight the key items of information of interest to readers—and make sure these items are clearly aligned with each other. As this model indicates, write down your objectives first and then make connections to supporting positions and action steps. For example, see how the following simple letter of request follows this pattern.

Deductively Organized Letter of Request

	Dear Customer Representative:
Purpose:	Please send us demographic information on consumers in New York, New Jersey, and Pennsylvania. We are conducting market research and these materials will help us prepare a market test.
Analysis and Data:	Specifically, we need information which breaks down the population by age, income, and number of residents per household in each major metropolitan area.
Action Steps:	Enclosed is a check for $327. This covers the $100 per state fee ($300), plus $27 for shipping and handling fees.
	Please ship these reports via Express Mail so they arrive no later than July 16.
	Thank you for your prompt attention to this request. If you need additional information, please call me at (812) 555-4475.

You can organize almost all messages you compose, including request, report, analysis, and proposal messages, using this model.

Model Outline for a Simple Request Memo

Purpose Statement:	Please send me information on the costs of Sunday newspaper advertising inserts for 1992-1993. We will use this information to evaluate the cost-effectiveness of the inserts as compared to alternative media.
Details/ Analysis:	Send annual totals for the number of inserts, the total costs, and the average size of the ads.
Action:	I look forward to receiving this information by May 22. Call me at x-3456 if you have any questions or concerns.

Model Outline for a Report Message

Purpose Statement: I am writing to report what I have learned from attending the Speech Tech 92 Conference. I attended to learn if new speech technologies can help our company meet current communications objectives.

Details/ Analysis: Extensive use of voice mail can help the company meet both domestic and international communication objectives.

Voice recognition systems, on the other hand, offer little value to the company at this time.

Action: I will continue to research this area and to update interested company managers.

Model Outline for an Analysis Message

Purpose Statement: This memo evaluates the success of the Welcome Wagon Coupon Campaign. Its objective is to convince consumers who have moved to switch to Brand X.

Details/ Analysis: The Welcome Wagon Campaign was successful. It exceeded target objectives for reach and switching and was inexpensive to administer. Details follow.

Action: We will conduct follow-ups to see the extent to which consumers have sustained loyalty to Brand X.

We will also investigate using this approach with additional brands.

Model Outline for a Recommendation Memo

Purpose Statement: This requests authorization to hire two part-time secretaries for the Audit Department. This assistance will help the department meet key short-term business objectives.

Details/ Analysis: The two part-time secretaries would work 20 hours per week at $8.75 per hour for six weeks.

(continued)

Company experience indicates approval of
this proposal will have three important
benefits. Leasing part-time office help will

1. Allow the office to meet immediate schedules and deadlines.
2. Cost less than using overtime.
3. Meet departmental objective of adding no
new full time employees.

Action: May we have your approval to sign a contract
with Kelly by May 1?

CLARIFY YOUR PURPOSE

Once you have made a simple outline of your message, work to
develop each part.

Begin by determining a precise thesis for your message: an organizing idea that indicates both the topic and the type and timing
of the response you want from your audience (the What and the
When), as well as the reasons you have prepared the message (the
Why).

Defining the What, the Why, and the When lends focus to your
efforts, helping you decide how to select evidence and arguments
to prove your point and how to arrange the rest of the message.

This book strongly recommends beginning memos and reports
with your thesis. Putting your main point up front gets readers off
to a fast start in understanding the relevance and significance of
your communication. And it meets their need to begin mentally
responding to your document as soon as they begin reading it.

For example, the first line of a memo beginning, "I am working
on the Shrink Wrapping Task Force" frustrated its reader because
it gave him no insight into how he should respond to it. In fact, it
invited this caustic response in the margin: "I'm so happy for you,"
whereas its revision, "This summarizes the results of a test to determine the relative effectiveness of the ABC and XYZ shrink wrapping machines" drew a positive response because it immediately
communicated the point of the memo.

Similarly, in the letter on the following page, the reader must
read five sentences of the original before finding answers to the

What and Why questions, and does not find an answer to the When question.

Letter with Delayed Thesis Statement

```
We at Wayside Pools are a new pool company. We started
in business last spring. We are now attempting to expand
the variety of products we offer customers. We have been
impressed with your company's professionalism in our
initial contacts with you and want to further investi-
gate ways of completing mutually advantageous deals with
you.

Thus, we would greatly appreciate it if you would give
us some assistance on a matter for which you are ex-
tremely well qualified. We need information on your new
line of electrostatic pool filters, which, if they meet
our needs, will be included in our line of products
(What and Why). (93 words)
```

Below is the probable reaction of readers on a sentence-by-sentence basis

Sentence-by-Sentence Analysis	Typical Reader Reaction
We at Wayside Pools are a new pool company.	How nice.
We started in business last spring.	O.K. What do you want?
We have been impressed with your company's professionalism in our initial contacts with you and want to further investigate ways of completing mutually advantageous deals with you.	Good to know. Great. Exactly what do you want?
Thus, we would greatly appreciate it if you would give us some assistance on a matter for which you are extremely well qualified.	What do you want already? I wonder how long you'll stay in business if it takes you this long to answer customer questions.
We need information on your new line of electrostatic pool filters, which, if they meet our needs, will be included in our line of products.	At last. Good, we might make some money. When do you need this information?

By contrast, notice how much more "reader-friendly" the revised version of the letter is than the original. It immediately answers three questions: what do you want? why do you want it? and when do you want it?

Letter with Immediate Thesis Statement

```
Please send us literature on your new electrostatic pool
filter (What). We read an enthusiastic review of it in
Poolside Magazine and are considering adding it to our
line (Why). So we have time to include your product in
our new brochure, send us this literature by March 1.
(When). (47 words)
```

Sentence-by-Sentence Analysis	Typical Reader Reaction
Please send us information on your new electrostatic pool filter.	Will do! I should be getting up-to-date brochures next month.
We read an enthusiastic review of it in *Poolside Magazine* and are considering adding it to our line.	That's great!
So we have time to include your product in our new brochure, send us the literature by March 1.	Can do! I have time to send this client our most recent literature which is scheduled to be delivered by February 1.

Given their importance in helping readers immediately understand the point of your memo, work carefully to develop the What and the Whys of your message.

DEFINE THE "WHAT" OF YOUR MESSAGE

Your message should be designed to make it easy for readers and listeners to find an answer to two key What questions: "What is this about?" and "What do you want me to do in response to this message?" In defining the What, compose a precise subject line and a first sentence that concisely and accurately answers these two key questions. You indicate to readers what type of message response you want in your subject line, in your first verb, and in the first sentence of your message.

Compose a Precise Subject Line

Since readers read documents from top to bottom, what you write first sets up expectations in readers' minds of how you will be developing the rest of the document. Thus, subject lines are important because they first inform readers of how they are expected to react to your message. Good subject lines announce the topic and purpose of your document. They should be both concise and precise, preferably beginning with words that immediately indicate the purpose of the message.

For example, compare how much easier it is to understand the point of documents which start with concise and highly descriptive subject lines than either brief, nondescriptive subject lines, or subject lines that include so much information that they burden readers' ability to understand exactly what they are to do in response to the message.

Make Subject Titles Concise and Highly Descriptive

Message Type	Brief and Less Descriptive	Concise and Highly Descriptive	Overly Complicated
Request	1993 Annual Report Need	Request for customer satisfaction survey results, 1991–1992	Customer satisfaction survey results, 1991–1992, request for your departmental assistance
Inform	Receiving Functions	New procedures for receiving purchases	Detailed instructions to be followed receiving packages in the future
Inform	Purchasing Agents	Positions available for purchasing agents	Purchasing agent: positions available in current year
Analyze	Sometimes Analysis	Analysis of the effect of Sometime's restage on Pretend's market share	Devastating impact of Sometimes restage on Pretend's existing market share
Propose	HP 3000 Computer	Proposal to purchase a HP 3000 computer system	Recommendation to purchase: HP 3000 computer, monitor, keyboard, and related peripherals

So readers can easily find them, subject lines are often written in all capitals and underlined. For additional emphasis, center and position them at the top of the page. Using boldface and slightly larger type may also help make subject lines easy to find.

On Your Own   Select the best subject line from each of the following.

1. **a.** Subj: Status Report
   b. Subj: Findings to date of the International Purchasing Task Force
   c. Subj: Status of the efforts of the International Purchasing Task Force to bring down the costs of purchases through global comparison shopping.

2. **a.** Subj: Recommendation to purchase six ABM 3000 laptop computers for use by the company's twelve field auditors
   b. Subj: ABM 3000 Computers
   c. Subj: Proposal to purchase six ABM 3000 laptop computers

3. **a.** Subj: How to Install SpellPerfect Software on a Macintosh
   b. Subj: Detailed Procedures Describing Computer Installation of SpellPerfect Software for MacIntosh Computers
   c. Subj: Software Installation Procedures

How did you do? Did you select 1b, 2c, and 3a as subject lines that struck a good balance between clearly introducing the thesis of the message and conciseness? Did you find 1a, 2b, and 3c contained too little information to properly inform readers of the thesis of the document? And that 1c, 2a, and 3b contained too much information?

Write First Sentences That Clearly Indicate How You Want Readers to React to Your Message

In addition to writing good subject lines, write a first sentence that precisely predicts the type of reaction you want from readers. In particular, be sure that the first verb you use clearly indicates which of the four types of messages you are writing. Note in the graphic on the facing page how a clear thesis allows readers to immediately begin asking key questions about the message, thus heightening its relevance to readers. The rest of your memo or report should be designed so readers can easily find answers to their questions.

Write Effective Opening Sentences

Message Objective	Purpose	Message Types	Example	Reader Questions
Request	to request information to request cooperation	Requests for information, cooperation, or response to a requst	Please send me a detailed report of the steps you took in response to the breakdown of the main office heating system.	What information do you want? Why do you want it? When do you need it?
Report	to transmit information	Compliance reports Policy manual Procedural Memo Meeting summary Thank you letter Notification memo or letter	This report describes the chronology of events surrounding the breakdown of the main office heating system.	What organization objectives does this information serve? Is the chronology correct? Is anything left out? Is anything recorded in incorrect order?
Analysis and Evaluation	to analyze the meaning of information by drawing inferences from it. to evaluate information in terms of the company's ability to meet its objectives	Key learnings memo New concept report Causal analysis Evaluation of test results Progress report Feasibility study Trip report	This analyzes the reasons for the breakdown of the main office heating system. This evaluates the effectiveness of the response of the maintenance team in handling the breakdown of the main office heating system.	Is the causal analysis correct? Is the proper weight given to each causal factor? Are any key causes left out? Are incorrect causes included? Are reasons supported by good facts? Do I agree with this evaluation? Are the correct criteria used? Are they properly weighted? Are alternatives omitted?
Proposals	to recommend changes in the status quo	Proposals Recommendation memos Letters of Recommendation Sales letters Business plans	This recommends the purchase of a preventive maintenance contract from ABC Heating and Cooling to cover all main office heating and cooling systems.	Exactly what do you want? How does this contribute to a company goal? How does this benefit the department? Why are you sending this to me? How much does this cost? Is the money in our budget? What are the alternatives? Who else agrees with this decision? When will this be implemented? How will this be implemented?

On Your Own   Select the best of the following first sentences.

1. **a.** I have become highly frustrated with numerous mistakes in data inputting that seem to occur so often and to take so long to correct.
   b. I am writing to request your feedback on a plan to improve the accuracy of the data input into the Customer Satisfaction Information File.
   c. This is to inform you that the level of errors of data inputted to the Customer Satisfaction Information File has to be reduced if we are to be able to justify collecting and interpreting the data at all.

2. **a.** This provides an overview of observations of how consumers view the backup copy of Product X.
   b. This report analyzes the results of 25 one-to-one interviews designed to determine the effectiveness of Product X backup copy.
   c. The Copy Analysis team travelled to Boston to observe interviews on the effectiveness of Product X backup copy which BK Associates conducted on 6/14/93.

Did you select 1b and 2b as the best first sentences? Did you find 1a and 1c to be too negative as well as unclear as to what response was requested? Did you find 2a less precise than 2b and 2c to be too indirect?

DEFINE THE "WHY" OF YOUR MESSAGE

After defining the What of your message, develop the Why. You indicate the Why by aligning your What with both an immediate and a company objective. As Peter Drucker has pointed out in his discussion of Management by Objectives, this synchronizes your purpose with the larger company purposes to which it contributes. This is especially important when your message is communicated to audiences who are not directly connected to a project and are, therefore, unaware of how it fits in with other company objectives.

To clarify these connections, picture your objective as part of a cascading flow of objectives. In communicating upwardly, relate the What of your objective to the How of a higher level objective.

Higher level:

What is wanted   Why it's important   How we will get it

Lower level:

What is wanted   Why it's important   How we will get it

Defining a higher level company Why shows your supervisors that you have a clear understanding of the relationship between what you are doing and how it relates to larger company purposes. Clarifying objectives is important because you will receive positive responses to the extent that you can demonstrate how what you are doing helps your readers more effectively achieve their objectives within the organization.

Likewise, in writing to those who directly report to you, clarify the relationship between what they are doing and the objectives you are striving to achieve in your position. This is significant in light of research which shows supervisors and their direct reports often differ radically on what they perceive as the key priorities for their jobs.

A useful approach to clarifying goals and objectives is write out What, Why, Why statements as illustrated below.

Write What, Why, Why Statements

Your What	Your Why	Higher Level Why
apply for a position	you desire a career in this field with this company	your excellent education, experience, and personal qualities precisely meet the criteria the company has for position
request that oral skills seminar participants and their managers fill out seminar evaluations six months following the seminar	to improve oral skills training by determining if it has met its stated objectives over time	to upgrade skills of employees by offering training that is effective, relevant, and sustained
summarize key learnings from attanding a Color Analysis seminar	to learn ways of more effectively measuring consumer perceptions of cleanliness	to develop a superior understanding of consumers and their laundry needs
recommend purchase of equipment	to fit more paper in less space on the towel roll	to save money on warehousing and distribution, and to increase amount of product per foot of shelf space

This exercise helps you write effective openings. For example, in writing a letter of application for a job, you might begin a rough draft using the previous information.

"I am applying for the position of proofreader advertised on April 11 in the *New York Times*. [What and When] I have long planned for a career in publishing. [Why] And as I demonstrate in this letter and in the attached resume, my education, experience, and personal qualities precisely meet the criteria listed in the ad." [Why]

Also note how well answering questions in What, Why, When order helps you write a draft of a thank you note.

Dear Ms. Jones:

Thank you for meeting with me to discuss the Sales Engineering position at ABC Computer Technology *(What)*. Our interview convinced me of two things: (1) my past experience as a sales representative as well as my master's degree in engineering are excellent preparation for this position *(Co. Why)*, and (2) a sales engineering position at ABC offers the challenges and opportunities I am seeking in a career *(Personal Why)*. I will call you next Monday to follow up. Please contact me at 555-555-5555 should you want to speak to me sooner *(When)*.

Be Sure Your What and Why Answer the "So What" Question

After writing a draft of a What and a Why, examine your opening sentences to make sure they are relevant to Company and reader concerns. For example, consider these opening sentences.

Opening That Fails to Answer the "So What" Question

"Two industry trade articles provide some perspective on how Mega Corporation views itself from a financial point of view. The articles appeared in the January 1993 *Finance Digest* and the September 1992 *Investors Review*. Details follow."

Providing only a vague What and no Why, these sentences fail to answer the "So What" question. The reader has a choice of not reading further or of hunting through the rest of document trying to find out the relevance of these trade articles to company objectives.

Significantly, the author rewrote this passage to make it more relevant to the reader interests.

Revised Opening That Clearly Answers the "So What" Question

"This analyzes the capital budgeting strategy of Mega Corporation and explains how this strategy enables Mega to consistently underprice our cough and cold products. This analysis is based on two recently published interviews with Mega's Chief Financial Officer."

This revised opening attracted the reader's interest immediately and focused the author's efforts on explaining the relationship between Mega's capital budgeting and pricing strategies and their impact on his company.

In addition to writing clear What and Why statements, include relevant When statements in your opening paragraph. Adding the When helps readers plan the timing of their response to your message.

Readers appreciate it when you put the What, the Why, and the When up front because it gets them off to a fast start in understanding the relevance and significance of your communication. Thus, a good way to write a draft of your thesis is to list the answers to key reader questions, such as "What is this about?" "Why is it relevant to me and to others in the company?" "How and When do you want me to respond?"

The chart below describes the key questions on readers' minds when they first consider a memo or letter and the techniques you can use to answer these questions.

Organizing Reader-Friendly Documents

Reader Questions When Initially Reading a Document	Technique for Answering Reader Questions
What's the point of this?	Compose a precise subject line
What does it have to do with me? What do you want me to do in response to this message?	Write a first sentence that indicates how you want reader(s) to respond.

(continued)

Reader Questions When Initially Reading a Document	Technique for Answering Reader Questions
Why is this relevant to my objectives and to company objectives?	Write 1–2 sentences clarifying why your discussion is relevant to your company role, your reader's role, and the company's objectives
When did this happen? When do you expect me to respond?	Include relevant dates in the opening of your message

On Your Own   Fill in the chart below. Write out five thesis statements, one for each of the following types of documents. You may choose your own topics or select the ones suggested below.

Your What	Your Why	Higher Level Company Why	When
Discover request info on how many employees would use an on-site exercise facility			
Report summarize monthly sales figures			
Analyze analyze the results of a home product test of a compact vacuum cleaner			
Evaluate evaluate eight locations for a midwest distribution center			
Propose recommend the purchase of a new milling machine			

ORDER YOUR ARGUMENTS

Once you've developed a purpose statement, develop a strategy for organizing arguments in the body of your message. This step is important because a logical sequencing of arguments will signal readers that you are a clear thinker; an illogical order will suggest an incomplete and disorganized thought process. Recording and ordering key body points in outline form helps you see the "big picture" of your memo, allowing you to determine if your argument is both logical and clearly aligned with your purpose statement. This technique also makes it easier to check whether your major points are developed in parallel structure.

Your choice of order depends on the nature of the material you are presenting. For example, trend analysis logically lends itself to ordering by chronology; a description of equipment suggests ordering by component.

Typical organizational patterns for arguments include ordering by importance, chronological organization, ordering by component, and comparison-contrast. Sometimes a general-to-specific pattern works best, with an overriding "umbrella" point stated first, followed by a series of more specific proofs of that point. Examples of each follow.

Lead from Strength in Action Memos

Lead off with the most important argument, followed in descending order by additional arguments. This technique suggests to readers your sense of priorities—your analysis of the relative importance of the key drivers of the business. When deciding on the order in which to present arguments, keep in mind both your priorities and those of your readers.

Given that readers typically can retain no more than 5–7 points at one time and prefer less, limit the total number of points in the body to 3–5. As one company manager told me, "if your strongest three or four arguments do not impress me, additional weaker points may only detract from the impressiveness of your argument."

Order of Importance

Objective
To report the results of a survey on the relative importance of variables driving rug-cleaning purchasing decisions

Key Learnings
1. Customers purchase rug cleaning services primarily on price. *[most important]*
2. On-time and responsive customer service is the second most important customer criterion in selecting a rug cleaning business. *[second most important]*
3. The performance of the service, including the image of competence presented by the company, also contribute to customer decisions about which rug cleaning company to select. *[third most important]*

Order by Chronology in Explanatory Memos

Chronological organization is best for historical reviews, procedural reports in which procedures are numbered by the order in which they occur, and status reports in which the author reports (in order) what has been accomplished, what is being done, and how this work relates to future plans.

Chronological Order

Objective
To explain procedures for installing and stocking lighted beauty care display boxes

Procedures
1. Gain approval of location for lighted display cases from store owners.
2. Obtain cost-effective bids from at least three licensed, bonded electricians.
3. Be sure the electricians follow the manual instructions precisely during installation.
4. Arrange products neatly in the display boxes.

Status Report

Objective
To report the status of departmental projects

1. Completed projects
2. Work in progress
3. Initiatives to be started next month

Order by Umbrella Point Followed by Specific Subpoints in Analysis Memos

Often when you develop an argument, you want to first state a key point and then expound upon that point in more detail in specific subpoints.

Analysis Memo Ordered by Umbrella Point Followed by Specific Subpoints

Objective
To communicate the importance of antitrust considerations on writing style

---

Analysis
1. Oral and written communication are increasingly being used against companies in antitrust cases. (umbrella point)
2. Words that suggest secrecy, such as "Confidential" and "For Your Eyes Only," have been used to indicate a company's illegal motives. (proof of first point)
3. Words that suggest market dominance have also been used against companies in antitrust suits. (further proof)

Order by Component or Comparison/Contrast in Descriptive Memos

Component, or spatial, organization is best for reports divided by geographical region and for descriptions of buildings or equipment. Comparison/contrast organization works well when reporting both positive and negative results about a single topic.

Geographical Description	Component Description
Objective	**Objective**
To report sales by region	To describe components of ABC Computer
Sales Results	**Components**
1. Eastern region	1. Disk drive
2. Southeastern region	2. Monitor
3. Midwest region	3. Keyboard
4. Western region	4. Mouse

Comparison/Contrast

Objective
To transmit the results of 800-number comments on liquid hand soap

Findings
I. Areas of agreement among all age groups:
   - clear labelling of product benefits
   - attractive packaging
II. Areas where perceptions differ by age:
   - 16–25: price is too high compared to bar soap
   - 26–49: more attractive than bar soap on kitchen and bath counters
   - 50–65: advertisement positively appeals to their traditional values
   - 65+: pump is too difficult to work

On Your Own What pattern of organization would you use for each of the following?

1. Similarities and differences in competing products
2. Major claim in a lawsuit and supporting subclaims
3. Description of equipment
4. Steps in a process
5. Reasons in support of a recommendation

How did you do? Did you select: (1) comparison/contrast; (2) umbrella point; (3) component; (4) chronological; (5) lead from strength?

LIST YOUR ACTION STEPS

Finally, outline action steps. To do so, organize the details of the next steps of your document in a separate graphic, as illustrated.

Write the objectives in the first column and then highlight appropriate steps, responsibilities, and timing in the columns to the right. This will help ensure your action steps are both relevant and complete.

Action Steps Outline

Objectives	Steps	Responsibilities	Timing
1. Understand consumer needs	Do concept test Do prod test of X	Market Research, J. Collins Prod Testing, P. Smythe	May 1990 May 1990
2. Evaluate consumer acceptance of new formula	Do prod test of X + oat bran	Prod Testing, L. Perry	June 1990
3. Evaluate consumer perception of Prod X vs. Prod Y	Do survey Do comparative product testing	Market Research, M. DuBois Prod Testing, J. Breemer	June 1990 July 1990

Note how this outline can stand alone as an action paragraph, stressing objectives or steps, or can be used in full sentence format, stressing timing and responsibilities.

Clear, Easy to Follow Action Steps Paragraph

Action Plan
By May 30
- J. Collins, Market Research, will place concept tests, to see if advertising copy reinforces the benefits consumers most want in these cereals.
- P. Smythe, Product Testing, will test the new Prod X recipe with a group of consumers to determine what they like and dislike about it.

By June 30
- L. Perry will test consumer acceptance of Prod X cereal with oat bran added.
- M. DuBois, Market Research, will complete survey comparing consumer perceptions of our current product to Prod Y, the market leader.

By July 30
- J. Breemer, Product Testing, will run a blind product test specifically asking consumers whether they prefer Prod X or Prod Y, and why.

SUMMARY

Outlining your ideas into Purpose, Analysis/Data, and Action Steps helps you organize your ideas in a reader-friendly pattern, one which logically orders information so that reader questions are answered in the order in which they are raised in their minds. To prepare a preliminary outline of your message, first jot down ideas for the opening, the body, and follow up. Then develop each section, clarifying a purpose statement, ordering the points of the body, and ending with action steps. Once you have developed a rough outline of your entire argument, select a pattern consistent with your purpose with which to organize your main points. These simple steps will give you a clear outline from which to write a first draft of your message and lend focus to your plan for gathering information, the topic of Chapter 3.

Exercise Outline a newspaper or magazine article on a business strategy. Write one or two sentences about company objectives, strategies and their supporting data, and implementation steps. *The Wall Street Journal, Business Week,* and *INC* are good sources for this assignment.

CHAPTER 3

Plan the Content of Your Message

To write or speak clearly and convincingly depends upon asking the right questions and finding the right answers. In fact, my interviews revealed a consistent theme—that managers like best those documents which reflect a careful and systematic analysis of facts and meanings—and like least those which suggest a haphazard or incomplete gathering and analysis of key facts and issues.

This chapter describes a challenging three-step process which has proved to be an efficient means of producing logically argued and coherently organized messages, sensitively adapted to the needs of readers and listeners. In this system, you shift your attention from content to audience and back again. For simple documents, you can do this analysis on a single piece of scratch paper, using the intuitive methods first discussed in this chapter. For more complex analyses, you will need to explore and record information carefully and systematically, employing a variety of analytical tools. While you will not want to use all of these methods for each message you prepare, you will find each useful in helping you better understand the information and analysis needs of your audience.

The three steps are as follows:

Gather information. Gather and record data to make sure you understand the realities of the situation you are investigating.

Analyze your position from the reader or listener's point of view. See if you have satisfactorily answered key questions and employed the types of arguments and evidence most preferred by key decision makers.

Evaluate your data. Determine what additional information you need to gather, analyze, and evaluate to meet reader or listener needs.

GATHER INFORMATION

Write down everything you learn and keep it recorded on paper, cards, or a computer disk stored in a centralized file. Putting ideas on paper will help you see how they relate to one another and determine how complete your information search is. On some issues, you are the expert, on others you will have to gather information by doing research, surveys, and interviews. At this stage, favor quantity over quality. Learn all you can first; sort and discard later.

Use Brainstorming Techniques to Generate Ideas

Generally, the easiest way to begin gathering information is to brainstorm: to tap your mind by asking such questions as, What are the key issues at hand? What has been my role with regard to these issues? What have been my readers' roles with regard to them? What do we need to know about this topic?

Two intuitive techniques, freewriting and mindmapping, will help you quickly find initial answers to these questions. Freewriting and mindmapping are "stream of consciousness" techniques that encourage open-minded thinking without committing you to any ideas. As such, they are excellent antidotes to writer's block.

Freewriting To successfully freewrite, write down everything that comes into your mind. Do not analyze, edit, or criticize ideas. Be spontaneous. Use free association to develop ideas. Put a time limit on yourself of 10 to 20 minutes so you do not run out of steam and begin repeating yourself. Then take a few minutes to analyze and organize your thoughts.

Below is an example of freewriting composed by a collections agent for a cable television company. Once she completed her focus sheet, she took out a piece of paper and jotted down everything that came into her mind, without crossing out anything.

Example of Freewriting

I have to write a letter to the most obnoxious person! He threatens to sue us!!!!! if we take out his cable and yet he has pirated it from us and I have checked the records and there is no evidence he called to get the cable installed or that he ever paid a single bill. I am going to tell him that we are going to cut off his cable service (I'd like to cut off something else, ha ha). We'll haul him into court and then he'll get a taste of his own medicine. And he'll pay a minimum of $100 in fines plus payments to us plus court expenses for his trouble. Of course, if he agrees to enroll and pay up all back payments as well as for installation costs, then we will, of course, greet him as a new member of our cable family! Ha. Ha.

This passage was transformed into the following letter.

Letter Based on Freewriting

This letter is to inform you that by having an unauthorized cable line in your home, you are in violation of the law. You are subject to a $100.00 fine as we have indicated in our televised public service announcements. [What and Why] We have checked our records thoroughly and find no documentation that you ever requested that cable be installed in your home or that you have paid any usage fees. [Data/Analysis]

Your service will be disconnected on October 2, 1992 [When] and you will be notified by mail of your court appearance.

Should you decide to pay for current and past use of our services, please call us at 555-5555 before we disconnect your cable. We will send a customer representative to your home to enroll you in our cable program and to discuss a payment plan. [Follow Up]

On Your Own Practice freewriting. For example, take 10 minutes to write down information that would be relevant for an oral or written communication for which you are responsible, such as writing a letter or memo, conducting a job interview, leading a committee meeting on a topic of your choice, or preparing for a performance improvement interview. Then examine and summarize your information into a set of notes that will help determine what information you should gather and what issues you should discuss.

Mindmapping   A second technique many find useful in generating ideas is mindmapping, a graphic form of freewriting in which you relate thoughts to one another schematically on a piece of paper. To mindmap, draw a circle with a central idea in the middle. Then jot down ideas as they come into your mind, including them in circles rotating on spokes coming out from your central idea.

Mindmapping works because it encourages you to write down ideas in brief phrases, rather than full sentences, thus allowing you to record ideas as rapidly as they come into your mind. It also encourages you to see relationships as you jot down ideas next to the ideas to which they are related. Once you have finished a mindmap, organize your ideas under logical categories, using your mindmap as a guide. Below is a mindmap written by a research scientist followed by the draft he generated from it.

Example of a Mindmap

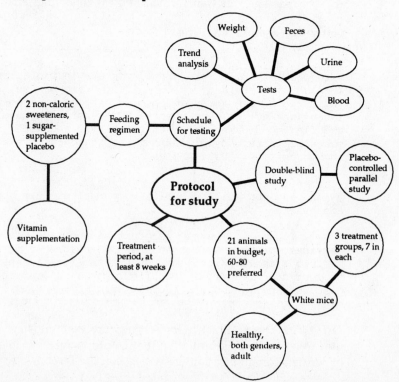

This mindmap served as the basis for the following passage:

Passage Developed from a Mind Map

We propose conducting a double blind test, concurrent with a placebo-controlled parallel test to determine the effects of the use of noncaloric sweeteners as sugar substitutes in the diets of white mice. [What and Why] The study will be conducted in compliance with good clinical practices as outlined by the FDA. Details concerning the subjects, treatment regimen, and testing schedule follow:

Subjects: Twenty-one healthy adult male and female white mice will be enrolled and randomly assigned to three treatment groups.

Treatment regimen: The groups will enter an 8-week treatment period during which they will consume a nutritionally balanced controlled diet providing three meals a day. The three groups will be using noncaloric sweetener A, noncaloric sweetener B, and sugar. The group receiving sugar will consume 20% more calories than those consuming the noncaloric sweeteners. All diets will be vitamin supplemented.

Testing schedule: The animals will be tested at the start of the study and every two weeks thereafter for a total of five tests. Weight, feces, urine, and blood will be analyzed and the results subjected to trend analysis.

On Your Own Draw a mindmap to help you see relationships between ideas and information. For example, you might draw a mindmap in getting ready to lead a meeting. The mindmap will help you determine what issues you should discuss and what information you and others should bring to the meeting.

Conduct Research

Many messages that you prepare will require you to conduct research, going beyond simple intuitive methods like freewriting and mindmapping. In some cases, you will want to read widely, especially reviewing files, reports, and records, such as previous documents on the issue on which you are writing and related documents previously sent to the same department. Some managers find it useful to conduct interviews and hold group meetings as additional ways to gather information. Whenever you are gathering information, ask yourself two questions. Is this information relevant and useful? Is this information accurate and unbiased?

Below is an example of an information search conducted by a research scientist preparing an important report for a regulatory agency. He gathered information through reading, library research, interviewing, and meetings.

Gathering Information through Research

Reading The scientist first reviewed the four previous studies he and his colleagues had completed on this project including "A 28-day Oral Safety Study in Rats," "Mouse Feeding Study: Impact on Rate of Weight Gain," "Dose Response Study," and "Subchronic Fortification Study." He also read related correspondence to evaluate the government agency's past response to company submissions. This gave him a clear sense of his audience's expectations, based on what they had read before. He also found historical information to include in the background section of his report.

Library Research His library research included reading articles from *The Journal of Toxicology; The Journal of Biological Chemistry; The Journal of Nutrition; The Journal of Lipid Research;* and *The American Journal of Physiology.* He photocopied relevant articles and stored them in files under appropriate categories for the type of research he was conducting.

Interviewing He talked to coworkers, especially those who had written on similar issues, as well as his predecessors on the job. He called relevant customers, suppliers, and professional colleagues to determine what additional information and questions his research should contain and address. He addressed issues of concern to himself as well as contextual issues regarding their histories with these issues.

He asked questions to reveal more information, including interviewee attitudes toward the study. To generate a positive response to the interview, he also offered to trade information, so both parties would come away with valuable data.

In each case, he expanded his research effort by asking "Who else should I speak to?" He recorded this information on a To Call list, as illustrated.

To call list:
Dr. David Brand, Los Angeles School of Medicine, Los Angeles, California
Dr. Joseph Wilson, American Health Foundation, Valhalla, New Jersey
Dr. Michael Simms, Director of Biomedical Research, American Institute of Health, Washington, D.C.

Meetings When he found significant boundary problems existed between research departments that shared ownership of this issue, he called a meeting of members of departments responsible for safety, toxicology, and nutrition to determine how to best resolve potential areas of dispute.

As this example illustrates, researching company files and secondary sources, conducting interviews, and calling meetings are all important ways of identifying the facts you need for inclusion in your memos and reports.

ANALYZE INFORMATION

Invest time in analyzing and evaluating your information. Information does not speak for itself: to clarify its significance to your audience, interpret it in terms of your organization's objectives, current situation, and future action plans.

This section discusses six useful techniques for interpreting information. The first two—drawing flowcharts of complex relationships and using classification to analyze information—are "logical" approaches, which aid you in understanding the dimensions of an issue by breaking it into smaller parts.

The other four help you analyze data "psychologically," permitting you to see information through your readers' eyes. These are:

1. Using mental rehearsal to view your ideas from your audience's point of view and developing matrices to help you;
2. Testing ideas against audience priorities;
3. Interpreting what the information you have gathered means to your organization's ability to meet its goals; and
4. Determining whether you are presenting evidence your audience will consider valid.

Draw Flowcharts to Clarify Complex Relationships

Beyond informal picture drawing like mindmapping, a more disciplined technique, flowcharting, is also useful for clarifying relationships.

Flowcharts help you analyze a process by breaking it down into its parts. For example, an office manager was asked to discover ways of improving the procedure for the payment of accounts. To get the "big picture," she wrote each step horizontally and the substeps vertically below each major step. This allowed her to view the entire operation chronologically. With this big picture, she developed a series of questions about each step and its corresponding substeps to see where procedures could be improved or streamlined. (See page 41 for Flowchart Analysis.)

Use Classification to Analyze Information

Classifying information into component parts both helps you determine what topics to cover and clarifies relationships among topics.

Classification When you have a lot of data to analyze, put "like" concepts into "like" categories.

Do this test: On the basis of _____,
_____ can be divided into _____ groups.

For example, in a company working to lower the cost of goods, including delivery, an accountant divided total delivered costs into three categories: fixed, semivariable, and variable. He found that the largest fixed cost was rent; the largest semivariable costs were labor, indirect labor, fringe benefits, material handling, repairs, maintenance, and energy; and the largest variable cost was sales commissions.

This analysis led her to examine ways of reducing costs in each category.

Similarly, a marketing analyst examined ethnic groups on the basis of country of origin. For example, Spanish-speaking consumers were classified as Cuban, Puerto Rican, Mexican, or Central/South American. They also were classified by area of concentrated residence, including Southern California, Texas, Florida, New York/New Jersey, and Chicago. This analysis helped determine the best locations for Spanish language marketing programs, as well as how to tailor the appeal of these programs to the needs of the different cultural backgrounds of each Spanish-speaking group.

Flow Chart Analysis

Example: Improving the Procedure for the Payment of Accounts

Receive notice of non-payment of account → Complete written notice → Put new information on computer → Check with appropriate department → Check with post office → Put new information on computer → Inform account of actions → Issue new check

Receive notice of non-payment of account →

Complete written notice
- Describe order
- Find I.D. number of account
- Check original paperwork

Put new information on computer
- Check original entry
- Add new information to entry

Check with appropriate department
- Call department
- See if materials were received
- See if materials fulfilled conditions of order

Check with post office
- Have tracer put on any mail not yet received

Inform account of actions
- Call
- Write
- Inform when new check will arrive

Issue new check
- Cancel old one, if necessary
- Send check certified mail
- Receive return receipt

On Your Own

- Draw a flowchart of a complex process to clarify the interrelationships of its parts.

- Use classification as a way of better understanding how to market to ethnic minorities. For example, how could Asian consumers be subdivided? Black consumers? How do these classifications help you develop a stronger marketing plan?

Answer these questions:

- How could a human resource manager use classification to better understand how to tailor a benefit program to the needs of employees?

- How could an engineer use classification to explain to management the pro's and con's of three different approaches to producing a jumbo-size candy bar?

Look at Your Message from Your Audience's Point of View

Communication theorist Roderick Hart has observed that to achieve your own objectives and also communicate persuasively to a particular audience requires you to take a "dual perspective," one in which you look at the situation from your own point of view and from that of likely readers and listeners. This becomes particularly important when you are communicating with people from different functions or at different levels in the organization. Thus, once you've recorded and analyzed some of your own ideas for your message, shift to considering the information needs of your readers and listeners. Effective ways of understanding readers include using the journalist's seven questions, and constructing three graphics: an audience priorities matrix, a key learnings table, and an evidence analysis matrix.

Use the Journalist's Seven Questions   One of the most effective ways to generate information and, at the same time obtain insight into your audience, is to conduct an imaginary dialogue with readers, asking them the journalist's seven questions: Who, What, When, Where, Why, How, and How Much? Then write down your answers and anticipate the likely responses to them.

This exercise provides you with two benefits. First, by articulating answers to key questions, you find which ideas need more clarification and which need more proof.

Second, visualizing reader and listener responses will direct you toward some kinds of information and away from others. Since you can select many arguments and provide a wide array of evidence on your subject, you can use an imaginary dialogue with readers to guide and limit your choices.

For example, imagine you are announcing a new policy for paid absences for authorized medical appointments. You have jotted down ideas in the following rough draft and are now shifting your attention to your audience.

Memo Which Leaves Many Questions Unanswered

Subject: Time off work for medical appointments

Employees are allowed to request time off with pay for medical appointments. They may do this for a period of no more than two hours. Specific procedures must be followed to qualify for the paid absence. Employees must obtain Form 3050, Request for Paid Medical Appointment, from the manager of their departments. All information on Form 3050 under the heading Employee Information must be filled in. And your immediate supervisor must approve the request by signing his name directly below yours on the form. Paid medical appointment absences are limited to four per year.

What are the questions readers will ask? As outlined below, using the journalist's seven questions helps you determine what additional information you need to include.

The Journalist's Seven Questions

- Who
  —Who is eligible for this benefit?
  —Does taking children or elderly relatives to appointments qualify?
  —Who authorizes paid medical absences?
- What
  —What types of medical appointments are covered?
  —What forms need to be filled out?
  —Under what circumstances can this benefit be denied?
- When
  —How much advance notification does the company require?
- Where
  —Are visits covered to physicians who are located outside the immediate vicinity?

- Why
  —Why is the Company offering this benefit?
- How
  —How does one apply for this benefit?
- How much
  —How many hours are allowed for paid appointments?
  —How many paid leaves are authorized per year?
  —How is the pay calculated?

On Your Own Re-read the Medical Benefit rough draft. See how many of the above questions are answered and how many are not. What information is missing from the rough draft? What additional information would you include? Revise the draft incorporating answers to unanswered questions as well as making other needed improvements.

What changes did you make? Why?

Compare and contrast your revision to the one that follows. What differences did you find? Which do you prefer? Why?

Memo Which Answers the Journalist's Seven Questions

To: All administrative and technical employees
From: Payroll Department
Date: June 1, 1993.

Subject: Paid Time Off for Medical Appointments

The ABC Company is happy to announce a new benefit for all administrative and technical employees: paid time off for medical appointments. [What] ABC is offering this benefit in response to the results of a recent survey, in which this benefit ranked first of 10 proposed benefit options. [Why] You may apply for paid time off for medical appointments any time after June 15. [When]

Listed below are the policies and procedures governing this new benefit.

Policies
1. You will be paid for up to two hours of time off for medical appointments.
2. You may be paid for as many as four appointments per year.
3. Medical appointments include visits to licensed medical practitioners, including physicians, dentists, psychiatrists and other counsellors, optometrists,

chiropractors, and podiatrists. Reimbursement applies only to visits to medical practitioners included in the company health insurance network.

4. Visits for dependent children who are under 18 and living at home are included. Visits for any other children or adults are not included.

5. You must give your manager 48-hours notice of the appointment so that he or she can plan for your absence.

6. Reimbursement will be at your normal hourly rate. You will not be reimbursed
   a. for time away from the company premises in excess of two hours, or
   b. for appointments for which you have not complied with company policies or for which you have not submitted proper verification.

Procedures
1. Obtain form 3050, Request for Paid Medical Appointment, and form 3051, Verification of Medical Treatment, from the manager of your department. Examples of completed sample forms are attached.

2. Complete form 3050 by filling in all the information requested in the section headed Employee Information.

3. Ask your immediate supervisor to approve your request by signing the form immediately below your signature.

4. Complete form 3051 and have a doctor or nurse date and sign it. Return form 3051 to the Personnel Office immediately upon your return to work.

Use the Journalist's Seven Questions When Writing Complex Memos and Reports

When you are writing a detailed memo, report, or proposal, ask yourself a longer list of questions. Conduct an imaginary dialogue with your readers, using questions such as the following as a guide.

Questions Typically Asked in Preparing for a Complex Document

What: Specifically what do you want?
          What role do you want me to play?
          What is the "fit" between what you are reporting and other company initiatives in this area?
          What are the precedents for this?
          What are the alternatives?
          What is corporate policy?
          What impact will this have on marketing? Innovation? Physical resources? Productivity? Company image? Social responsibility?

What objections do you anticipate? What risks and constraints exist?

Why: Why will the Company benefit from this information?

How: How does this relate to long-term, intermediate, and short-term company objectives?
How will this be implemented? Do we have the technology to support the action steps? If not, can we obtain or develop it?
If we proceed with the action steps, how will this affect our personnel? Our control system?

How much: How much will this cost in time? Money?
How much training or recruiting is required?

When: What schedules do we need to meet?

Who: Who else has concurred with all or part of this analysis? Who else is affected by this?

Where: Which location(s) are involved?

On Your Own   Mentally rehearse your responses to readers and listeners to a message by answering the previous questions. Write down significant insights which will help you clarify your logic and improve your audience analysis.

DEVELOP AN AUDIENCE PRIORITIES MATRIX

A second way to gain insight into likely reader reactions is to develop an audience priorities matrix. This matrix will help you determine which arguments will most likely be persuasive to readers and listeners. It does so by helping you evaluate information in light of those key questions decision makers consistently expect to see addressed. They are:

- Is it worth doing?
- Is it on target, aligned with other company objectives?

- Is it cost effective?
- Is it feasible?
- What are the risks and how can we manage them?

Worth doing refers to proving that the information you are reporting is essential to the effective performance of your department. For example, anything having a significant impact on the company, including increased profits, volume and share; increased productivity, reliability, safety and security; improved customer and consumer satisfaction; or improved morale would normally be categorized as worth doing.

On-target refers to showing an alignment between what you are doing and company goals. Often you demonstrate this relationship when you state a higher level Why in the opening paragraph of your document.

Cost effectiveness is a demonstration that resources have been effectively leveraged in achieving goals.

Feasibility refers to showing that what you are discussing has worked or can work, can be implemented with relative ease and speed, will be acceptable to those who are affected by it, and reflects a long-held or highly desired organizational competence.

Risk discusses real and potential limitations of the approach you are discussing, including external threats, such as competitors and government agencies, and internal constraints, such as budget limitations, internal opposition, lack of technology, and lack of human skills.

One seminar participant, a sales manager, outlined a complex report using these five criteria, as illustrated in the following table. This procedure helped him to determine what content to use in a report in which he proposed a sales promotion plan which offered high-volume purchasers up to 20% free product.

Proposed Action: A Sales Promotion Plan Targeted at Large Hospitals

Hierarchy of Objectives	Key Decision Factors *[worth doing, on-target, cost-effective]*	Why It's Achievable *[will work]*	Constraints *[risk]*
Author:	achieving quarterly share, volume, and profit objectives for hospital division	• high immediate impact • easy to understand • fast implementation • excellent incentives to purchasing agents	• end results depend on hospital purchasing agents' commitment and cooperation

(continued)

Hierarchy of Objectives	Key Decision Factors *[worth doing, on-target, cost-effective]*	Why It's Achievable *[will work]*	Constraints *[risk]*
Division:	short-term volume, profit and share; budget implications; personnel implications; confidence that plan will work; plan's cost effectiveness	• easy to measure • within budget • endorsed by Sales reps • low maintenance cost	• relatively high start-up cost • additional paperwork
Company:	short & intermediate term share, profit and volume trends; alignment with broader company efforts with these products and this market	• will work because we will be only company making this deal • sales message in line with overall product strategy	• modest long-term benefits • competitors may copy

Specifically, the sales managers decided that the three key benefits he should stress were the ability to meet quarterly sales, profit, and share goals; alignment with other company efforts in this area; and fast, easy implementation.

It also allowed him to determine what areas of risk he had to address, including providing incentives to motivate compliance from hospital purchasing agents and justifying—as an investment with an outstanding return—the incremental spending requested.

As the following example illustrates, analyzing his argument through his readers' minds allowed this writer to develop an opening statement, an audience-sensitive rationale for his argument, and a plan for addressing risks.

Outline Generated by Key Learnings Table

The Sales Department recommends a promotion plan for Prod X targeted at large hospitals. [What] This program, which will offer up to 20% free product for volume purchases, is projected to generate 10% incremental volume during the next six months, as well as an additional $65,000 in quarterly profits and an 0.2 increase in share. [Why]

This cost-effective plan will be funded internally and is well-aligned with company efforts to focus sales efforts on the large hospital market. [Cost, Why]

Rationale:
1. **This program is worth doing:** it will help the company achieve its quarterly share, volume and profit objectives.

2. **This program is opportunistic:** it can be implemented quickly and simply before competition can respond.
3. **This program will work:** it contains incentives to assure the participation of hospital purchasing agents.

Issues:
Start-up costs offset by volume, profit, and share gains.

Nonproprietary, high-volume purchases by hospitals will remove program incentives to purchase copycat programs by competition.

On Your Own   Develop a visual similar to the previous one in which you outline an argument on behalf of an action plan.

DESIGN A KEY LEARNINGS TABLE

Another way to consider information from your readers' point of view is to design a key learnings table. It helps you determine which Whys to use for each argument. To design a key learnings table, analyze your information from three perspectives—your objectives, lessons learned from past experience, and the actions the company should take in response to what you have learned. This process will allow you to interpret information in ways that are responsive to audience experience and concerns—and later will help you coherently develop your argument.

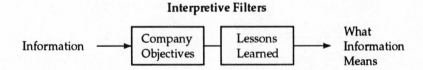

Interpretive Filters

Information → Company Objectives → Lessons Learned → What Information Means

Key Learnings Table

Information	Objective	Lessons Learned	What It Means
Future standards require half as many effluents per gallon of wastewater as present standards	To bring chemical discharges within present and future EPA limits	Investments in forward looking environmental citizenship pay strong dividends both in building morale and in developing positive on-going relationships with external agencies	The ABC plant will need a 30% reduction in effluents to meet 1995 standards

For example, the previous analysis helped the Regulatory Department plan a draft of a memo, including an opening paragraph that read as follows:

Effectively Positioned Opening Paragraph

"The Regulatory Committee has analyzed ABC's waste water compliance record and has concluded that ABC needs to plan now for ways to reduce effluent per gallon by at least 30% in the next two years [What]. This will bring ABC into compliance with 1995 EPA standards [Why] and continue our outstanding record of forward looking environmental citizenship [Why]. Details of our analysis and data follow."

Similarly, the Key Learnings Table below helped its author develop persuasive "whys," based on company experience, for both benefits of his proposal.

Key Learnings Table

Information	Objective	Lessons Learned	What It Means
Customer X owns the senior segment of the market and perceives young families as its main growth market.	To improve sales of Pretend to Customer X	Sales are most efficiently generated by targeting efforts to the largest consumer segments Customer commitment is best delivered when Sales can offer a portfolio of product advantages.	Pretend's copy and product packaging should be refocused to appeal to both seniors and affluent young families

Effectively Reasoned Outline of a Proposal

Reco:
Refocus Pretend's copy and packaging to appeal to both senior citizens and young families.

Rationale:
1. The program will increase purchases by Customer X (because)
   - the new copy and packaging is designed to better appeal to Customer X's most important consumers and
   - experience shows customer commitment is best delivered when Sales can offer a portfolio of product advantages.

2. The program is cost-effective (because)
- sales are most cost-effectively generated by targeting efforts to the largest consumer segments.

On Your Own Develop a key learnings matrix to help you determine what information you gathered means in terms of your organization's objectives and past experience.

ANALYZE YOUR EVIDENCE

Once you have tested your ideas against audience priorities and experience, do the same for qualitative and quantitative evidence. Different readers respond to different types of evidence. Some prefer reference to company experience, some prefer test data, and others respond well to expert testimony and qualitative data. The Evidence Evaluation Table below and on page 52 lists the strengths and weaknesses of four types of evidence.

Ideally, in complex memos you will present a variety of evidence to support your position. This will allow you to capitalize on strengths and minimize weaknesses inherent in each type of argument. For example, most readers would agree to an action plan supported by evidence that the company has succeeded in similar endeavors in the past, statistical analyses projecting highly positive outcomes, and expert testimony supporting the likely success of the program.

Evidence Evaluation Table

Type of Evidence	Example	Strengths	Weaknesses
Comparison	Based on lessons learned "We can increase share in detergents by packing them in compostable packaging . . . when our company developed environmentally safe propellant dispensers, it increased market share by x%"	Appeals to company pride; shows readers the relationship between past and future successes; based on real experiences; can be replicated	analogy must be based on comparable situations
Statistically Verified Analyses	results of a survey or large size sample; "Results of random sampling of 2000 users reveal . . ."	controlled test; proven statistical significance; reliable results	expensive time-consuming slow

(continued)

Type of Evidence	Example	Strengths	Weaknesses
Qualitative Data	expert testimony "Hudson Institute predicts"	fast, inexpensive informed judgment	may not be objective
	focus groups "Consensus of two focus groups reveal"	often accurate	limited reliability
Judgment	anecdotal evidence intuition, reasoning "12 letters indicate that"	sometimes right fast, inexpensive	little reliability; difficult to defend

EVALUATE THE ADEQUACY OF YOUR INFORMATION

At the end of your initial information search, ask yourself four questions. What did I find? What does this information mean? What additional proof do I need? What relationships need clarification? Then make out a Need to Know and Understand chart to follow through on your evidence search. An example of a Need to Know and Understand chart is shown below and on page 53.

By organizing your search for information this way, you won't be asking people to provide you with information that you will not be using, thereby improving the organization's use of time and focusing your search only on information relevant to your message.

Need to Know and Understand Chart

Objective: to determine if a new product can be successfully marketed

Question	Sources	Responsibility	Timing
What patterns of behavior do our actions stimulate among competitors?	Past & present advertising managers	H. L. Pagnozzi S. D. Small	12/1/91
How have competitors reacted in the past to company initiatives?	Market Research Dept Sales Dept	T. Pizzaro J. L. Swiggart	12/2/91 12/2/91
Can we focus more effectively on target purchasers?	Market Research	M. M. Stock	12/9/91

(continued)

Question	Sources	Responsibility	Timing
Do we have a precise idea of who the target purchaser is?	Psychographics Inc.	J. Jefferson	1/28/92
What are industry trends in sales and profits?	Distributors	H. Jones	2/1/92
How does the company compare with others on volume, share, and profit?	Finance Dept	C. Backhouse	2/1/92

On Your Own   Develop a need to know and understand list for a research report you are planning.

SUMMARY

To produce a convincing argument, you need to ask the right questions and find the right answers. For most simple messages, you can use the intuitive methods discussed early in this chapter. For more complex messages, carefully following this three-step process of gathering, analyzing, and evaluating information, though seemingly time consuming, is an efficient way of producing logically argued and well-documented arguments.

Once you've planned your message by analyzing the situation, clarifying your objectives, gathering information and analyzing your audience's likely response to it, you are ready to compose a complete outline of your message, one that uses highlighting techniques to make it easy for readers to follow the logic of your argument.

Exercise   Generate information for a report or presentation. Use at least one technique from each of the following groups.

1. Freewriting
   Mindmapping
   Flowcharting

2. Classification
   Research

3. Journalist's seven questions
   Audience priorities matrix
   Key learnings table
   Evidence analysis table
   Need to know and understand chart

CHAPTER 4

Highlight Your Message

Visual design makes an important first impression on readers; in fact, a Purdue University study revealed that readers look at the design of a document before they read its text. To illustrate, try this test. Look at the two memos shown on pages 55 and 56. Which would you prefer to read first? The one highlighted to make skimming and scanning easy, or the one that confronts you with paragraph after paragraph of uninterrupted text?

If you are like most readers, you selected the highlighted memo as superior. An effectively highlighted layout produces three benefits: it makes your documents inviting to read; it increases the speed with which readers process information; and by directing readers to ideas and their support, it helps readers locate data and understand their significance.

In well-designed documents, readers can easily conduct both "big picture" and "detailed picture" analysis. They get an accurate big picture by first skimming and scanning highlighted information; they get a detailed picture from a word-for-word reading of the document. Effective highlighting will also allow you to more easily check the logic of your argument. In essence, the physical design of messages aids clarity, conciseness, and organization by illuminating ideas and relationships difficult to express in writing alone.

Memos, letters, and reports without highlighting force readers to hunt for information and make it more difficult for them to determine the sequence of thought underlying an argument.

Memo Without Highlighting

To: Regional and District Sales Managers
From: J. Jones, Vice President for Sales
Date: April 1, 1993
Subj: Exciting New Lease Option

Beginning May 1, 1993, we are offering an exciting new lease option that can turn those "I'm from Missouri" prospects into customers! With the new "Guaranteed Performance Lease," your customers can now try out our products for 90 days without obligating themselves to our standard lease terms of three years. The only obligation during the first 90 days is to make the normal monthly lease payments while using the equipment. Also, customers must return the equipment, freight prepaid, if they choose not to continue the lease.

Surveys reveal that 65% of nonpurchasers indicated the long-lease commitment as their single largest reason not to buy. As one respondent wrote on a survey, "I don't want to be stuck for three years with a piece of equipment that we may not use enough to justify the expense."

Our company is the first in this field to offer the "try before you buy" deal. It will give customers one more reason to lease our equipment rather than a competitor's.

The lease rate factors have been increased 3% to offset the costs of this program. Customers must notify us in writing if they want to cancel during the 90 day period. On day 91, the standard lease terms automatically go into effect. A one-page "Guaranteed Performance Lease Addendum" to our standard contract is the only additional paperwork involved. The 90 days begin on the day the customer receives the equipment.

Now is the time to go back to those customers who turned us down and give them the chance to experience the superior benefits of our equipment, all in a risk-free environment! Within the week you will receive promotional materials to support this program via intercompany mail.

Good luck! Call me at 555-3906 with questions and customer feedback about this program.

Memo With Highlighting

<hr>

Subj: The "Guaranteed Performance Lease"

To: Regional and District Sales Managers
From: J. Jones, Vice President for Sales
Date: April 1, 1993

Beginning May 1, 1993, we are offering an exciting new lease option that can turn those "I'm from Missouri" prospects into customers!

The New Guaranteed Performance Lease

With the new "Guaranteed Performance Lease," your customers can now try out our equipment for 90 days without obligating themselves to our standard lease terms of three years. The only obligation during the first 90 days is to make the normal monthly lease payments while using the equipment. Also, customers must return the equipment, freight prepaid, if they choose not to continue the lease.

Why It Will Work

- **This plan removes the single largest barrier to purchase.** Surveys reveal that 65% of nonpurchasers indicated the long-lease commitment as their single largest reason not to buy. As one respondent wrote, "I don't want to be stuck for three years with a piece of equipment that we may not use enough to justify the expense."
- **This plan allows us to offer a unique, high-value customer benefit.** Our company is the first in this field to offer the "try before you buy" deal. It will give customers one more reason to lease our equipment rather than a competitor's.

The Technical Details

- The lease rate factors have been increased 3% to offset the costs of this program.
- Customers must notify us in writing if they want to cancel during the ninety day period.
- On day 91, the standard lease terms automatically go into effect.
- A one-page "Guaranteed Performance Lease Addendum" to our standard contract is the only additional paperwork involved. The 90 days begin on the day the customer receives the equipment.

How To Use This Option

Now is the time to go back to those customers who turned us down and give them the chance to experience the superior benefits of our equipment, in a risk-free environment! We will be sending you promotional materials to support the program by intercompany mail within the week.

Good luck! Call me at x-3906 with questions and customer feedback about this program.

To help you learn how to highlight documents effectively, this chapter discusses four highlighting techniques—headings, lists, boldface, and indentation. Each serves an important role in clarifying meaning. Your use of them should correspond to reader expectations and the logic of your argument.

HEADINGS

Headings are the most important form of highlighting: they help readers gain insight into large bodies of information. As a reader scans a memo or report, headings, including the subject line, serve as the "table of contents," giving a quick overview of the document and outlining the sequence of thought behind it. They also make information easier to find by indicating to readers where particular types of data appear in the message. Effectively written headings are precise, logical, easy-to-find, and consistent.

Use Precisely Worded Headings as "Macro-Organizers"

Headings help readers effectively scan documents only when they serve as accurate and concise announcements of the information that follows them. Note how readers receive a much clearer idea of the content of a message when scanning the precise heading than they do with imprecise headings.

Use Precise Headings

Imprecise	Precise
Issues	Existing vs. Proposed Procedures
	Decisions Reached
	Issues Requiring Further Discussion
Discussion	Reasons for Recommendation
	Risks
	Alternative Solutions Rejected
	Why This Plan Will Work
Details	Service Options
	Payback Analysis
	How to Implement this Program

Use Both Idea and Generic Headings

Many companies use a consistent set of generic headings, such as Background, Findings, Conclusions, Recommendation, Follow-Up, and Constraints to indicate the nature of the argument being proposed. To people familiar with them, these generic headings serve as important insights into the writer's thinking because they reveal the place of information in the hierarchy of the author's thought.

For example, Conclusions at one company at which I conducted interviews are always an evaluation of results; Findings are interpretations of what data means; Recommendation indicates that the What and a brief How of a proposal are being discussed; Rationale predicts that the Why's will be discussed, and Implementation where the How will be described in detail. When readers within this company see these headings, it tells them both the type of information that follows and often the level at which the author has interpreted the information, an important insight into the nature of the argument.

On the other hand, idea headings—headings which announce the topic discussed in the information following the heading—are almost always superior for simple documents, such as monthly reports, as well as letters and reports addressed to external parties. Use the chart below to help you decide which types of headings to use in messages to different audiences.

Decision Matrix for Using Idea and Generic Headings

	Idea Headings	Generic Headings
Type of reader	external to company; internal receiver of simple reports	internal to company; receiver of complex reports
Type of document	simple report or letter	complex analysis requiring development of an argument
Representative headings	Sales by Region Phase I Results ABC's Product Line	Key Learnings Conclusion Indicated Action
Criteria	predicts content; key word in heading repeated in first sentence of text following it	predicts treatment of content; demonstrates a sequence of logical thought, often with numbered, indented full sentence underlines in the Body.

You can achieve the best of both approaches by combining idea and generic headings. Instead of Results, you can write Results of Product Safety Tests; instead of simply writing Background, you can write Background: The Lessons of Previous Product Recalls.

LISTS

While headings serve as "macro-organizers," allowing readers to observe the organization of major ideas in a document, lists serve as "micro-organizers," highlighting key details. For example, notice how much easier it is to understand the following action steps when they are put in a list format. This format immediately indicates to readers where one idea ends and the next begins.

Paragraph without List Format

`Action Steps`
AA Consulting will independently test each of our products. The review will include overall product functionality, ease of use, and clarity of instructions. AA will summarize their findings in an oral presentation to the executive board on June 1. The presentation will be accompanied by a written report and a video presentation. I will repackage this presentation to include the product modifications recommended by the executive board, and send it to our plant managers nationwide. It is anticipated that I will send this modified presentation by July 1. I will communicate with the plants to gain feedback about the suggestions and to ensure that each plant implements needed changes.

Paragraph Revised into List Format

`Action Steps`
1. AA Consulting will independently test each of our products. The review will include overall product functionality, ease of use, and clarity of instructions.
2. On June 1, AA Consulting will summarize their findings in an oral presentation to the executive board. The presentation will be accompanied by a written report and a video presentation.

3. I will repackage this presentation to include the modifications recommended by the executive board and send it to our plant managers nationwide by July 1.

4. I will communicate with the plants to gain feedback about the suggestions and to ensure that each plant implements needed changes.

As you can see, a list format is easier to follow. It tells you where one point begins and another ends, and it makes the chronology of steps clearer to readers.

To make lists easy to find and read, number each point to indicate sequence or rank. If you do not want to indicate sequence, use asterisks, bullets, or dashes to separate each item. Do not run words under numbers or bullet points in lists. When you have room, include a line of white space between each point.

Also be sure that each item or sentence put in list format is written in parallel structure, so that each point begins with a noun, a verb, or other consistently used grammatical construction.

BOLDFACE AND UNDERLINING

Boldface and underlining are also important forms of highlighting. They are best used solely to highlight information such as headings, learnings, findings, and reasons—items which can stand on their own when scanned.

Use Boldface or Underlining to Highlight the Logic of Your Argument

A key to the ability of memo writers to reveal the logic of their positions is to boldface or underline key topic sentences, in many ways interchangeable techniques. Note how in the following examples on page 61 you can scan the overriding rationale of the memo which employs boldfacing.

Boldfacing also helps readers understand the logic of your argument by encouraging scanning of toplined inferences, separate from the reasoning and data that support them. This gives readers an understanding of the Big Picture, allowing them to more immediately see the relevance of details during their word-for-word reading.

Without Boldface

Objective
To gain approval to replace preglued film with on-line
gluing of cardboard cartons

On-line gluing will save money. The savings result from
the lower cost of glue as compared to tape. Our analysis
of the European experience indicates a savings of $.50
per 100 cartons. A similar savings in the United States
would result in $37,500 annual savings.

On-line gluing will also better guarantee the integrity
of the contents of each box. This will result from the
improved adhesion on-line gluing produces. Product
stress tests indicate gluing the cardboard to itself
produces a 50% better bond than tape, allowing for less
movement within the box.

With Boldface

Objective
To gain approval to replace preglued film with on-line
gluing of cardboard cartons

- **On-line gluing will save money.** The savings result
  from the lower cost of glue as compared to tape. Our
  analysis of the European experience indicates a savings of $0.50 per 100 cartons. A similar savings in
  the United States would result in $37,500 annual
  savings.

- **On-line gluing will better guarantee the integrity of**
  the contents of each box. This will result from the
  improved adhesion on-line gluing produces. Product
  stress tests indicate gluing the cardboard to itself
  produces a 50% better bond than tape, allowing for
  less movement within the box.

INDENTING

A fourth important form of highlighting is indenting. Use headings
in conjunction with indenting to reveal hierarchies of thought. Giv-
en that readers read from left to right, a heading that begins at the
left margin is more emphatic than one that is indented several spaces.

Readers can tell from the visual design that indented points are subpoints of larger points.

Note how difficult it is to evaluate the logic of the following outline when it is not indented.

Report Lacking Indenting

ABC Sales Results
Region A: Overall sales were up 50% in this region.
These results were driven by a strong promotional program conducted during the first six weeks of Oct-Dec.
period.
North: This region experienced a 45% increase.
South: This region experienced a 50% increase
Region B: Overall sales were down 12% in this region,
largely due to competitors' aggressive promotion and
special pack activity.
North: This region experienced a 5% increase. The disappointing results are largely due to a competitor's special pack promotion which induced many of our consumers
to switch to the competitive brand.
South: This region experienced a 20% sales decrease,
largely due to a competitor's high-value coupon initia-
tive, which led to dramatically reduced sales of our
product.

Report Using Indenting

ABC Sales Results
Region A: Overall sales were up 50% in this region.
          These results were driven by our strong pro-
          motional program conducted during the first
          six weeks of Oct-Dec. period.

North: This region experienced a 45% increase.
South: This region experienced a 55% increase

Region B: Overall sales were down 12% in this region,
          largely due to competitors' aggressive promo-
          tion and special pack activity.

North: This region experienced a 5% increase. The
          disappointing results are largely due to a
          competitor's special pack promotion activity
          which induced many of our consumers to switch
          to the competitive brand.
South: This region experienced a 20% sales decrease,
          largely due to a competitor's high-value
          coupon initiative, which led to dramatically
          reduced sales of our product.

SUMMARY

The visual design of a document creates an important first impression on readers. In all but the simplest memos and letters, plan your use of highlighting techniques, including headings, lists, indentation, underlining, and boldface. Wise use of these techniques will make your document more inviting to read, help readers understand the logic of your argument, and allow readers to locate and retrieve information quickly.

Using the format and highlighting techniques discussed so far will help you organize most simple documents effectively. For highly complex documents, you should organize your information into a planning matrix, the topic of Chapter 5. It is a highly efficient way of checking the logical consistency of your argument.

Exercise #1 Find a 1–2 page unhighlighted memo or report you have written or received. Use the highlighting techniques recommended in this chapter to improve it.

Is your revised document more inviting to read? Easier to skim and scan? Is the logic of its organization improved? Are ideas and relationships more effectively illumined? Are there other ways the revised document significantly differs from the original?

Exercise #2 Use highlighting techniques to improve the clarity, scannability, and appearance of the following letter:

```
ZigZag Collectibles
8044 Montgomery Road, Suite 450
Cincinnati, Ohio 45236
   Attn: Ms. Marybeth Mulligan


                          12 July 1993.

Dear Ms. Mulligan:

We are pleased to propose an advanced writing skills
class at ZigZag Collectibles.  We have an excellent
history of meeting the writing needs of corporate execu-
tives and are confident we can provide the expertise you
are seeking at a highly competitive fee.

The proposal below describes our program, estimated
fees, and mutual responsibilities for this engagement.
```

As prework, each participant should submit 5-6 documents typical of both their most common and most challenging assignments. These assignments may be from current and past positions. Our consultants will read and evaluate each document in advance of the seminar. Seminar exercises will reflect the types of documents submitted as prework. To keep your costs to a minimum, our proposal assumes that you will reproduce and bind a copy of the master workbook for each participant. Optionally, we provide workbooks for $65 each. We also request that you make sure the prework documents arrive in our offices by August 1.

The class will consist of two four-hour segments. The first segment will teach participants principles of good document design, including primacy, recency, chunking and toplining. It will also introduce participants to techniques for writing complex documents. Exercises will cover letter and memo writing and planning complex documents.

Participants will receive extensive individual feedback on the documents they have submitted for review and be given the opportunity to revise them in class. They will be asked to outline and revise one document between sessions.

During session two, participants will continue work on writing complex documents and discuss using graphic aids, such as tables and charts, and they will work on style, including how to write for a multicultural audience.

We will teach this class on August 15 & 22 1993 so that we have sufficient time to review documents and tailor the materials to ZigZag's needs. Mark Friend, Ph.D., and Richard Miller, MBA, will review the prework documents. Mr. Miller will conduct the classes. Total fees are $975.

Marybeth, I enjoyed speaking with you and am honored that you have again asked us to prepare a proposal for teaching writing skills to ZigZag executives. Please call me if you have any questions about this proposal or about other courses we offer.

Sincerely,

Dr. Mark Friend

Suggested Revision How did you do? Did you use a centered and underlined subject line to orient your reader to the purpose of your document? Did you use headings to allow readers to scan your document and gain insight into the order in which you introduce topics? Did you use indentation to reveal a hierarchy of ideas and lists to highlight important ideas? Did you use boldfacing and underlining to highlight important points. Compare your revision to the one below.

Possible Solution

```
ZigZag Collectibles
8044 Montgomery Road, Suite 450
Cincinnati, Ohio 45236
  Attn: Ms. Marybeth Mulligan
```

```
                                             12 July 1993.
```

Proposal for Advanced Writing Skills Seminar

```
Dear Ms. Mulligan:
```

We are pleased to propose an advanced writing skills class for ZigZag Collectibles. We have an excellent history of meeting the writing needs of corporate executives and are confident we can provide the expertise you are seeking at a highly competitive fee.

The proposal below describes our program, pedagogy, schedule, estimated fees, and mutual responsibilities for this engagement.

Program: An Advanced Writing Skills class for Zig Zag executives.

Schedule: We will teach this class on the mornings of August 15 and August 22 1993.

Prework: Participants should submit 5-6 documents typical of both their most common and their most challenging assignments by August 1. These assignments may be from current and past positions. Our consultants will read and evaluate each document in advance of the seminar. Seminar exercises will reflect the types of documents submitted as prework.

Course Design: The class will consist of two four-hour segments.

Session One: During session one, participants will
- Learn principles of good document design, including primacy, recency, chunking and toplining.
- Learn techniques for writing complex documents. Exercises will cover advanced letter and memo writing techniques.
- Receive extensive individual feedback on the documents they have submitted for review and be given the opportunity to revise them in class. They will be asked to outline and revise one document between sessions.

Session Two: During session two, participants will
- continue work on writing complex documents;
- discuss using graphic aids, such as tables and charts; and
- work on style, including how to write for a multicultural audience.

Fees for prework evaluation and class: $975

Instructional Responsibilities: Mark Friend, Ph.D., and Richard Miller, MBA, will review the prework documents. Mr. Miller will conduct the classes.

Client Responsibilities: To keep your costs to a minimum, our proposal assumes that you will reproduce and bind a copy of the master workbook for each participant. Optionally, we provide workbooks for $65 each.

Marybeth, I enjoyed speaking with you and am honored that you have again asked us to prepare a proposal for teaching writing skills to ZigZag executives. Please call me if you have any questions about this proposal or about other courses we offer.

Sincerely,

Dr. Mark Friend

CHAPTER 5

Use a Planning Matrix to Organize Complex Documents

Have you ever written a draft of a long report and dreaded re-reading it? Did it seem intimidatingly long and difficult to comprehend? Did you find yourself unable to answer questions easily such as "Is my argument clear and logically coherent?" "Will readers understand exactly what objectives this report is trying to accomplish?" "Does this document effectively communicate insights about our current ability to achieve these objectives?" "Does the data prove what I say it proves?" "Is my argument complete—have I followed up on every point of analysis with logical action steps?"

This chapter will show you how to organize information into a planning matrix to help ensure the clarity and consistency of your argument. Second, it will show you how to use the "Because, Based On, Therefore" test to evaluate the logical adequacy of your argument.

OUTLINE WHAT YOU KNOW IN A PLANNING MATRIX

A planning matrix uses a column and row format to help you focus on developing a clear alignment between objectives, findings, and action. This is the key to producing a coherent report, one in which each section flows logically from the one preceding it. Headings, lists, and underlining are used to highlight and clarify key relationships.

As the following example illustrates, a matrix organization is superior to the traditional outline because it allows you to answer different questions reading down and reading across.

Reading across you can see if each objective is aligned with a point in the body and if there are action steps that logically flow from the analysis, steps positioned so that they clearly indicate how they will help the company achieve the stated objectives.

Reading down, you can see if the objectives make sense as a group, if the body makes sense as a whole, and if the action steps, taken together, are appropriate follow-ups given your objectives and analysis.

Example of a Planning Matrix for a Status Report

Action objective: to improve line efficiency by remedying the key bottleneck, the filling machinery

Company objective: to improve plant productivity by improving equipment, cost-effectively and within budget

Sub-Objectives	Analysis/Data	Actions	Constraints
To have a smooth uninterrupted flow of product into containers	Current filling machine is subject to frequent breakdowns, causing work stoppages and costly repairs.	Investigate purchase of new equipment; compare on key criteria.	Downtime to install new equipment.
	Current filler has been out of use for an average of 110 hours per year due to repair requirements. Repairs costs average $1,200 per year and are escalating.	Buy new equipment, refurbish and store current equipment for emergency use.	
To meet projected increases in product demand	Current machinery cannot meet projected capacity increases. Increases projected to exceed capacity by 25% in 2 years, excluding breakdowns. [insert calculations]	Buy filler equipment with six heads to replace current four-head design.	

(continued)

Sub-Objectives	Analysis/Data	Actions	Constraints
To be able to change over quickly from one product to another	Current equipment takes too long to changeover to handle a variety of product viscosities.	Buy equipment that has fast changeover capability.	Time to train staff to operate new equipment.
	New products will be of varying viscosities which require one-hour changeover times on current equipment.		Downtime during startup verification process.
To stay wintin current year equipment budget	Sufficient funds exist in current capital budget to purchase improved equipment	Find equipment that best meets criteria for capacity, change-over and cost.	
	$50,000 remains in the current year budget, of which $35,000 has been alloted to improve equipment capabilities.		

Once you have finished a planning matrix, you have already taken a significant step toward writing an opening draft of your memo or report. Notice how some of the most difficult parts of writing are accomplished in this outline. For example, the objectives section of this outline helps you write an effectively organized opening. Your draft might read:

We are writing to update you on the status of the Plant Equipment Task Force. [Action Objective] Our team's purpose is to increase plant productivity, cost effectively and within budget, by improving current equipment. [Company objective] Our first project has been completed: an analysis of the impact of the filling machinery on line efficiency. We found that current machinery significantly impedes productivity in three areas: reliability, capacity, and versatility. [Results] We have developed an action plan to replace the filling machinery using current year equipment funds. [Follow-up]

Similarly, the body paragraphs and action steps can flow almost directly into your first draft. In fact, to write the rough draft you would only have to fill in background and constraints to clarify your analysis.

And you might use the matrix to compose the following action steps section.

Action Plan

1. We have appointed a task force to locate a filling machine that meets the following criteria: total delivered cost of $30-50K; proven reliabilty; high versatility; and sufficent capacity to meet projected capacity requirements for the next five years. The task force members are J. Fisher, (chair), L. Minges, and P. Perraro. They have set a July 15 deadline for completing this analysis.

2. Once the task force has evaluated alternative filling machines, it will examine how to manage installation and training issues with minimum downtime to the company.

To develop effective planning matrices, follow these rules:

Rules for Developing Planning Matrices

1. Write down all of your arguments and evidence, organizing them concisely into appropriate categories, such as objectives, findings/data, constraints, and follow-up steps. Omit background, methods, and information not central to your argument. You may add these sections afterwards.

2. Fill in gaps where linkages are unclear.
   - Provide relevant evidence for every point, and a point for each grouping of relevant evidence.
   - Revise each toplined point until you are satisfied it accurately predicts the evidence that follows it.
   - Be sure each objective is followed by reasoning and evidence and each point has an action step that is clearly related to a stated objective. Sometimes a single action step is a logical response to a number of findings. Similarly a number of Findings may relate to a single objective.

3. Read your outline vertically, in columns, asking these questions:
   - Do objectives make sense together?
   - Is the body logically coherent?
   - Do action steps make sense together?

4. Read your outline horizontally, in rows:
   - Is there an objective for each point?
   - Is each point followed by good reasoning and evidence?
   - Is there an action step that connects the meaning of each point to an objective?

5. Revise until you are confident you have outlined a coherent argument.

CHECK YOUR MATRIX FOR LOGIC AND PERSUASIVENESS

Once you have finished organizing information into a planning matrix, test your outline for logic, using the "because, based on, therefore" tests. The following figures illustrate this concept graphically for Key Learnings, Analysis, and Recommendation memos.

Key Learnings Memo Logic Flow

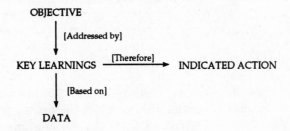

Analysis Memo Logic Flow

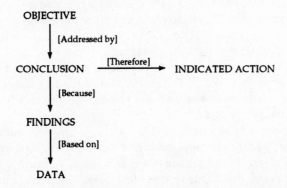

Recommendation Memo Logic Flow

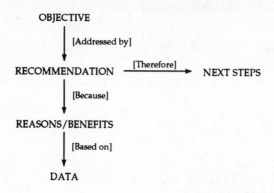

OBJECTIVE

[Addressed by]

RECOMMENDATION   [Therefore]   NEXT STEPS

[Because]

REASONS/BENEFITS

[Based on]

DATA

In essence, this test requires you to make explicit logical connections between your points. To make sure arguments make sense, apply this test to recommendation and analysis memos: can I say "because" prior to each of the toplined Whys that follow and have an argument that makes sense in terms of company and reader objectives? If not, then the toplines must be rephrased so you can. This technique is also useful as a way of ensuring parallel structure and persuasive positioning of the phrasing of the toplines.

For example, if you have recommended that your company hire an additional material services administrator, you might initally write down as a reason "recent customer satisfaction surveys indicate our customer approval rating has declined from 75% to 40%." When you apply the "because" test, you realize that this statement is a fact rather than a reason. This insight will encourage you to rephrase your reason as "Hiring an additional administrator to address customer questions and concerns is an instrumental step in raising customer approval ratings to the 75% company objective."

Additionally, each set of data should be checked by the "based on" test. This assures that each inference is actually based on good argument and evidence. After each topic sentence, mentally insert the words "based on" into the paragraph. If the language that follows makes immediate sense and proves the point made in the topline, then a logical connection between data and inference has been made. If not, then the data has to be rewritten so the connection is immediately clear.

For example, if you have justified hiring a full-time administrator because it will help raise customer approval ratings, you need to prove that point with persuasive reasoning and accurate data. So you might argue that "Our research indicated the precipitous drop in our customer approval ratings from 75% to 40% resulted from current representatives not having enough time to return calls within 24 hours of receiving a request or complaint. As the calculation below indicates, adding one additional customer service representative would permit all calls to be returned in one day or less." In essence, the "based on" test reminds you of the importance of providing sound data and clearly relevant argumentation to support your arguments.

Finally, apply the "therefore" test, asking yourself if each action step is logically related to both your stated objectives and the analysis and evidence you have presented. For example, if one of your objectives is to see if a new product appeals to the 16–25-year-old target audience, and you have evidence that indicates many in this group dislike the packaging graphics, you need to follow through with steps to address this problem as part of your follow-up analysis, such as "The Brand team will convene two focus groups, one with a representative group of 16–20-year-olds and one with 21–25-year-olds, (1) to evaluate the precise reasons for the disapproval of the packaging graphics with these age groups, and (2) to determine if alternative packaging graphics better appeal to this target market."

The easiest way to conduct the "because, based on, therefore" tests is while you are assembling your planning matrix, as illustrated on pages 74 and 75.

SUMMARY

In short, to organize a complex document effectively

- Organize your information into a planning matrix, using highlighting, including headings, lists, and underlining to outline your argument. At the end of this chapter, you'll find generic planning matrix templates for Key Learnings, Analysis, and Recommendation memos.

- Analyze and evaluate your evidence and challenge the logic of your outline using the Because, Based on, Therefore tests. Then revise your matrix until you are satisfied you have produced a logically coherent and well-documented argument.

If you have done these steps well, your first draft of a complex memo or report will easily flow from this outline.

Using the "Because, Based On, Therefore" Test in a Planning Matrix

General Objective: to improve Brand X's market share by increasing the portfolio of advantages X offers consumers

Action Objective: to conduct consumer research to enable Brand X marketing team to better understand consumer needs

Conclusion: Brand X will better meet consumer needs if it has a stronger taste, a darker color, and a natural process for decaffeinating the Decaf brand.

Detailed Objectives	[Because] Findings	[Therefore] Actions Steps
1. Understand consumer reaction to taste of Brand X: ■ Actual product tests	1. Consumers prefer the stronger taste of ABC to Brand X's mild flavor: **[based on]** a. Consumer rankings of comparative products in in-home tests b. In-store interview results	1. Send report to Brand noting consumer choice.
2. Evaluate consumer acceptance of Brand X product claims: ■ Concept testing ■ Formula testing, visual inspection	2. Consumers associate a darker coffee with the richer, stronger flavor they prefer: **[based on]** a. Consumer rankings of comparative product attributes b. Consumers ranked the Expo recipe second only to STR's Gourmet brand, while the regular and Bask recipes ranked fifth and seventh. Expo has the darkest color of all Brand X coffees; STR's Gold the darkest of all coffees tested.	2. Send results to product development. Suggest retesting Expo with new name, darker color.

Detailed Objectives	[Because] Findings	[Therefore] Actions Steps
3. Evaluate consumer preferences on other attributes:	3. Young, single women are most likely to purchase a stronger, darker Brand X, especially if packaged in dark-brown foil: [based on]	3. Develop psychographic profile of this target group.
a. Gender	a. Women prefer strong coffee more than do men, and would be most likely to switch.	
b. Packaging	b. The dark brown foil package produced the most favorable comments among all tested.	Work with packaging on dark foil packaging.
c. Age	c. Consumers aged 16–35 are most likely to switch to a darker, stronger recipe, switching primarily from cola beverages.	
4. Evaluate Brand X Decaf separately: ■ Paper and pencil survey	4. Consumers who drank decaf will switch to obtain a coffee with natural decaffeination: [based on] ■ Brand Y leader for health, not taste reasons	4. Investigate using water-filtering decaf system.

Exercise   Test the logical adequacy of each of the pairs of arguments below. Explain the reasoning behind your decisions.

1. **Determine which of the arguments below best meets the "because" test.**

Analysis of Results of Product Stress Test

Conclusion: Polyethylene packaging is inferior to cardboard for shipping and stocking widgets.

[because]

1. Polyethylene was selected as a test material because it is 40% cheaper than cardboard packaging.

2. Customers have complained about products packaged with polyethylene.

3. The polyethylene package is likely to show wrinkles

1. Polyethlene is twenty times more likely to tear than cardboard packaging

2. Customers returned ten times more product in polyethylene bags than in cardboard boxes.

3. Show tests reveal that rigid cardboard boxes are more appealing to consumers than are wrinkled and often crushed polyethylene bags.

2. **Using the "because" test, determine which of the arguments below is most logical and persuasive.**

Recommendation: hire an additional material services administrator.

[because]

1. Other company offices have gotten increases in staffing.

2. Recent customer satisfaction surveys indicate our customer approval rating has declined from 75% to 40%.

1. The increased business and administrative workload justifies an additional adminstrator.

2. Hiring a new manager is an instrumental step in raising customer approval ratings to the 75% company objective.

3. The cost of temporaries is extremely high.

3. The company can hire a full-time maintenance administrator at no additional cost to the current system of hiring temporary help.

3. **Using the "based on" test, determine which of the following arguments is most relevant to the point it is to prove.**

A mailer to pregnant teens with histories of drug abuse will persuade many to practice drug abstinence during all nine months of pregnancy.

A mailer to pregnant teens with histories of drug abuse will persuade them of the importance of drug abstinence during all nine months of pregnancy.

[based on]
Similar mailings on the importance of abstinence from smoking led to a significant 15% reduction in low birth weight babies. The mailings reached 33% of all pregnant teen smokers attending school.

[based on]
Smoking has been associated with low birth weight of babies born to teen mothers. And low birth weight is a key indicator of a number of serious infant illnesses.

Follow-up research revealed a 59% decrease in smoking among those who received the mailing accounting for the subsequent reduction in low birth weight babies. We predict a similar result from a targeted campaign to pregnant drug users.

Key Learnings Memo Outline

Action Objective:

Company Objective:

Specific Objectives	Background	Key Learnings	Action Steps	Risks
		1. _____ (based on)		
		2. _____ (based on)		
		3. _____ (based on)		

Analysis Memo Outline

Action Objective:

Company Objective:

Specific Objectives

Background

Conclusion
(because)

Findings

1. _____
   (based on)

2. _____
   (based on)

3. _____
   (based on)

Action Steps

Risks

Recommendation Memo Outline

Action Objective:

Company Objectives:

Specific Objectives

Background

Recommendation (WHAT)
(because)

1. _____

(based on)

2. _____

(based on)

3. _____

(based on)

Implementation (HOW)

Risks

Alternative
Solutions
Rejected

Request for Approval

PART II

WRITE YOUR MESSAGE

CHAPTER 6

Write the First Draft

Once you have designed an excellent outline of your document, one which permits you to see logical connections among objectives, reasoning and evidence, risks and action, you are ready to write a first draft. Your immediate objective should be to get a first draft done as quickly as possible so you get a sense of the whole from which you can generate improvements to the draft.

QUICKLY WRITE A FIRST DRAFT

With your outline in front of you, write a first draft from top to bottom. If you cannot think of the right word or right idea, go immediately to a new paragraph or a new section, then come back and fill in those sections you left incomplete. Sometimes you write most effectively when you come back and fill in a section because the sentence or section makes more sense to you once you have finished and have a clear idea of how it fits into the whole.

Resist urges to revise as you write the initial draft; don't worry about misspellings or poorly constructed sentences. Your objective is simply to record your ideas on paper; your successive drafts will refine and improve your early efforts. In fact, you should set a time limit for yourself for writing this draft. Under the pressure of time, you are much less likely to stop and edit than if you proceed without such a self-imposed limit.

REVISE YOUR DRAFT PARAGRAPH BY PARAGRAPH

The remainder of this chapter will show you how to review drafts of each section of the memo, including opening, background, methods, body, risk, follow-up, and action step paragraphs. Chapter 7 discusses how to compose tables, graphs, and charts. Chapter 14 includes numerous models of completed memos, letters, and reports.

Write an Opening Paragraph that Concisely Summarizes Your Document

Complete a draft of your opening paragraph by adding information to the What, the Why, and the When you believe is needed to concisely summarize the entire document. Such information might include timing, results, follow-up, concurrences, benefits, costs, and attachments, as the following examples illustrate. In sum, this "strategy"paragraph should concisely and accurately summarize the entire document, getting readers off to a fast start in understanding the relevance and significance of your message.

Discovery and Report Memos: WHAT, WHY, WHEN, Plus Other Information, Such as Attachments, Needed for a Clear Summary

---

Discovery Memo: Please send me, by March 1, one copy of the 1991, 1992 and 1993 Shareholder Satisfaction surveys. [What and When] I will incorporate the results into a report on Stockholder Relations that my department is preparing for distribution at the Board of Directors meeting in June [Why]. A preliminary outline of the report is attached.

Report: This summarizes agreements reached at a meeting of the Murray Hill Engineering group on May 29, 1991. [What and When] The meeting was called to determine if Analogy better meets MHE hardware needs than the current ABC ATs. [Why]

The group decided that Analogy is the superior product and recommended setting up a test system at the Murray Hill substation. [Results] Details follow.

Analysis and Evaluation Memos: What, Why, When, Results, Follow-Up, Plus Other Information Needed for a Clear Summary

Analysis Memo: I am writing to report the results of an air quality test conducted the week of April 3 in the Ipswich laboratory. [*What, When, and Where*] Its purpose was to determine if the use of ventilators would reduce airborne dust levels at the Lexington plant. [Why] Results indicate ventilators significantly reduce dust levels [*Results*]. A test to confirm this finding will be fielded at the Lexington plant the week of May 4. [*Follow Up*] Details follow.

Evaluation Memo: This discusses the status of the Promotion Effectiveness Report (PER) project. [*WHAT*] We conducted this test to see if PER would help Salted Snacks evaluate the effectiveness of its promotion methods. [*Why*]

Results to date are disappointing. As currently conducted, PER is of little value in measuring promotion effectiveness. [*Conclusion*].

By March 1 [When], we will complete the test using the most stable measures with Taco Chip data. At that time we will also evaluate the use of two outside vendors as an alternative to PER. [*Follow Up*] A sample PER is attached. [*Attachment*]

Proposals: What, Why, When, Benefits, Costs, Concurrences, Plus Other Information Needed for an Accurate Summary

Proposal: The National Sales organization recommends a telemarketing effort behind the C-Mark national introduction in April 1990. The effort will consist of a teaser mailing followed by telephone sales calls to 12M nonusing and switching accounts. [*What and When*]

Our objective is to gain sales and share by offering C-Mark in a functionally superior design and size. [*Why*] We project $3MM in new C-Mark sales and a share of growth of 1.5 basis points. [*Benefits*] The $200M cost of this effort is included in the current brand appropriation budget [*Cost*] A. Gibson, J. Herbold, and P.B. McDonald agree. [*Concurrence*]

Review your Opening Paragraphs for Completeness and Consistency Given the all important nature of the opening paragraph, take time to make sure it is both complete and concise. To do so, put an imaginary box around it. Then ask yourself: "Does it clearly orient your readers to your thesis? Does it indicate its significance to the company? Does it concisely and accurately summarize the entire document?"

In addition, because this paragraph sets up reader expectations for the rest of the document, ask yourself the following additional questions: "Is there too much information? Too little? Does this opening precisely predict the rest of the message?" If not, review the discussion below and make appropriate changes to your document.

Beware of Including too Much Detail in the Opening While it is valuable to compose introductory paragraphs as a concise summary of the entire document, beware of writing opening paragraphs that include information that does not help readers gain a broad perspective of the key issues involved in the document.

For example, evaluate the following opening paragraph. Ask yourself if it adequately summarizes key issues or if it focuses too much on implementation details.

The Sales Department recommends that Pretend conduct a national coupon event with Sometimes during February 1993. Specifically, we have been offered the opportunity to deliver 10 million $.20 off any size Pretend coupons to 15% of households at a cost of about $200,000, including redemption. [What] Pretend will be in-packing the coupon in its 9 ounce size. The coupon values will be announced to consumers on the Sometimes package [How].

This passage fails to meet significant reader needs. It omits information about why the company will benefit from this proposal, who else agrees with it, and whether the money for it is in the current budget or will need to be authorized as additional funding. On the other hand, its last two sentences include too much implementation detail. This information belongs in the Body of the document, because it becomes relevant to readers primarily after the author proves the plan is sound: that is, that it is feasible, has significant benefits, is on target with overall company strategy, and is cost effective. Once readers agree these key points have been proven, then they are ready to determine if the implementation plan is an effective one.

A better opening would be:

The Sales Department recommends that Pretend conduct a
national coupon event with Sometimes during February
1993 [What and When]. The program will deliver ten million $.20 off any size Pretend coupons to 15% of house-
holds at a projected cost of $200,000, including redemp-
tion. [Expansion of What, Cost] Previous experience
indicates this program will conservatively translate
into a 6% increase in quarterly volume and similar increases in share and profit. [Benefit] The project will
be funded internally and is supported by both Pretend
and Sometimes brand management teams. [Funding, Concur-
rence] Details follow.

Beware of Including too Little Information in the Opening Paragraph

Similarly, opening paragraphs that con-
tain too little detail force readers to hunt through the document to
find answers to questions they'd prefer to see answered in an opening summary.

Consider this opening paragraph,

This is in response to Mr. Jones' request on recent
pricing trends for advertising in Sunday supplements.
[What and Why] The review covers 1978-1992. [When]

This paragraph forces the reader to find answers to key questions elsewhere in the memo. For example, most readers would
appreciate knowing early on why Mr. Jones requested the study
and, briefly, what its results were and what actions the company is
taking in response.

Notice how much more responsive the revision is to reader
needs:

This report summarizes the results of a study Mr. Jones
requested to determine if recent price increases in the
cost of advertising in Sunday supplements were justified. [What and Why] The review, which covers 1978-1992,
revealed that prices increased far faster than did the
costs of producing the Sunday supplements. [Conclusion,
When] I have forwarded this report to the Purchasing
Department for use in future negotiations with relevant
suppliers. [Follow-up]

Use a Forecast in Long Documents

In addition, in reports
four pages or longer, a forecast of the entire document is necessary;
in extremely long reports, an executive summary may be required.

EXAMPLE: The following presents: (1) an overall vision
for Pretend; (2) realistic financial objectives for
Pretend over the next three years; (3) the strategic
framework by which the Pretend team will operate; and
(4) a specific program designed to meet set objectives.

Write Background Paragraphs that Clearly Link the Opening with the Body

After reviewing your opening paragraphs, compose the Background
section. Your background paragraphs should both further orient
readers to the content of the memo and also serve as a smooth
connection between the opening and the body of your message.

Background paragraphs serve four important purposes:

1. They provide a concise summary of historical facts that clarify
   why the memo is being written.
2. They link the current document to previous documents the reader has received on the topic.
3. They provide a context for the memo, which is particularly useful for those not intimately acquainted with the details of the
   topic being discussed.
4. They "set up" the rationale in recommendation memos, objectively describing the current situation in terms which make it
   easy for readers to see the advantages of the recommended
   changes.

Background paragraphs, being historical, should be objectively
positioned, focusing on facts. Normally, they should not forward
an argument or refer to the future state of the company.

Begin background paragraphs with a topic sentence which predicts the rest of the paragraph's development. In addition, write
them so their relationship to both the opening and body paragraphs
is clear. For example, the background paragraph below, while relevant to the thesis of the memo, is not positioned to reflect the
author's strategic objective—to show that new copy can build the
business—nor is it clearly linked to the recommendation paragraph.

Example of an Unfocused Background Paragraph

Objective: to gain approval for a new copy strategy for
the entire Sometimes line of products

Background
The existing "rockin and rollin" copy has shown no significant advantage of Sometimes in delivering key acne
prevention benefits. Overall growth in the segment behind this copy has been flat for the past two years,
primarily due to strong competitor heritage advantages
and aggressive expansion of herbal lotions.

Recommendation
We propose changing copy for the entire line of Sometimes products to focus on the theme of "clear skin
improves sex appeal," using supermodels Hunk Smith and
Blaire Benson as spokespersons.

By contrast, note how the background paragraph below has
been written to make a smooth, logical, and persuasive progression
from the objective—to gain approval of a new copy strategy—to the
body of the document.

Example of a Strategically Positioned Background Paragraph

**Objective: to gain approval for a new copy strategy for
the entire Sometimes line of products**

Background: How good copy builds business
Company experience indicates that a well-conceived and
executed copy strategy can grow Sometimes share. For
example, past 6-month share for Sometimes with Jojoba
increased 22% behind "Christy Smith" copy. This copy was
the result of progress we have made in uncovering key
insights motivating our teenage target audience—the
single largest homogeneous group of acne lotion users,
representing 60% of category volume (index 159 vs. population).

The current "rockin and rollin" copy strategy, by contrast, has shown no significant advantage of Sometimes
in delivering key acne prevention benefits. Overall
growth in the segment behind this copy has been flat for
the past two years, primarily due to strong competitor
heritage advantages and aggressive expansion of herbal
lotions.

Recommendation
We propose changing copy for the entire line of Sometimes products to focus on the theme of "clear skin
improves sex appeal," using supermodels Hunk Smith and
Blaire Benson as spokespersons.

Compose Easy-to-Understand Methods Paragraphs

In memos where methods are described, such as reports on the results of experiments, market research, or surveys, a distinct methods section typically follows Background.

- **Methods should be described in list format.**
  This allows readers to easily follow the steps of the method should they wish to replicate the test.
- **Methods should be written in the passive voice.**
  Writing in the passive voice (with the object rather than the subject starting the sentence) also produces an objective tone—suggesting that if the test is replicated, the same results will occur.
- **Methods should be described concisely.**
  The actual test methods should be described concisely in the body of the report, with more detailed descriptions attached.

Example of Methods Paragraph

Objective: to test the ability of Prod X to remove stains from linen and silk ties

Methods
1. Sixteen linen and sixteen silk ties were preheated in either spaghetti sauce or barbecue sauce for 50 minutes.
2. They were then washed with recommended usage of Prod X.
3. Each tie was examined by an independent laboratory for stain removal.
4. Trained raters classified the cleaning of the stains as either satisfactory (95-100% stain removal) or nonsatisfactory (less than 95% stain removal).

Write Scannable Body Paragraphs

If the opening serves as an appetizer to the document, the body constitutes the main course. You prove your case here, expanding on What you have found and Why it is significant, as well as presenting the Data underpinning your position. In all but the simplest memos, develop this section as an argument.

Paradoxically, although you report most of your evidence in the body, research indicates it is one of the least carefully read sections of most memos.

Typical readers scan this portion of a document. Even readers who give memos a thorough analysis typically skim—then scan—the body first before coming back and reading it in detail. Therefore, it is essential that you make this section easy to scan and make its logic extremely clear from scanning alone.

Two techniques—writing paragraphs in What, Why, Details format and underlining key sentences to give readers the ability to scan the logic of the argument—will allow you to compose bodies that are clearly understood both from a scan and from a careful reading.

These methods work because they help readers accomplish three important objectives: to scan through an entire argument efficiently, to understand the overall logic of an argument, and to see immediately the relevance of data to the writer's position.

Topline Topic Sentences   Readers can easily scan memos in which the thesis of each paragraph is distilled to one simple, telegraphic topic sentence. This sentence clarifies, as appropriate, the What or the Why or both, and is underlined. The remainder of the paragraph amplifies that point with facts and logic.

That is, paragraphs begin with the point to be proven, followed by a clarification of the relevance of the point, and then details proving the point. This might best be illustrated by viewing paragraphs as inverted triangles in which you present the WHAT followed by the WHY—the most significant information first—followed by relevant details.

This technique prevents undercommunication, writing without answering the three key questions of What, Why, Proof.

It also inhibits overcommunication because when you start with a thesis, a what and a why, you provide only the data necessary to prove your thesis.

On Your Own   Compare and contrast the two versions of the body of a memo which summarizes the results of a meeting. The first does not use toplining and is not organized in What, Why, Details order, while the second one is. Which do you find easier to scan? To understand? Which is more persuasive?

Meeting Summary, Inductively Organized

Objective: to define ways in which the Systems Engineering Laboratory could help sales close orders

1. Sales pointed out, and we agreed, that the laboratory does not have its systems connected and operational most of the time; that is, it is not kept in a "customer ready" state. Sales can call in from a customer's office asking for a demonstration; and if we have other priorities, we delay getting the lab ready to the point where the sales representatives seldom call for this service any more.

   In essence, Sales made the point that the laboratory would be used more if we kept it up to date, operational, and customer ready. To do so, we agreed to define the expected lab conditions and content and then investigate designating a coordinator for the lab who would be responsible for maintaining it in a customer-ready condition.

2. The other issue we discussed was the reluctance of potential customers to come to Detroit to actually see the product in the laboratory, especially at the early "preselling" stages. Customers are most likely to buy when they get "hands-on" experience in our laboratories. This would be especially useful early in the process before they have either eliminated us from consideration or have sought out a number of bids from competitors.

   When we offer to take them to the Detroit laboratory, customers object to the time and expense lost to send several people away from the office for one or two days and paying their travel expenses. We discussed what it would take to actually move the laboratory to the customer. We thought it would be feasible to move a duplicate lab—on a rotating basis—to each of our six regional sales centers, and agreed to investigate setting up a demonstration project in the Lexington sales center to test the idea. We chose Lexington because it is the closest sales center to Detroit and because it has the smallest sales base of the regional centers, thus offering the least complexity of the other five alternatives. (290 words)

Note how the second example is more concise because it provides only the details necessary to prove the stated thesis. Note also how reframing the toplines in What, Why, Details order helps the writer focus on solutions rather than problems—thus projecting a more proactive image of both the sales and Systems Engineering team members.

Revised, Toplined, Deductively Organized Meeting Summary

Objective: to define ways in which the Systems Engineering Laboratory could help sales close orders

1. <u>We agreed to investigate the feasibility of designating a laboratory coordinator who would be responsible for keeping the Systems laboratory in a customer-ready state</u>.

    Sales pointed out its reps will bring customers to our laboratory on a regular basis only when we can assure them that we can immediately deliver a professional presentation of the benefits of our system. [why] Currently, our lab does not have its system connected and operational most of the time. [data]

2. <u>We also agreed to investigate rotating the laboratory to each of the six regional sales centers, starting with a pilot project in Lexington</u>.

    This will allow sales to give potential customers a realistic demonstration of the benefits of our system at a greatly reduced cost to customers in time and money. [why] Sales experience indicates "hands-on" product demonstrations are a key to customer "buy in" in the often critical early stages of a sale. Customers are currently reluctant to visit the laboratory because they do not want to incur the expense of sending several people to Detroit to experience a full-scale product demonstration. [data]

    If we proceed, we agreed Lexington would be the best test site because of its smaller sales base and proximity to Detroit. [how] (174 words)

As the illustration demonstrates, the combination of toplining and highlighting encourages readers to scan the body of the memo, helping them see the logical structure of the argument. With the logical structure clearly in their minds, they can go back to read the memo for details, on a point-by-point and word-by-word basis.

Evaluate Each Paragraph for Logic and Evidence   For this form of toplining to work as an accurate scan of the document, the following criteria must be met:

1. Toplines are clearly relevant to objectives highlighted in opening.
2. Toplines make sense when read in sequence.

For example, the following right hand example violates both norms. The objective statement in the opening leads to reader expectations that each toplined learning will indicate a way of expanding merchandising at Fruit Market. The toplined sentences do that only indirectly in the poorly written example. Likewise, the toplines do not flow well in sequence in the poorly written examples. By contrast, in the well-written one, they flow logically into one another when scanned.

clearly aligned with objective, logically sequenced toplines

weakly aligned and connected, difficult to scan toplines

`Objective: to learn what action plan our company should follow to expand merchandising at Fruit Market Inc.`

Key Learnings

1. ABC should prove that its product mix appeals to Fruit Market's core markets: the retired segment and the young family segment.	1. Fruit Market's marketing goal is to attract young familes that are fuelling Florida's explosive growth rate.
2. ABC also needs to show that its products will generate strong consumer demand, independent of featuring, at Fruit Market.	2. Fruit Market will not stock a variety of brands unless there is strong consumer demand for that specific brand.
3. ABC should sponsor promotions that move fruit as well as its own products.	3. Tony Frizone, produce manager, suggested we consider that he and his buyers are first and foremost "produce" people.

In addition, in order to make sure your argument meets tests of both reader understanding and good proof, your paragraphs should meet three additional tests.

3. Topline predicts all the information that follows it.

4. First sentences of data section provide immediate proof.

5. Evidence positively proves point.

Note how the poorly written document fails to meet these tests.

1. The topline does not predict key information about retired purchasers being the biggest Fruit Market customer. Readers will thus be unprepared for this information when they read the rest of the paragraph.
2. The first sentence is only tangentially relevant to the topline; it indicates neither Why nor How Fruit Market is marketing to young families, thus failing the "because" test.
3. Its first data, concerning the growth rate of Florida, does not prove its toplined claim, failing the "based on" test.

Clear, Relevant, Positive Proof	Unclear and Incomplete Relationship of Proof to Toplined Claim
ABC should prove that its product mix appeals to FM's core markets: the retired segment and the young family segment.	Fruit Market's marketing goal is to attract young families that are fuelling Florida's explosive growth rate.
FM will view ABC products more favorably if we align them with its marketing strategy. [Why] Specifically, we can show that our 120-oz jug is a good fit with their "young families" program while plus calcium lemonade could support an impactful program targeted at preventing osteoporosis in senior citizens. [application]	Florida's the fastest growing eastern state. [data] FM recognizes that they own the retired segment and will continue to cater to this group. [data] This suggests an opportunity to use the 120 oz jug for a "young families" program and to implement an impactful seniors program targeted at seniors on behalf of plus calcium lemonade. [application]

Write Further Discussion Paragraphs

The Further Discussion section of a document is a place to discuss issues that have not as yet been addressed.

Constraints/Risks A key issue frequently discussed here is risk. After reading about the key reasons to do something, readers are ready to see the limitations of the approach. As a rule of thumb, accompany statements of risk with plans that show you have a means to minimize them.

Example of a Constraints Paragraph

```
ABC is at slight risk from price competition in this
market [What]. We can manage this risk because (1) we
are pricing our product at levels comparable to the
generics and (2) we can achieve target margins and prof-
its at these price points because packaging, manufactur-
ing, and distribution efficiencies have significantly
reduced costs [Why].

Given our low prices and the already slim margins of
competing products, the generics have little room to
sustain price cuts. As a result, our current entry into
this market is projected to be much more successful than
our previous entry, which we withdrew in response to
deep price cuts from generics [Estimate of signifi-
cance].
```

Alternative Solutions Rejected Alternative solutions rejected are also discussed after the body, generally in memos where the reader is expecting to see a different solution than the one offered.

Example of an Alternative Solutions Rejected Paragraph

```
We will not be sending you any double-sided display
cases as we have not as yet found any that meet ABC's
aesthetic standards.
```

Write Follow-up Paragraphs

The follow-up section of a memo is important to completing the logic of your argument. The How, Implementation Steps, are discussed here, since it is only after knowing What is being discussed and Why it is important that readers want to consider the details of implementation.

The action steps must flow logically from all that have preceded them. They must be closely related to the objectives and the argument of the memo. This section should answer three questions: Who does What? When? and Why? including specific data on steps, timing, and responsibilities.

Action steps should be written in list format, so readers can clearly see where one step ends and another begins. Put burdens on yourself and on readers to follow up on action steps, using accessibility statements to encourage others to carry out the steps for which they are responsible and to keep in touch with you on the subject.

Example of Action Steps Paragraph

Action Steps
1. I will draw up a purchase order and circulate it to committee members by March 18.
2. Members are to suggest improvements to the P.O. and submit them to me by March 21.
3. I will send the revised purchase specifications to A. Jackson of purchasing by March 25.
4. A. Jackson has agreed to solicit phone bids from six suppliers and send the committee a report by March 30.

Call me at 555-1234 with concerns or questions.

SUMMARY

To write a good first draft, follow a two-step process. With your outline as a guide, put a rough draft on paper without stopping for revision. This will allow you to view your document as a whole. Then review and rewrite each paragraph to complete your first draft. View each in terms of its function to the reader. Make sure:

- opening paragraphs concisely summarize and forecast the entire document.
- background paragraphs clearly link the opening and body paragraphs.
- methods paragraphs are arranged in a list format.
- body paragraphs are scannable and deductively organized.
- further discussion paragraphs identify and address key reader concerns, including risks and alternatives.
- follow-up paragraphs answer the Who does What? When? questions.

Exercise Write a complete draft of the memo or report you organized in a planning matrix.

CHAPTER 7

Prepare Tables, Charts, and Graphic Aids

Tables, charts, and graphics are often central to clarifying meaning in memos, reports, and proposals. When done well, they aid clarity, conciseness, and organization by illuminating ideas and relationships difficult to express in writing alone. Thus, using them effectively can be important to producing a positive impression on your readers.

This chapter first discusses the value, types, and placement of graphic aids, and then presents guidelines for using tables, charts, and information matrices.

VALUE OF GRAPHIC AIDS

You can use graphic aids to:

- Clarify complex and detailed information and relationships
- Emphasize important information
- Save space when communicating a large body of organized information

- Serve as a summary source for future reference, especially since readers remember images better than words
- Aid in rapid recall of information, yielding immediate access to data

My interviews revealed that managers across functions put a high value on graphic aids, and a surprisingly large number said they typically read the tables and graphics included in a memo before they read the text.

Well-designed graphics are appropriate to both readers and objectives. They need to be composed and edited just as carefully as text. Your challenge is to be aware of the kinds of graphics available to you, their appropriate uses, and the guidelines for the effective design of each.

TYPES OF GRAPHIC AIDS

A variety of graphic aids are available to you. Tables are by far the most frequently used graphic aid in business writing, because writers can use them to organize a good deal of information into a small space. Charts, graphs, exhibits, and information matrices are more commonly used in appendices to reports and as visual aids in oral presentations.

Types and Uses of Visual Aids

Tables:	**organized arrays of numerical data**
Charts, graphs and exhibits:	**pictorial representation of numerical data listings, maps, drawings, etc.**
Information matrices:	**organized arrays of verbal information**

PLACEMENT OF GRAPHIC AIDS

Where to place a graphic aid depends upon its size and the type of information it contains. Data central to your argument should be included in the text, rather than conveyed only in an appended exhibit. Insert "need to know" graphic information that is less than one-third page long into the text. Put larger graphics with important information on the next page of the text. Put graphics with "nice to know" information at the end of the document.

Where to Place Graphic Aids in a Document

		Type of Information it Contains	
		1	2
		INFORMATION CRITICAL TO SUPPORTING THE LOGIC OF THE DOCUMENT	BACKGROUND, SUPPORTING DETAILS NOT OF INTEREST TO MOST READERS; "FYI"-TYPE INFORMATION
Size of Graphic Aid	LESS THAN ONE-THIRD PAGE	Insert into text	Separate attachment at end of document
	ONE-THIRD PAGE OR LARGER	Use separate page. Insert immediately after page containing lead-in	Separate attachment at end of document

WHEN TO USE TABLES

Using tables is your only choice if a great deal of numerical information is discussed, if space is at a premium, and where numerical precision is important. Tables can organize the most data clearly, can show up to five relationships, and take up relatively little space. Tables are best used for collective purposes—the orderly display of collected data.

Better than any other graphic, tables concisely display the complete picture of a situation. Although they are rarely inappropriate, the limitation of tables is that they do not reveal relationships as immediately as graphs.

Given the emphasis put on concise memos and precise numbers, tables are almost exclusively the graphics used in the texts of memos and reports of the companies where I interviewed managers. Below are listed a series of guidelines for designing easy-to-understand and follow tables. Most of these guidelines also apply to the design of pictorial graphics. Each stresses a common principle: you need to both design tables from which readers can easily retrieve information and also provide context, background, and perspective to clarify what data mean in terms of achieving company objectives.

Guidelines for Composing Tables

1. **Develop Tables that are Self-Contained Yet Tied to the Text** Develop tables so they meet two reader objectives: they make sense when read alone and also are preceded by text that allows them to fit logically as part of the full text. (See Table 7–1.) To achieve these goals, label tables clearly.

   - provide fully descriptive titles for all graphics, tell what you are showing or comparing, over what time period your data applies, and what unit of measure is being used.

   - label columns and rows in tables, and vertical and horizontal indices in pictorial graphics, such as bar and line graphs.

   - cite sources, when not obvious.

Table 7.1   Sources of Lexington Plant Sales, 1989–1990

	1989	1990
Sales totals (units)	50,000	60,000
Percent from inventory	40	25
Percent from production	60	75

Source: 1989–1990 Plant Annual Report

2. **Provide Lead-ins to Graphics That Both Evaluate and Analyze the Data That Follows** This will provide a road map to readers of the graphic, directing them to pertinent information and connecting it to your explanation of what the data mean.

   In general, text is best for evaluating and analyzing information, whereas graphics are best for reporting information and showing its relationship to other information. Note in the following example how numbers are interpreted to determine whether a coupon book was effective at changing the purchasing habits of consumers who had moved. The text first evaluates the data, then provides analysis to support the data, including an estimate of its significance. Only then is the raw data presented in table form so readers can see how it supports the preceding analysis. This organizational pattern is identical to the What, Why, Details pattern we suggest you use when composing each paragraph of your messages.

Findings

1. *The Welcome Train Coupon Book (WTCB) was ineffective at generating increases in past 3-month usage among consumers who had moved.*

There were no differences in past 3-month usages even among consumers who had moved within the past year. This suggests targeting movers within 12 months of the move may not be an efficient way to get consumers to switch brands.

Welcome Train Coupon Book—Past 3-Month Purchase %

	Group 1 Movers		Group 2 Movers		Control Group	
	Cpn	Not Cpn	Cpn	Not Cpn	Cpn	Not Cpn
Prod A	36	39	48	40	33	33
Prod B	45	42	41	34	41	38
Prod C	27	24	22	19	22	21
Prod D	48	45	46	48	49	51

3. **Design Tables so that Headings Reflect Logical Groupings of Information** Note in the following before and after examples how much easier readers can follow the logic of the headings of the revised version. In sharp contrast to the original, information in the revised table is grouped under clear headings arranged in a column and row format, clearly relating the three time variables—baseline, test, and follow-up—to the test variables of consumption and weight.

Before: Table Lacking Clear Headings

Exhibit 3 Sequence of Noncaloric Sweetener Consumption and Weight Analysis for a Single Subject in the Mouse Pilot Study

6/01/92 to 8/31/92	Consumed a total of 1 gm of noncaloric sweetener over this entire period
8/25/92 to 8/31/92	Three baseline weights of mouse on 8/25, 8/28, 8/31
8/31/92 to 9/09/92	Consumed 20g noncaloric sweetener/day for 10 days beginning 8/31; weighed on 8/31; 9/6; and 9/9
12/20/92	Final weighing. No noncaloric sweeteners consumed since 9/09

After: Table with Clear Column and Row Headings

Exhibit 3   Sequence of Noncaloric Sweetener Consumption and Weight Analysis for a Single Subject in the Mouse Pilot Study

Period	Noncaloric Sweetener Consumption	Dates of Weighings
Baseline Period 06/01/92 to 08/31/92	Total of 1 gm for entire period	8/25, 8/28
Test Period 08/31/92 to 09/09/92	Total of 20 gr. noncaloric sweetner consumed	8/31*, 9/6, 9/9
Follow-up Period 09/01/92 to 12/20/92	None	12/20/92

* before consuming noncaloric sweetener

4. Use Reduction and Underlining Sparingly Do not reduce numbers to the point where they become difficult to read, or use so much underlining it clutters your table, as illustrated in the hard-to-follow table below.

<u>March/April/May 1992 Business Results</u>
<u>(Indices vs. Year Ago)</u>

<u>Shipments</u> <u>(Avg. per March-May '92)</u>	<u>AM'79</u> <u>Share</u>	<u>Consumption</u>
841.4 (114)	18.6 (107)	1355 (114)

<u>AM92 Merchanding Results</u>
<u>(Indices vs. year ago and balance 1991-92)</u>

	<u>Share</u> <u>Feature</u> <u>100 retail calls</u>	<u>Level</u> <u>Lineage</u>	<u>Feature</u>	<u>Lineage</u>	<u>May displays for</u> <u>Lineage</u>
ABC	12.3 (65)	13.5 (75)	33.0 (77)	1225 (68)	11 (69)

5. Design Tables so Readers Can Quickly Find Relevant Information Readers need to immediately find the data in tables that have been discussed in the text of the report. To illustrate the difficulties readers can have when tables are not designed for easy retrievability, do the following exercise.

On Your Own Evaluate both the textual and the design problems in the monthly report that follows. Answer these questions as an aid to your evaluation:

1. Does the opening paragraph provide a good summary of the entire report?
2. Can you easily scan this report? Are analyses of what data mean easy to find and to retrieve?
3. Can you easily find and evaluate the actions the brand is taking in response to the data it has presented?
4. Does the table conform to principles of good document design?

Based on your answers to these questions, suggest ways this report and the table in it could be improved. Compare your revisions to those that were made in the "After" version of this report.

"Before" Report

Subj: Cigarette Category Share Results, January-February 1993

This report summarizes January-February 1993 category share results.

		ABC Results		
		vs. prior 2-mos	vs. prior 6-mos	vs.
	JF'89			YAG
HERO	21%	22%	20%	113%
Meth	10	11	9	2
Reg	11	11	11	11
WAYNE	30	27	27	31
ROANOKE	38%	36%	39%	42%
Mkt grth	-2.0%	-1.8%	-1.4%	-2.0%

MARKET—In Jan-Feb '89 total cigarette market was down 2.0% compared to one year ago.

HERO—Hero's share is up 8% vs. year ago, but -1% vs. previous period. The loss traces largely to a government report questioning the safety of menthol flavoring of cigarettes and partly to a pricing disparity, with menthol costing $.02 per pack more than regular. We are rebuilding our menthol business by beginning with a joint regular/menthol merchandising strategy and by continuing our focus on joint merchandising and couponing activity.

WAYNE—Wayne share is down 1% vs. year ago and up 3% vs. previous period. Share growth so far has been fueled by the Jumbo carton introduction, although business remains driven by the regular carton (90% of sales). In addition, a pricing disparity of $2.00 per carton has hindered share growth. We are introducing the Jumbo carton on an international basis in June, given its national success. To address pricing, we will implement a $3.00

per-carton cash refund to supplement an already strong promotion plan.

ROANOKE—Roanoke's share was down 4% from year ago but up 2% from the previous period. This increase from previous period reflects higher spending levels ($10.00 per case) resulting in a strong pricing advantage versus Wayne and parity with Hero. Additionally, targeted couponing hurt both Hero and Wayne.

MARCH–APRIL FORECAST—We expect a total share of 50% with Hero share accounting for 22% of the market and Wayne declining to 28%, due to reduced spending prior to the international rollout of the Jumbo carton in June.

"After" Report

Subj: ABC Cigarette Category Share Results, Jan-Feb 1993

This analyzes January-February 1993 cigarette category share results as they compare with previous results in the past year. Overall, our share of 51% (5) was up 1% versus year ago, and down 2% from the previous 2-month period. We forecast a 50% share in March-April 1993.

Recent Share Trends for Cigarette Category

		JF'89	vs. prior 2-mos	vs. prior 6-mos	vs. YAG
1.	HERO	21%	22%	20%	13%
2.	Meth	10	11	9	2
3.	Reg	11	11	11	11
4.	WAYNE	30	27	27	31
5.	TOTAL ABC	51%	49%	47%	44%
6.	ROANOKE	38%	36%	39%	42%
7.	All other	11	15	14	14
8.	Total other	49%	51%	53%	55%

Total Market Growth in Cigarette Market

		JF'89	vs. prior 2-mos	vs. prior 6-mos	vs. YAG
9.	Mkt Grth	-2.0%	-1.8%	-1.4%	-2.0%

Analysis	Action
MARKET In JF'89 the total cigarette market (9) was -2.0% vs. year ago, largely because of a decline in the 16-24 old age group.	We will continue to analyze the influence of age demographics on our market.
HERO Hero share (1) at 21% is +8% vs. year ago, and -1% vs. previous	We are rebuilding our menthol business by introducing a

period, a decline attributable to a loss in menthol (2) business.

The loss traces largely to a government report questioning the safety of menthol flavoring of cigarettes and partly to a pricing disparity, with menthol costing $.02 per pack more than regular.

WAYNE

Wayne share (4) of 30% is +3% vs. previous period, reflecting growth behind a Jumbo carton introduction and share is -1% vs. year ago because of pricing disparities.

Share growth so far has been fueled by the Jumbo carton, although business remains driven by the regular carton (90%). In addition, a pricing disparity of $2.00 per carton has hindered share growth.

ROANOKE

Roanoke's share (6) of 38% was +2% versus previous period, due largely to increased advertising and promotion. Roanoke's share is -4% vs. year ago.

The gain versus previous period reflects higher spending levels ($10.00 per case) resulting in a strong price advantage vs. Wayne and parity with Hero. Additionally, targeted couponing hurt both Hero and Wayne.

joint regular/menthol merchandising strategy and by increasing our focus on couponing to attract price conscious users.

We are going to introduce the Jumbo carton on an international basis in June, given its national success. To address pricing, we will implement a $3.00 per-carton cash refund to supplement an already strong promotion plan.

MARCH/APRIL FORECAST We project a total share of 50%, with Hero share accounting for 22% of the market, and Wayne declining to 28%, due to reduced spending prior to our increased spending behind the international rollout of the Jumbo carton in June.

Here are some of the principles of good design you may have identified.

a. **Design text and tables to make it easy for readers to understand the relationship of the data in tables to company objectives, the data in the text, and projected action steps.**

Opening: the revised opening better meets reader needs for a
concise summary of the entire document because it
summarizes the report's most important information,
including a forecast for the next monthly period. By
contrast, the opening of the original simply states
the topic of the report and immediately introduces
the table to readers, leaving them with little focus on
what the information means.

Body/   since the body of the original is only marginally high-
Action   lighted, readers find out little information when they
Steps: scan it. For example, they cannot quickly find out
key Whys nor can they easily find what steps the
company is taking in response to these results. By
contrast, readers can easily find this information in
the revised version.

b. **Group comparable data together; highlight key numbers and
ideas. Number or letter columns or rows to make information
easier to retrieve.** This makes it easier for readers to make logical comparisons and transitions among categories of data. To
group information, provide logical breaks in spacing rows, and
use second and third tiers where appropriate.

For example, in analyzing the after document, you probably observed that information is more logically arranged than in the
original. ABC's products are grouped together and totalled separately from the rest of the market as well as from information
on growth in the cigarette market. In addition, lines of white
space separate the three tiers of information, visually reinforcing
the three categories of information.

In addition, in the revision,

- **Sideline headings** clearly indicate where the results of each
cigarette brand are discussed.

- **Underlined and toplined paragraphs** allow readers to scan
both key results and an interpretation of why those results
occurred.

■ **Parallel columns of action steps next to key points of analysis** allow readers to see, when reading across, what action is being taken in response to each result; and when reading down, what total set of action steps are being undertaken by Brand groups.

c. **Highlight key numbers if they are discussed in the text and would be difficult to find in a table.** Note how in the revised Wayne Cigarette Monthly report the sales of Menthol and Regular Hero cigarettes are indented to indicate they are a subset of total Hero sales. You may also use boxing, underlining, or boldface to highlight key numbers.

d. **Number or letter columns, rows, or both in complex tables.** This makes it easier for readers to locate relevant information. See how much more quickly readers can find tabular information when the text tells them exactly which row to read.

On Your Own   Revise a table from a memo or report you have received so it better meets the tests of clarity, relevance, emphasis, and easy retrievability.

6. Explain Numbers Clearly   Take particular care in reporting numbers. To give readers adequate information to understand what your numbers mean, use the following guidelines.

Guidelines for Using Numbers

1. **Use an appropriate, recent base period**: six months to a year for results that are stable; monthly or bimonthly when results are trending up or down significantly. This will allow readers to see an accurate version of what has happened.

Stable results
Results prior to product tampering scare
JJ 88   JD 88   JJ 89   JD 89

Volatile results
Results following product tampering scare
JF 90   MA 90   MJ 90   JA 90   SO 90   ND 90

2. **Use actual numbers and clarify them with percentages comparing them to other results.** This will put the results in perspective. For example, a report that 1,600 cases were shipped daily as a result of a new schedule is put in perspective when readers are

informed that this total is 15% above the average of the previous schedule.

3. **Footnote items which help explain results.** For example, if share and shipment have risen dramatically during a time of substantial price reduction, the price reduction should be footnoted.

4. **Examine trends as well as averages.** In many instances, trends will be far more significant than averages, as the following example illustrates.

```
Volume declined an average of 1.3% in 1990 for all
cloth diaper brands. This decline is largely a re-
sponse to the declining birth rate, especially among
those who purchase premium brands.
```

5. **Use up-to-date cost numbers; identify the source of information.** Cost figures should be recent, not more than 90 days old. Sources of information should be identified.

On Your Own   Read the paragraph below. What additional information would you gather? What additional insight would you lend to it?

```
The category has lost volume in the past year, probably
in response to EPA reports of the negative environmental
effects of chlorine bleach. In addition, results indi-
cate a major loss of share for ABC cleanser since XYZ
introduced Prod X with an anti-clog nozzle in April
1992. ABC experienced an erratic pattern of recovery,
with share increases in response to periodic high-value
coupons and share declines subsequent to couponing
events.
```

Compare your revisions to those suggested below:

Suggested revisions:

- Show annual category volume results before and after EPA report, including a calculation of percentage loss. Footnote date of original EPA report.

- Show 2-month share and volume results for ABC cleanser for 1992. Footnote timing of introduction of Prod X as well as of ABC high-value coupons. Use percentages to clarify degrees of gain and loss.

- To give perspective to the issue, (1) show results of company responses to similar situations in the past, and (2) cite expert testimony or results of consumer research to document claim that EPA report and Product X delivery systems led to category and ABC share declines.

WHEN TO USE CHARTS AND GRAPHS

Charts or graphs are generally more effective than tables when:

- You have sufficient space to include them
- Relative relationships are more important than precise values
- You want to demonstrate a simple relationship in a way that is immediately comprehensible. Pictorial graphics typically become increasingly confusing the more data and more relationships that you attempt to demonstrate.

Guidelines for Charts and Graphs

This section first provides specific insight into individual types of pictorial graphics. It discusses when to use charts and graphs followed by a chart that describes the most commonly used pictorial graphics, the objectives for which their use is most appropriate, and the rationale explaining why this graphic works in these situations. (See table on pages 110 and 111.)

VALUE OF INFORMATION MATRICES

The information matrix, a highly valuable, often underused visual, combines text with a tabular format. These graphics often work better for clarifying complex relationships than conventional linear text, because they allow readers to answer different sets of questions depending on whether they read down or across, as illustrated on page 112.

For example, in reading down the first two columns of the Tasty Bar three-year business plan, the reader gets a sense of the strategic flow of the business plan. In reading down the third and fourth columns, the reader can see the tactical coherence of the strategic implementation and the expected results. When reading across rows, the reader sees on a yearly basis the relationship between a strategy, tactics, and expected profit.

In addition, the ABC competitive positioning matrix shown on page 113 is used to summarize information in a competitive analysis

Major Chart Forms

If You Want to Show	Use This Graphic	It Works Because It	Picture of Graphic
relationships that form a larger structure, such as the flow of materials, the progress of a project, or reporting relationships	flowchart	• reduces the number of sentences needed to explain a process • allows readers to concentrate on one step at a time • helps readers distinguish relevant from irrelevant information	Design Build Test Ship
how things get done over time	time chart bar chart line graph	• places actions visually in a chronological sequence; effectively shows relationships of concurrent actions	Feb Mar Apr May
ranking of quantitative information	bar chart	• groups numbers by category, allowing readers to see immediately how numbers compare	A B C D E 1960 1970 1980 1990 Market Shares
trends of growth and decline over time	line graph; combination line/bar chart; stacked bar chart	• clearly shows trends over time, including degree of growth or decline	Revenue Cash Flow 0 Expenses

110

Major Chart Forms (continued)

If You Want to Show	Use This Graphic	It Works Because It	Picture of Graphic
changes of component parts as part of total	stacked bar chart	▪ shows total as full bars, components as subdivided bars	
percentages, shares, proportions	pie chart stacked bar chart	▪ immediately shows proportions of parts to the whole	
correlation	scatter chart	▪ shows how a change in one set of data affects a second set of data	
frequency distribution	bar chart line graph	▪ shows frequency of distribution over time intervals.	
industry or product position	positioning matrix	▪ shows relationships of two variables in a matrix format; can be particularly effective in displaying size differences	Product Price / Distribution outlets (A, B, C, D)

Tasty Bar Three-Year Business Plan

Fiscal Year	Strategic Elements	Planned Initiatives	Volume Potential
1992/93	Leverage historical product and user strengths	■ Revised brand strategy to focus on "Low cost" product strength and "Kids Love It" copy ■ Development and shipment of Tasty Bar "S" With Peanut Butter	+19%
	Spend to the business	■ Initiate Top 40 Program ■ Air "Kids Love It" copy in districts comprising 80% of volume	
1993/94	Leverage historical product and user strengths	■ Ensure existing Tasty Bar user conversion to and new user trial of Tasty Bar "S" product ■ Develop and ship Tasty Bar "H" product improvements	+4%
	Leverage user candy needs	■ Implement "low cost/kids love it" creative exploration into copy	
	Spend to the Business	■ Improve distribution/trade support among top 40 accounts	
1994/95	Leverage historical product and user strengths	■ Garner new user trial of Tasty Bar "H"	+10%
	Spend to the business	■ Expand high-district sales media test	

Analysis of Current Competitive Position For ABC

Areas of Competition	Who Has the Advantage?		Priority Action Needed	
	ABC	Competitive Brand	Build Advantage	Eliminate Disadvantage
1. Positioning (What the brand stands for that provides the basis for consumer choice)				
2. Product Performance Product Aesthetics				
3. Package Performance Package Aesthetics				
4. Copy				
5. Media				
6. Distribution/Shelf Space				
7. Price				
8. Feature				
9. Display				
10. Delivered Cost				
11. Support				
12. Volume/Market Share				

report. Reading across answers the questions: is the product a winner on this criterion? Does the company have the appropriate response? Reading down answers questions about the total standing of the product across criteria and the total package of offensive and defensive actions the brand is taking in response to its analysis of its situation. In short, it highlights the key information readers want to know: where does the product rank on key variables and what is the company going to do in response?

SUMMARY

Readers often pay more attention to graphic aids than they do to written text. So good writers take as much care in preparing tables, charts, and information matrices as they do in preparing written text. In particular, be sure your graphic aids are:

1. Appropriate to both your readers and your text, and are designed so they can be easily found and easily understood
2. Self-contained, yet tied to the text
3. Introduced by lead-ins that explain the significance of the information in the graphic
4. Designed so readers can easily find relevant information.

Exercise   Read the information below and summarize it in an information graphic.

One useful way to gain insight into the nature of Tasty Bar users is to use psychographics, defining user demographic characteristics by paired insights into the kind of people who eat Tasty Bars as compared to the kind of people who eat competitors' bars.

The Tasty Bar consumer is typically a teen or older than 45, whereas consumers of competitive bars generally fall in the 18–44 age range. Tasty Bar consumers typically live in small to mid-size areas, such as small towns, rural areas, and suburban communities. Family income typically is less than $20K per year and often the father is the sole breadwinner. Consumers of competitors' candy bars are typically affluent urbanites with two-career families.

In terms of personality, Tasty Bar consumers are "we people," traditional, conservative, friendly, approachable, comfortable, practical, family-oriented, responsible, and not status conscious. By contrast, consumers of competitor bars tend to be "I people," experimental, pretentious, extravagent, independent, innovative, and status conscious.

Socially, Tasty Bar consumers are involved in family and community activities, enjoy casual social engagements such as picnics and bridge clubs, vacation in the same spots, shop in mid-range stores, and drive a Chevy. Consumers of competitive bars typically are involved in self-oriented pursuits, such as yoga or decorating, attend intellectual events, explore new places, and drive a Volvo or BMW.

Tasty Bar consumers are casual, conventional, neat, and unpretentious; whereas consumers of competitive products are flamboyant, overstated, trendy, wild, extravagant, elegant, and for one competitor's bar, frumpy.

How did you do? Compare your answer to the one following.

Psychographic Analysis of Tasty Bar Consumer

Who is the Tasty Bar Consumer?	Who is Not?
Age	
■ 45+, teen	■ 18–44
Demographics	
■ Lives in small to mid-size midwestern town, suburban or rural area	■ Urbanite
■ Lower middle/middle class (less than $20K in family income)	■ Affluent
■ May work	■ Career-oriented
Personality	
■ Traditional, conservative	■ Fly-by-night or experimental
■ Friendly, approachable, comfortable	■ Aloof or pretentious
■ "We" person	■ "Me" person
■ Practical	■ Frivolous or extravagant
■ Wants good value in candy	■ Flamboyant, glamorous or sexy
■ Wants to fit in	■ Stands out
■ Candy is an expression of love	■ Candy purchases are a means of self-expression
■ Family-oriented	■ Independent
■ Responsible, attentive	■ Innovative

(continued)

Who is the Tasty Bar Consumer?	Who is Not?
Socially	
▪ Involved in family and community activities—PTA, school board, church	▪ Involved in self-oriented pursuits
▪ Enjoys casual social affairs that focus on family—school functions, picnics, bridge clubs	▪ Attends stuffy, intellectual or formal engagements
▪ Shops at mid-range department stores	▪ Shops at boutiques or Saks Fifth Avenue
▪ Vacations at same spot	▪ Interested in exploring new places
▪ Drives a Chevy	▪ Owns a Volvo/sports car
Personality Orientation	
▪ Becoming	▪ Dowdy/frumpy
▪ Casual/informal	▪ Formal/elegant
▪ Moderate	▪ Extravagant
▪ Conventional	▪ Trendy
▪ Neat	▪ Wild
▪ Simple/comfortable	▪ Elaborate/overstated
▪ Unpretentious	▪ Flamboyant

Exercise Revise Table 7–2 for use as a stand alone exhibit. Its objective is to analyze national trends by brand and by size, with a particular focus on the 24 oz. and 2 lb. large sizes.

Table 7–2 Margarine Share Trends by Size (Denver Market)

	JFM'90	OND'90	AMJ'91	Index (AMJ'91 vs. JFM'90)
Total Zep	22.0	25.8	21.9	100
Total Creamy	17.4	11.3	15.0	86
Total Cinderella	16.1	13.6	21.6	134
Total Smith's	0.0	0.0	4.1	N/A
Total 10-ounce**	35.1	31.6	42.6	121
Total 16-ounce**	14.0	13.8	15.3	109
Total 24-ounce**	4.2	3.2	2.9	69
Total 2-pound**	2.1	1.9	1.8	86
Zep 24-ounce	2.1	2.0	1.8	86
Zep 2-pound	1.2	1.2	1.1	92
Creamy 24-ounce	1.2	0.8	0.6	50
Creamy 2-pound	1.0	0.7	0.7	70
Cinderella 24-ounce	0.9	0.4	0.5	56

* Smith's measured from JFM'91 introduction
** National Brands

How did you do? Compare your revision to the one that follows.

After:

Table 7–3   Margarine Share Trends (Denver Market)

Analysis: National brands have grown share 13% over the last nine months with Cinderella making the largest gains. Large size brands declined significantly in volume across brands.

	(A) JFM'90	(B) OND'90	(C) AMJ'91	(D) Index (AMJ'90 vs. JFM'91)
Overall Brand Shares—%				
Zep	22.0	25.8	21.9	100
Creamy	17.4	11.3	15.0	86
Cinderella	16.1	13.6	21.6	134
Smith's	0.0	0.0	4.1	N/A
Total National Brands	55.5	50.7	62.6	113
Shares By Size (National brands combined)—%				
10-ounce	35.1	31.6	42.6	121
16-ounce	14.0	13.8	15.3	109
24-ounce	4.2	3.2	2.9	69
24-ounce Zep	2.1	2.0	1.8	86
24-ounce Creamy	1.2	0.8	0.6	50
24-ounce Cinderella	0.9	0.4	0.5	56
2-pound	2.1	1.9	1.8	86
2-pound Zep	1.2	1.2	1.1	92
2-pound Creamy	1.0	0.7	0.7	70

PART III

EDIT AND REVISE

CHAPTER 8

Edit for Logical Consistency and Reader Trust

Once you have written a good first draft of a message, edit it to make sure that you have represented your position as clearly and accurately as possible. Do not regard editing as a chore—rather view it as a form of quality control that assures you that readers will not be distracted by seeming inconsistencies or by unclear or verbose expressions of ideas.

To edit effectively, put your memo or report aside and then come back to it. This will help put you in your reader's place so you can read your memo or report as if you were looking at it for the first time.

Specifically, pursue five objectives:

1. To make sure your argument is internally consistent
2. To gain reader trust
3. To project positive images of yourself, your department, and your company
4. To express your message concisely; and
5. To write to avoid litigation

This chapter discusses the first two objectives, logical consistency and reader trust; Chapter 9 discusses image and conciseness; Chapter 10 writing to avoid litigation; and Chapter 11 reviewing your memos and those of your coworkers.

EDIT FOR LOGICAL CONSISTENCY

Few things bother perceptive readers more than apparent logical inconsistencies. They suggest the writer is guilty of muddled thinking. While using a planning matrix will help you eliminate most logical flaws, make sure you have stated your objectives clearly and consistently, and also check the internal logic of your arguments.

Position Objectives Clearly and Consistently

As you revise your drafts, check to make sure you have positioned your objectives clearly and positively—and that your opening both accurately predicts and is consistent with the development of the rest of the message.

Position Objectives Clearly and Positively That is, be sure you clarify the proper cause-and-effect relationship between what you are doing and the higher level company objective to which it contributes. This will demonstrate that you clearly understand the relationship between your job and the overall company objectives to which it is to be aligned.

Notice in the example below how the initial statement of objectives does not show the causal connection between reach and building share at low cost, the ultimate brand objective.

Improper Positioning of Objectives
Our objective is to expand the reach of the Sometimes International program on a minimal budget and build the Brand's business.

By contrast, the revision makes the relationship explicit.

Proper Positioning of Objectives
Our objective is to build the Brand's business at low cost by expanding the reach of the Sometimes's International program.

Be Sure Your Opening is Aligned with the Rest of the Message Your opening statement suggests a path of development and follow-up action which the rest of the message must fulfill.

See how, in the following examples, inconsistencies between the opening statement and subsequent statements can puzzle readers. In the first example, the ultimate objective is stated in the opening and, only later, the means to that objective in the body. As a result, readers are forced to shuttle back and forth between these paragraphs to make clear causal connections between ideas. In the revision this cause-and-effect relationship is clarified in the opening paragraph.

Unclear Relationship of Original Opening and Recommendation Paragraphs	Clearly Revised Opening Paragraph
(opening) The objective of our efforts is to build trial and continuity among purchasers. (body paragraph) The study's goal is to determine the best number and value of coupons to build loyalty among consumers.	(opening) We request your approval of a series of tests to determine the best number and value of coupons for building long-term consumer loyalty. These learnings will help the Brand build trial and continuity among purchasers.

In the second example, the original opening paragraph is misleading. It does not tell readers it wants their approval, nor does it tell them that the new definition will be used for evaluating new product ideas. Readers find these requests in the final rather than the opening paragraph, and thus must now reread the memo to get a clear idea of whether the proposal merits support.

The revision, on the other hand, clarifies what the writer expects of readers in the opening paragraph, thus allowing readers to immediately see if the memo's evidence and argument support the recommendation.

Original Opening Does Not Predict Action Steps	Revised Opening Predicts Action Steps
This provides an overview of Brand and Agency thinking about what Pretend should uniquely stand for. We are planning to establish a distinct brand image for Pretend versus its premium competitors. (closing) With Management agreement, this definition for Pretend will provide guidance for future advertising and provide a basis for evaluating new product ideas marketed under the Pretend label.	The Pretend Team requests approval of a definition of a new distinct brand image for Pretend vs. its premium brand competitors. This definition will guide new advertising and provide a standard for evaluating new product ideas to be marketed under the Pretend name. (closing) May we have your approval of this new definition?

Check Each Argument for Internal Logic

In addition, test the internal logic of your argument. See if data actually support the inferences you have derived from them.

Alternative Inferences   Ask yourself if alternative inferences are better explanations of the data. Notice how different the appropriate action steps are depending on which explanation is used to explain the decline in summer output.

Different Inferences From Same Data

Stated Data	Inference	Alternative Inference
Output is higher in the winter, spring, and fall than in summer	The summer heat slows down the pace of work. We need to air-condition the plant.	Substitute workers are less efficient than the vacationing workers they have replaced. We need a better training program for temporary workers.

Intervening Variables   Check if intervening variables would prevent the cause and effect as you have described them. Ask if any key factors have been ignored.

Intervening Variables Can Limit the Validity of Conclusions

Data	Initial Conclusion	Intervening Variable
Dust levels remained the same with the new formula as compared with the old.	New formula failed to reduce dust levels in the plant.	Poorly calibrated instrumentation and operator error may mean the data are invalid.

EDIT TO GAIN AUDIENCE TRUST

In addition to making sure your argument is logically compelling, also make sure your argument is psychologically compelling, one that allows you to establish trust with your readers.

Establishing trust comes from an accurate understanding of reader needs and perspectives. Writing or speaking persuasively is harder than it initially appears, because as S. I. Hayakawa and other general semanticists have pointed out, meaning resides in people, not words.

For example, Deborah Tannen, author of *You Just Don't Understand*, shows in her study of male and female communication, writers and speakers "co-create" meaning with their audiences. Each interprets the meaning of verbal and nonverbal signals differently depending on such differences as gender, audience knowledge, interest, and expectations; message content; author's purpose; the situation in which the writing or speaking is done; and the medium through which the message is communicated.

To achieve your own objectives and also communicate persuasively to a particular audience requires you to take a "dual perspective," one in which you look at the situation from your own point of view and from that of likely readers and listeners. This becomes particularly important when you are communicating with people from different functions or at different levels in the organization.

Meaning Resides in People, Not Words

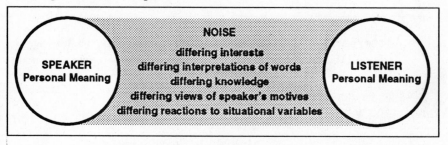

You initially analyzed your audience when filling out your planning sheet. Go one step further as you edit initial drafts of your messages. To develop as accurate a picture as possible of your audience, take an inventory of their roles, responsiblities, expectations, and preferences.

Specifically answer these questions:

1. What are the needs of my primary and secondary readers and listeners? The chart lists seven common needs, consistent with the findings of three highly regarded psychologists, Maslow, Herzberg, and McClelland.

2. How does my position relate to theirs?

3. What issues do they expect to see discussed? Is my audience favorable, neutral, or hostile to my thesis?

4. What are their stylistic preferences? What cultural differences should I take into account?

For simple messages answer these questions briefly; for complex issues, answer them in more detail on a chart similar to the one which follows. Use your answers to help revise your memos, so that they best meet your readers' psychological needs.

Audience Analysis Inventory

Who Is My Audience?
Key decision makers:
Potential readers and listeners:

What Are Their Needs?
Power
Image
Achievement
Affiliation
Safety
Security
Procedural Order
Other

How Does My Position Relate to Theirs?
What are our similarities and differences with regard to:
Function
Objectives
Organizational roles
Visions of the future

What Issues Should I Discuss?
Knowledge of topic
Interest in topic
Predisposition on this subject
Expectations about what you will write

What Stylistic, Historical, and Cultural Considerations Should I Take into Account?

Diction:	Technical language or simple words?
Tone:	A passive, impersonal style or a forceful, conversational tone? Direct or indirect opening? Formal or informal approach?
Length:	An absolute one page limit? Or longer, if justifiable?
Appearance:	Boxed summary at top of page? Large or small typeface? Wide or narrow margins? Crossouts or perfection?

The remainder of this chapter illustrates how to edit for audience analysis. Specifically, it illustrates how to use your knowledge of readers to revise opening paragraphs, where trust is first established.

Who Are My Listeners and Readers and What Are Their Needs?

Your readers and listeners will vary according to their needs. Some will look at messages and ask themselves how they relate to their relative power within the organization. The primary concern of others will be its effect on the people in the organization. Some will view your message through a task-oriented focus: how it relates to getting jobs done. Others will be concerned that a proper procedural order is followed or that safety and security needs are met.

Understanding your audience is crucial in these areas as the following case study illustrates.

Case Study One   In this case study, the author is responding to a request for information. The initial letter is filled with the language of rejection, words such as *unfortunately, regret, but*, and *limited*. And it does not respond positively to the reader's request: that the literature requested will be sent at a future date.

The author revised the document to meet the key reader expectation: to receive answers to questions about the pool cleaner immediately and to provide the writer with the full information as soon as possible. In addition, by removing the negative words of the original, he improved the tone of the letter.

Example One: The Language of Rejection

Before
I am writing to respond to your March 3 letter in which
you express an interest in H-530 pool cleaner. Unfortunately, I regret to inform you that we are out of all
literature on H-530, but I am sending you related information which may be of limited assistance to you. I hope
this answers your needs.

After
I will send the literature on H-530 pool cleaner you
requested in two weeks, as soon as I receive a fresh
supply. If you need specific information sooner, please
call me at 555-1111 and I will be happy to answer any

questions to the best of my ability. Under separate cover, I have sent related literature on the safe use of pool cleaning chemicals.

Case Study Two   In the second case study, a people-oriented sales manager is writing to an achievement and task-oriented vice president for sales. When he read his initial draft, the sales manager realized the vice president would view it as unjustifiably optimistic, focusing on short-term tactical thinking, rating human factors too highly, and reflecting intuitive rather than strategic thinking.

His revision is much more strategically focused and rationally argued, using data and causal reasoning to support its conclusion.

Example Two: Adapting to Reader Needs

Before

We believe we can reach a 10 share in Memphis by May 31. We have a good plan, an enthusiastic sales staff, and a superior product. We are having a sales meeting to really motivate each sales person to do his or her best in making this plan a major success.

After

To reach the company objective of a 10 share in Memphis Region 26 by May 31, sales has developed a plan of action similar to one that we successfully employed in the Houston market. We will employ three strategies: deep-cut feature pricing, product sampling, and sponsorship of a Nascar race. Past experience indicates these techniques can significantly and cost effectively increase share by increasing trial and reach.

This consumer-oriented stategy is designed specifically to offset the distribution, trade dollar, share of voice, and display advantages of the two market leaders with the trade.

How Does My Position Relate to Theirs?

Look at the relationship of your position to those receiving your message. Going through and considering objectives, personal roles, functions, divisional roles and visions will help you see issues through your audience's eyes, thus allowing you to better show the relationship of your objectives to audience objectives. In particular, it will help you position your message so it is most appealing and useful to your audience. For example, it can help you know what types of issues to discuss, as well as what level and type of information the person expects to receive.

Case Study Three   In the following case study, a management accountant wanted to convince upper management that brands should be charged for the additional warehousing, distribution, and set-up costs of special display packaging. He submitted the draft below to his manager.

His manager returned the memo for revision, pointing out that it was not well-adapted to the likely responses of those affected by it, responses such as: why should key decision makers care whether or not these costs are equitably distributed? Won't this plan add time and complexity to an already complex process and inhibit timely and creative responses to the initiatives of competitors? In short, if it isn't broken, why should we fix it?

Example Three:
Weak Adaptation to Audience Roles and Objectives

Before
My analysis indicates that warehousing and distribution costs are unjustly distributed among brands, depending on how often they use special display packaging to promote their products. To be equitable, accounting should be called upon to estimate the total additional cost of each special pack and assign those costs to the brands that incur them.

Upon reflection, the writer anticipated a number of key questions and objections and modified his writing in response to these issues. His changes included modifying his proposal to show sensitivity to the issues of time and complexity, showing a consensus among audit department employees, proving alignment with higher management objectives, and showing the plan worked successfully in other locations.

Example Three:
Improved Adaptation to Audience Roles and Objectives

After
The Audit department proposes assessing a standard fee of 50¢ per case to brands each time they use special packs to promote their products. This simple and easy-to-implement tool will help meet a key total quality

objective of more precisely assessing profits and losses for each brand. It does so by more equitably allotting costs across brands according to the warehousing, set-up, and distribution costs these brands incur through special pack promotions. Similar standard assessments are successfully used in our European facilities, where experience indicates they have produced significant company benefits.

What Issues Should Be Discussed?

Once you consider the relationship of your objectives to audience objectives, consider what your audience knows, feels, and expects regarding you and your topic.

In the following case study, a finance executive needs approval of the director of the Management Systems Division to purchase a personal computer. The MSD director is highly concerned with security, cost-benefits, and procedural order. He prefers a formal tone. Once aware of this, the finance executive changed the opening paragraph of her original proposal.

The revised opening more effectively engenders trust because it anticipates reader questions, providing a high level of detail concerning costs, paybacks, timing, concurrences, training, security, and departmental benefits. The author achieved a more formal tone by changing from the first to third person, using the passive voice in the second sentence, and employing formal diction, with words such as *sited, on line, negotiated, projected payback, in-house training,* and *concur.*

Example Four: Adapting to Reader Preferences

Before
I am writing to request approval of a purchase order for $3,200 to purchase an ABM 386 PC and XYZ financial analysis software. The computer will allow me to complete financial reports faster, more accurately, and more perceptively.

After
The Financial Analysis Department requests approval to purchase an ABM 386 PC and XYZ financial analysis software. The computer will be sited at the desk of J. Jones and put on line within 30 days of approval. Use of the PC will meet departmental objectives of faster, more accurate, and more detailed monthly reports. The department negotiated total costs of $3,200, with a projected

payback of 4 months. This total includes 16 hours of
training for Ms. Jones, including in-house training on
proper security procedures. R. Ragu (technical services)
has reviewed this proposal and concurs with it.

What Stylistic, Historical, and Cultural Considerations Should I Take into Account?

Plan your document so it conforms to the stylistic, historical, and
cultural expectations of key decision makers. Since organizations
operate in multicultural settings, your messages should take into
account such differences between audiences. Cultures differ among
countries, regions of countries, industries, business functions, and
organizational rank, to name some of the most prominent cultural
considerations.

In many organizations wide cultural gaps separate employees
in technical areas from the rest of the organization. Computer and
natural scientists, for example, are often viewed in the rest of the
organization as being narrow, impersonal, overly technical, and
lacking in human insight.

As part of your analysis, review documents and presentation
summaries that have been historically successful with your audience. This will allow you to better understand reader norms for
documents and presentations, including style, length, appearance,
graphics, use and types of evidence, organizational structure, re-
current themes, and positioning of arguments.

Below are before and after examples of introductions written
by a computer scientist. The first confirms many of the worst ste-
reotypes nontechnical employees have of computer scientists. The
revision is much more responsive to the needs of readers for brev-
ity, simplicity, and directness. It begins with a concise imperative
sentence clarifying exactly how readers are expected to respond,
followed by clear statements of Whys and Whens.

Example Five: Adapting to Stylistic and Cultural Differences

Before
In MIS literature, largely inspired by SHARE and PROLIX
guidelines on database management concerning the selection of information management systems, there has been
much discussion of the function and organization of
databased activities within for-profit and not-for-
profit organizations. In for-profit organizations, it is
generally recommended that decisions be decentralized by

division, but only within well-established corporate guidelines approved by a committee of business managers and MIS professionals. While this is a good guideline for companies in general, it needs to be adapted specifically to the needs of individual companies.

Currently, the company has no standard to govern the purchase of MIS equipment by department. Yet 6782 PCs have already been purchased with little or no thought to future needs and integration with other systems. For this, a task force has been formed which has generated specific criteria to which all departments will be expected to conform. Feedback on the findings concerning this issue, as discussed below, is respectfully requested.

After

Please review and evaluate the following guidelines concerning departmental purchases of personal computers. A team of top level business managers and MIS experts has developed them to ensure that future purchases of PCs meet the current and future needs of the departments purchasing them and are compatible with the PCs others in the company are purchasing. Send your comments to us by Friday, March 21. Your quick response will help us establish definitive guidelines by the June 1 deadline requested by Mr. Morris.

SUMMARY

Effective writers realize that their success depends upon both adapting messages to their readers' logical needs and to their personal needs and self-images, their positions in the organization, their knowledge and interest in the topic, and their stylistic, historical, and cultural preferences.

Editing for logic takes place on two levels:

1. Making sure your opening consistently predicts everything that follows. To do so requires you to "shuttle" from the opening to other points in the message to assure complete logical consistency.

2. Making sure causal connections are clear and convincingly supported by evidence. Using the "Because, Based On, Therefore," can help you achieve this objective.

Editing to gain reader trust requires you to edit your text so it conforms to reader expectations in tone and content. Filling out an

Audience Analysis Inventory will help you to better understand your readers' needs and expectations.

Beyond editing at the macro level for logical consistency and audience sensitivity, you also need to edit at the micro level, revising your messages so they meet two tests: to project positive images of you, your department, and your company; and, to be as attractive and concise as possible, the topic of the next chapter.

Exercise   Analyze the following opening sentences of letters written by a consultant to his immediate supervisor. Then revise the letter so it reflects business purpose much more effectively.

"Just a note I jotted on my laptop during a terrible flight on *People's Distress* six-seater to Albany. The ride was so bumpy I had to order two drinks just to contain my nerves! I will return to the office on Friday, after my meeting with our regional staff in Albany, to discuss the results of my protracted negotiations (see below) with Allied Reproduction on the purchase of photocopiers for the Oak Street Production facility. We talked about just about everything: price, training, service, and delivery! Their bid, the second lowest in total cost, was impressive."

Suggested Revision

How did you do? Did you revise it to take out the personal and negative language? Did you add information about the purpose and results of the consulting engagement? Here's one possible approach to revising this passage.

"I am writing to report the progress I made in negotiating a purchase of photocopiers from Allied Reproduction. Allied offered the second lowest cost bids for the six photocopiers to be placed in the recently leased Oak Street production facility. Key among the issues we discussed were price, training, service, and delivery. As I demonstrate below, Allied's total package is impressive and superior to that of Smith Business Supply, which submitted the lowest dollar bid."

The first passage—focusing on the writer's needs—conveys an unflattering portrait of its author and does not allow readers to immediately sense either the point of the document or how they are supposed to respond to it. Its personal and negative tone undermines the author's image of professionalism and objectivity. By contrast, the second passage is revised to focus on the key business questions the full letter answers and allows readers to immediately understand the relevance of the remainder of the letter's content to a business objective.

CHAPTER 9

Edit to Project Positive Images of Yourself and Your Company

Everything you write makes a statement about you and the organization you represent. Consequently, take care to edit your writing to project appropriate images of you and your department to readers and to protect yourself and your company.

Your writing should communicate four characteristics about your managerial ability.

Use Language that Projects Four Positive Images of Your Managerial Ability

Sincere, fair, and objective	perception that you are fair, sincere, reliable, objective, respectful of individual differences; perception that you respect your readers and coworkers, including those lower on the hierarchy than you
Authoritative	perception that you are forthright and intelligent; that you make empirically based decisions, focused on achieving a company, rather than a personal or ideological agenda

| Pro-active | perception that you are a doer who views the organization positively; one who sees problems as "opportunities for improvement" |
| Dynamic, confident, relevant, and concise | perception that you have expressed a complete and accurate grasp of subject matter, expressed directly and concisely |

WRITE IN A NATURAL, SINCERE STYLE

Using business jargon projects an image of stuffiness. Substitute natural sounding language for jargon.

Jargon	Natural
Pursuant to our agreement	We agreed
As per your request	As you requested
Attached please find	I have attached
Effective immediately	Starting now

Use Natural, Not Stuffy Language

Stuffy
Your inquiry concerning the Population 2,000 project has been duly noted by the director and sent to me for response. As per your request, attached please find a copy of our preliminary report on this topic.

Natural
We enjoyed reading of your interest in the Population 2,000 project. I have attached a copy of the preliminary report you requested.

Also avoid using ingratiating words. They often sound insincere and may also serve to reinforce an image of subservience.

Write to Communicate Sincerity, Not Subservience

Ingratiating Passages
ABC views it as an unequalled honor and privilege to offer a proposal to your excellent organization to complete its 1991 federal income taxes.

It is with the utmost gratitude that I accept your gen-
erous offer to serve as a member of the fifth annual
company picnic committee.

Revised Passages
We thank you for choosing ABC to complete your 1991
federal income taxes.

I accept your offer to serve on the picnic committee.

Use Personal Pronouns to Set an Appropriate Tone for Memos

Personal pronouns are indicators of the nature of the message you are writing and of how you view your relationship with readers. Many companies advocate beginning memos with the impersonal pronoun *this* to encourage writers to immediately stipulate a company oriented what and why.

Personal pronouns, such as *I, we* and *you*, which are used less frequently, also serve important purposes. For example, the pronoun *I* suggests a close personal relationship with readers and is especially useful in writing to direct reports. Similarly, *you* suggests a high level of familiarity and adds a personal touch when you are offering congratulations. *We* demonstrates that you recognize and appreciate the input of others and serves as a significant form of recognition.

Use Personal Pronouns Appropriately

this   **Use at outset of memos to immediately orient readers to your objective.**

This provides background to _____.
This report analyzes fourth quarter financial results.

I, my   **Use when writing personal notes to direct reports and peers, and when requesting authorization of relatively small changes.**

I enjoyed working with you on your sales
accounts last Friday. Below I summarize
our discussion on effective sales techniques.
Please authorize the expenditure of $25 to
purchase SpellChecking software for my PC.

You, your	Use in congratulating an individual and in asking for approval of proposals from supervisors.

Your report was outstanding.

May we have your approval to proceed?

I congratulate you and your coworkers on securing the Adams account.

we, our department	Use to give recognition to a group

We recommend using $25,000 of our budget to purchase XYZ financial analysis software.

We concluded that the ABC offer best meets our criteria for soap purchases.

The Audit Department requests approval to purchase DataBase III software.

Use Language That Respects Diversity in the Workplace

To be effective in an international business environment and at home in an increasingly multicultural work environment, learn to write with sensitivity toward others in your organization. This includes using gender neutral language; using references to religion, race, creed, or place of national origin only when they are relevant to your message; using neutral terms in writing about disabled employees; and using language that shows respect for coworkers.

Use Gender-Neutral Language   *Workforce 2000* predicts that two-thirds of new workers will be women, including a significant number of new managers. Women are now and will be filling virtually all positions that have previously been assigned to men. So your prose reflects the new realities of the workplace, be sure your messages contain gender neutral language, conforming to the guidelines below.

Use Gender Neutral Terms

Instead of:	Use:
stock boys	stock clerks
chairman	chairperson, moderator
foreman	supervisor
salesman	sales representative
watchman	security guard
mailman	letter carrier

Use the Appropriate Gender Pronoun When You Know the Gender of the Person Who Holds the Position

- The Comptroller signed her report with a flourish.
- The flight attendant buckled his seat belt in preparation for take-off.

Rewrite Sentences to Avoid Using Gender-Specific Pronouns

From: Each division manager will offer his opinion.
To: The division managers will offer their opinions.

From: Each researcher must file his results by June 20.
To: File your results by June 20.

From: Each auditor was assigned his own personal computer.
To: Each auditor was assigned a personal computer.

Avoid Awkward Constructions, Including "s/he," "he/she," "his/her." Limit "his or her" and "he and she."

From: The Task Force Director is responsible for beverage service to his/her office guests. She/he should not expect secretaries to prepare beverages for and serve them to her/his guests.
To: The Task Force Director, not secretarial staff, is responsible for preparing and serving beverages to office guests.

From: Every employee should be at his or her desk.
To: All employees should be at their desks.

Use Language That Shows Respect for the Contributions of Coworkers
Employees at all levels of an organization are sensitive to the terms used to describe them. To be respectful, avoid language which highlights the status of business associates. Instead use positive descriptors, including full adult names, and preferably ones that indicate how the people mentioned actually contribute to the organization.

Use Language That Describes Coworkers' Function Rather Than Their Status

Respectful Terms	Less Respectful Terms
Administrative and technical workers	Nonmanagement employees
Associates	Nonexempts
Business contributors	Hourly-wage personnel
Actual job title	
	Subordinate

Respectful Terms	Less Respectful Terms
Actual full name	People, as in "my people will meet with your people"
	Underling
Colleagues	Personnel
Coworkers	
Team members	
Actual job title	Boss; superior
team leader	
project head, supervisor	
coordinator	

Insensitive
Two of my clerical people, though hourly wage personnel, are outstanding subordinates.

Respectful
Brian O'Leary and Anita Tarentino, file clerks in the Accounting Department, will receive letters of recognition for their consistently excellent and timely work.

Condescending
Each year's fiscal review has been found to be a reasonably good improvement in the reduction of errors in the profit forecast over the previous years and, for this, the appropriate personnel are to be applauded.

Motivating
Congratulations for continually improving the accuracy of our annual profit forecasts. We applaud our finance department associates for their excellent work.

Use full adult names, preferably with job titles, when writing about employees. Avoid using nicknames as well as the phrases *girl*, *gal*, and *ladies* when referring to adult females, and *boy* when referring to adult males.

Use parallel phrasing in the use of names.

Highlights Status Differences
- Debbie and Bobbie, two *girls* from the office pool, have been transferred to Mr. Hall's office.
- Debbie B and Bobbie have been transferred from the office pool to Mr. J. Hall's office.

Shows Respect for Coworkers' Contributions
- Deborah Brown and Roberta Minelli, secretaries in the Systems Engineering Department, have been transferred to Jay Hall's office.

- Ms. D. Brown and Ms. R. Minelli, secretaries in the Systems Engineering Department, have been transferred from the office pool to Mr. J. Hall's Office.

Use References to Religion, Race, Creed, or Place of National Origin Only When They are Relevant to Your Message
In almost all cases, you will find such references to be irrelevant to achieving company objectives.

References to Religion, Race, or Origin Are Usually Inappropriate

Inappropriate
Moustafa Abdul, *native of Iraq*, will travel to Cairo to attend a meeting on The Statistical Quality Control Association.

Appropriate
Moustafa Abdul, quality control engineering manager, will travel to Cairo to attend a meeting of The Statistical Quality Control Association.

Use Neutral Terms in Writing About Disabled People
Neutral terms objectively describe a disability , thus showing respect for disabled people. Avoid terms that carry negative connotations, particularly those which suggest that the disability itself is the defining characteristic of the person described.

Use Language That Is Sensitive to Disabled People

Preferred Terms	Terms to Avoid
deaf, hearing impaired	deaf mute
wheelchair users	wheelchair bound, invalid, confined to a wheelchair
mentally challenged	retarded
emotionally challenged	mentally ill
multihandicapped	deformed
person with arthritis	arthritic
person with cerebral palsy	cerebral palsied
person with epilepsy	epileptic
paralyzed	paralytic

Insensitive
Ms. Jordan delivered an excellent speech even though she was *bound to a wheelchair*.

Descriptive
```
Ms. Jordan, seated in a wheelchair, delivered an excel-
lent speech.
        or
Ms. Jordan delivered an excellent speech.
```

USE CONCRETE, DESCRIPTIVE, AND OBJECTIVE LANGUAGE TO PROJECT AN IMAGE OF AUTHORITY

Using concrete, descriptive, objective language in messages helps reinforce an image of authority, a dimension of credibility made up of a number of components, including expertise, decisiveness, and impartiality.

Use Concrete Language to Reinforce an Image of Knowledgeability

Use direct language and precise data in memos, letters, and reports. This practice will indicate to readers that you are a knowledgeable and forthright coworker who makes empirically based decisions and, therefore, someone entitled to respect and consideration.

By contrast, tag questions, qualifiers (including parentheses!), disclaimers, and generalities undermine your image of authority by suggesting uncertainty about the value of your opinions, ideas, skills, and knowledge.

Replace Weak Language with Strong Specific Language

Weak statements	Strong, specific, data-supported statements
Tag question: The meeting is tomorrow, isn't it?	The meeting is tomorrow at 3:30, in the Wilcox Room.
Qualifiers: This provides an overview of insights from interviews (approximately 27 in total) conducted in Boston on 1/5/91 to get a little insight into Pretend's copy problems.	This summarizes results of 27 interviews conducted to assess the effectiveness of Pretend copy. PL Associates conducted the interviews in Boston on 1/5/91.

Weak statements	Strong, specific, data-supported statements
Disclaimer:	
It seems to me, and others might disagree, that this costs a bit too much.	The TLC bid is 20% above what we budgeted for this project.
Generality:	
Overall, we feel initial results are highly promising.	Initial results are 20% above project goals.

Use Language That Promotes an Image of Rationality and Objectivity

Aggressive language and punctuation can connote rigidity and emotionality. Such constructions include the use of *allness* and *ism* words as well as of forms of punctuation and highlighting which magnify the emotional impact of emotional language. In their place substitute specific information and conventional punctuation.

Allness Words   A concentration of *allness* words may indicate you have a predisposition toward rigidity and emotionality.

Allness Words include the following: *absolutely, always, certainly, completely, continually, constantly, decidedly, definitely, endlessly, entirely, eternally, fully, invariably, perpetually, persistently, positively, quite, surely, thoroughly, totally, utterly, undeniably, wholly, all, none, nothing, never.*

For example, note how the use of *allness* words, underlining, dots, and exclamation points suggest the writer has not viewed the situation objectively, whereas the revisions suggest a much more careful analysis of the details of the situation.

Make Factually, Not Emotionally Based, Claims

Exaggeration
```
This computer has never worked right!
      vs.
This computer has had to be repaired six times in the
last three months.
```

Inflexibility
```
ABC always promotes new products heavily.
      vs.
Historically, ABC has promoted heavily behind brands
believed to have broad national demand. It typically
promotes small or regional brands more modestly.
```

Emotionality

```
We are absolutely (!) convinced our source is . . .
totally reliable.
        vs.
Our source has consistently provided us with complete,
accurate, unbiased, and up-to-date information.
```

***Ism* Words** Overuse of *ism* words may undermine your image of objectivity and flexibility. Open-minded leaders consider a wide range of explanations of problems and a wide range of solutions to problems. Concentrations of *ism* words may suggest you are close-minded, viewing reality solely in terms of two opposing forces (sexism vs. feminism), ideologies (communism vs. capitalism), and doctrines (atheism vs. fundamentalism).

Note how much better the revised passages project an image of objectivity of the writer than does the original.

Replace *ism* Words with Descriptive Language

Exaggerated

```
Religious fundamentalists from the Tennessee Bible Belt
have originated all claims linking General Widget's
Saturna project to the symbols of Satanism.
```

Descriptive

```
Private investigators found that Rev. P. J. Arnot, pas-
tor of the Primitive Tabernacle, located in Marshall,
Tennessee, started rumors identifying the Saturna
project name with followers of Satan. Similar subsequent
claims to members of churches within a 100-mile radius
of Marshall were also discovered.
```

Emotional

```
Let me assure you that racism and sexism pervade our
public schools.
```

Objective

```
Data indicate discrimination against Black, Hispanic,
and female students in some local high school clubs. For
example, approximately 30 percent of Black and Hispanic,
and 40 percent of female applicants to the Gold Key Club
in J. T. Morgan High School were accepted compared to 60
percent of white male students.
```

To project an authoritative image requires you to write calmly and empirically, avoiding language and punctuation strategies that suggest you are wishy-washy or overly aggressive.

SUBSTITUTE POSITIVE FOR NEGATIVE LANGUAGE, WHEN APPROPRIATE

Use a positive vocabulary to build an image of proactivity. Positive language reflects a can-do attitude, as well as respect and enthusiasm for the work of your colleagues. You can achieve this image by writing in terms of a vision of the future and not reactively by focusing on past mistakes.

Transform negative phrases, which will lead readers to believe you do not respect them, into positive ones, which are more likely to motivate them.

Replace Negative Phrasing with Positive Phrasing

Negative phrasing	Positive phrasing
■ I bought you this word processor so you would *not waste* so much time cutting and pasting your reports together.	■ We acquired this word processor so you can get your reports done more quickly.
■ You made a good point; *however*, I will add that	■ You made a good point, and I will add that . . . .
■ You *only* have one child.	■ You have one child.
■ You *never* married.	■ You are single.
■ Your report was *quite* good.	■ Your report was well-researched.
■ *No* smoking	■ Please smoke in designated areas.
■ To *avoid* losing your place	■ To preserve your place
■ This pastry contains *no* fat.	■ This pastry is fat-free.
■ You *don't* have a B.A.	■ This position requires a B.A.
■ You *failed* to sign the report	■ Please sign the report.
■ To *avoid* further delay	■ To get this to you as soon as possible
■ To *reduce* errors in the forecast	■ To increase the accuracy of the forecast

Notice in examining the passages below what a more positive impression you gain of the author of the positively positioned strategy than you do of the one who positions his brand's strategy negatively. The positive approach suggests the author can work productively within the guidelines higher management has set, whereas the negative passage suggests a lack of commitment to the strategy selected—and it appears to be building in an excuse in case of failure.

Position Strategies Positively

Negative Positioning of Strategy

Sometimes International is *in need of* low cost exposure opportunities. Our budget *was cut 95% last year alone.* Essentially, we are operating on a *minimal, maintenance budget. However,* we have sought out ways of effectively getting the Sometimes message to a wider international audience at relatively low cost.

Positive Positioning of Strategy

Piggybacking our message on the back of Pretend product labels is an effective, low cost method of promoting Sometimes to an International audience.

Likewise, position benefits positively in proposals. Notice how much more persuasive the positively positioned passage is compared to the negatively positioned passage in the following example. In the original passage, all the reasons given are negative. In the revision the reasons are positive, clearly explain the benefits of the recommendation, and directly show its relationship to company goals.

Position Benefits Positively

Defensive Argumentation	Persuasive Argumentation
Rec: To hire an additional contract laborer in the warehouse for two months	To hire an additional contract laborer in the warehouse for two months
[because]	[because]
1. Company could fall as much as four weeks behind agreed upon delivery schedules.	It will allow the company to flexibly and cost-effectively meet agreed upon delivery schedules.
2. Current workers simply cannot handle the scheduled deliveries over this period.	Past experience indicates contract workers bring reliable performance to the workplace.
3. This is our peak delivery period.	It meets the company objective of adding no new permanent workers during the fiscal year.

WRITE TO PROJECT A DYNAMIC IMAGE

You create a dynamic image through good design, conciseness, clarity, directness, and variety. This section discusses several strategies for projecting a dynamic image.

Make Documents Inviting to Read

Documents should be as "dressed for success" as the managers who write them. While highlighting is of central importance, you also should check overall appearance, typeface, margins, reproduction quality, total length, paragraph length, and other variables that affect the "curb appeal" of your memo.

Overall Appearance   Make sure there are no erasures or inserts. Photocopies should be as clear as the original. Try to eliminate page breaks which interrupt the flow of the argument. Be sure text is centered on the page, and memos, letters, and reports are neatly folded into thirds so they make a positive impression when first opened by readers. Use good quality white paper and dark typewriter ribbons only.

Margins   Be sure at least a three-fourths inch margin surrounds your text. At a well-known consumer products company, one executive was famous for having developed a template with a heavy black line marked three-fourths inch within its boundary. Each memo submitted to this manager was placed within the template. If any text went over it, he returned it for revision and retyping.

Typesize   Use 8, 9, 10, or 12 point type for memos and letters. These most closely replicate normal typewriter typefaces and are neither too small to read, nor are they so large that they limit how much text you can fit on a page. When writing instructions, consider larger size type if you can fit them on one page.

Boxing   Also investigate boxing, which can highlight instructions as well as tables, executive summaries, and warning signs.

Typeface   Choose a serif type in preference to sans serif, and a combination of upper and lower case letters. Evidence indicates serif and a mixture of lower and upper case letters is easier to read in the text of memos, letters, and reports. By contrast, all capital letters and nonserif type typically are easier to read when used for headings and short phrases on visual aids.

Write Concise Documents

Overall Length   As Peters and Waterman point out in *In Search of Excellence,* many companies, following the lead of Procter & Gamble, are famous for insisting on one-page memos. Writing to cover information in one page has several advantages.

- **Improved reader access**
  Readers are more likely to read short documents when they receive them because they take less time to read.

- **Improved sensitivity to need-to-know information**
  A space limitation forces a writer to be more selective in choosing information—more likely to tell readers what they need to know instead of everything the writer knows.

- **Improved logical consistency**
  Readers and writers are better able to check the logical adequacy of shorter documents because they can isolate the major elements of a document—purpose, reasoning and data, and actions—that should be consistent with one another. The longer a document gets, the harder it is for readers to find the key elements, isolate them, and "shuttle" between them to check for their alignment with higher level goals.

The techniques for writing concisely, discussed later in this chapter, will help you limit the length of your documents. You also have to ask yourself if you have limited your argument to everything the reader needs to know, or if you have included nice to know information that could be excluded.

Of course, the one-page memo is an ideal that cannot always be met (even at P&G). In those cases, you need to effectively use other writing techniques, such as opening paragraphs that summarize the entire document, as well as highlighting that makes it easy for readers to understand your analysis and locate key facts supporting your reasoning.

Write Short Paragraphs

Paragraphs should normally be short, less than ten lines long. Paragraphs longer than this often look heavy and uninviting to read. They suggest the writer to be presenting unreasonably complex ideas. In addition, a long paragraph is likely to contain more than one point, and for coherence, should be divided into at least two paragraphs.

Note how much more difficult to understand the first passage appears to be. It reinforces the common perception that computer experts have difficulty communicating with their less computer literate coworkers. The revision, on the other hand, broken up into short paragraphs with headings, dispels that stereotype.

Break Up Long Paragraphs

Difficult to Read

There was considerable development of MIS data during the month. Improvements were made to the accuracy of estimated revenues for uninvoiced shipments. Manufacturing costs, which have formerly been stored as monthly unit costs, are now stored as both unit and total costs. This change permits weighted average costs to be easily calculated, using total cost and total production, over user-selected time periods. An initial set of raw materials business data now resides in the MIS. Included are fairly high-level summaries of raw materials shipments, prices, sales dollars, production, and inventory status. A standard structure is being implemented for storing cost data in the MIS. Accounting is reviewing the feasibility of establishing standard divisional operating-expense statements, which would be the source of such data for the MIS. Finally, work is nearly complete on a data upload capability to automatically move data prepared on HP150 personal computers to the MIS data base. This important capability will simplify the acquisition of considerable data which are currently prepared on PC's, including shipment forecasts and pricing P&L data.

Easy to Read
Development of MIS Data

MIS improved the data base in three areas:

Estimated Revenues for Uninvoiced Shipments: Improvements were made to the accuracy of estimated revenues for uninvoiced shipments. Manufacturing costs, which have been formerly stored as monthly unit costs, are now stored as both unit cost and total costs. This change permits weighted average costs to be easily calculated, using total cost and total production, over user-selected time periods.

Raw Materials Business Data: An initial set of key business data now resides in the MIS. Included are fairly high-level summaries of raw materials shipments, prices, sales dollars, production and inventory status. A standard structure is being implemented for storing cost data in the MIS.

Accounting is reviewing the feasiblity of establishing standard divisional operating expenses statements, which would be the source of such data for the MIS.

<u>Transfer of PC Data:</u> Work is nearly complete on a data upload capability to automatically move data prepared on HP 150 personal computers to the MIS data base. This important capability will simplify the acquisition of considerable data which are currently prepared on PC's, including shipment forecasts and pricing P&L data.

Write Concise, Easy-to-Follow Sentences

To use sentences to project a dynamic image, (1) use sentence combining techniques; (2) put the main clause first; (3) keep sentences short; (4) keep the subject-verb-object kernel together. These techniques also help produce clarity, conciseness, variety, and rhythm in sentences.

Sentence Combining and Sentence Breaking Variety and rhythm characterize good writing style. If you have written short, choppy sentences that fail to flow when read, combine them to improve their rhythm. On the other hand, break up sentences which are overly long into shorter, easy-to-follow sentences.

Combine Very Short Sentences into Longer More Coherent Sentences

Choppy and Wordy
I followed up on the letter sent to the ABC Veterinary. It was mailed on 8/25/91. I reiterated our concern with costs. I asked for cost estimates of both the trial study and the main study. Dr. Morgan called in his response. He promised to fax us an itemized list of the cost of all materials. He will send them by week's end. He is deferring the cost estimates for the studies. He wants to wait until the protocol has been finalized.
[9 sentences, 83 words]

Fluent and Concise
In a letter to ABC Veterinary, dated 8/25/91, I again requested cost estimates for both the trial and the main study. Dr. Morgan called to say he will fax us an itemized list of the cost of all materials by week's end. He promised to send cost estimates for the studies once he has finished the protocols for them. [3 sentences, 58 words, a 30% reduction]

Break Up Very Long Sentences into a Series of Concise Sentences

Long and Difficult to Follow
Once our laboratory has developed an appropriate liquid
diet, it will obtain six species of year-old philodendra
from Thornton Supply and will attempt to raise them on
this custom-made diet which they will be fed while
housed in custom-made containers, fitted with special
trays for appropriate feeding, for the duration of the
pilot study. [1 sentence, 59 words]

Fluent and Concise
Our laboratory will obtain six species of year-old
philodendra from Thornton Supply. We will raise them on
a special liquid diet we are developing. The philodendra will be fed from special trays and housed in custom-
made containers for the duration of the pilot study.
[3 sentences, 43 words, a 27% reduction]

Put the Main Clause First in Most Sentences and Keep the Subject-Verb-Object Kernel Together

Putting your main clause first and keeping the subject-verb-object
kernel together in sentences will allow readers to read your documents more quickly. Putting long subordinate clauses first and in-
terrupting the subject-verb-object kernel will slow readers down.

Putting the Main Clause First Helps Readers Understand Meaning More Quickly

Difficult to Comprehend
Main Thirty or more calendar days prior to the public
point hearing of the school board, or fifteen or more
withheld calendar days if the school board does not
until end schedule a public hearing, the proposal for a
of revised curriculum in Foreign Languages should
sentence: be submitted to the appropriate committee
for formal review.

Easy to Comprehend
Main point: Please submit your proposal for a revised
starts curriculum in Foreign Languages to the
sentence Curriculum Committee for formal review.

Details	**1.** If there is a public hearing, 30 days
highlighted	prior to the hearing;
for easy	or
retrieval	**2.** If there is no public hearing, 15 days
of informa-	prior to the scheduled meeting of the
tion	school board.

Write in the Active Voice Most of the Time

Sentences written in the active voice project an active image of the writer because they are shorter and more direct than passive sentences. Use of the active voice is particularly important for writing instructions because it emphasizes who should be doing the action. Note how much more clearly the responsibility for the audit is specified in the following examples of the active than in the passive voice:

Responsibility Not Specified
An audit should be conducted at the Morristown facility monthly. (10 words)

Responsibility Clear
Lyle Webb should audit the Morristown facility monthly.
(8 words, a 20% reduction)

To test for the active voice, (1) find the subject and the verb of your sentence and (2) see if the subject is the doer of the action expressed by the verb.

Active   Tommy kicked Bobby.
Passive   Bobby was kicked by Tommy.

Active   Mitchell approved the deadline extension.
Passive   The deadline extension was approved by Mitchell.

Use the Passive Voice in Special Situations

While you should use active voice in most instances, use the passive voice to avoid placing blame and to project an image of objectivity in scientific reports, especially when reporting methodology.

To Be Diplomatic

Diplomatic
Windows broken during the first shift were repaired prior to the start of the second shift.

Undiplomatic
The crew members who broke the windows while horsing around on break repaired them prior to the start of the second shift.

To Highlight the Objectivity and Replicability of a Test Procedure

Objective
16 cc of water were poured into the beaker.

Personal
I poured 16cc of water into the beaker.

Keep Sentences Short

Short sentences, those that are 16–25 words long, suggest an action-oriented personality. Long sentences suggest a more analytical and passive persona.

Following the previous guidelines for sentences and words, plus the following three rules, will help you keep your sentences short—and help you project a dynamic image to readers and listeners.

Use a Single Word in Place of "Doublings"   This will allow you to write more economically.

Replace these phrases . . .	with these . . .
▪ completely finish	▪ finish
▪ positive benefits	▪ benefits
▪ personal opinion	▪ opinion
▪ true facts	▪ facts
▪ past memories	▪ memories
▪ significant and important	▪ important
▪ collect together	▪ collect
▪ red in color	▪ red
▪ large in size	▪ large

Limit the Uses of Prepositions and Forms of "to be"   These types of words frequently signal that sentences are padded with extra words. The phrases "There is" and "There are," in particular, signal verbosity to many readers.

Before

There *are* three areas *in* which the performance of your division can *be* improved. (14 words)

After

Your division should improve its performance in three areas. (9 words, a 30% reduction)

Before

The area *of* Management *of* Information Systems *is in* need *of* a manager *of* personnel. (15 words)

After

The MIS Department needs a personnel manager. (7 words, a 56% reduction)

Substitute Short Expressions for Wordy Phrases

Frequently, you can substitute shorter phrases for longer ones, as illustrated.

Wordy Phrases	Concise Substitutions
in regard to	about
with reference to	
in the matter of	
with regard to	
after the conclusion of	after
subsequent to	
at the end of	
despite the fact that	although
as a result of	because
in view of the fact that	
owing to the fact that	
due to the fact that	
on the grounds that	
in advance	before
prior to	
previous to	
is of the opinion that	believes
in accordance with	by
by means of	
came into contact with	met
for the purpose of	for
in the event that	if

Wordy Phrases	Concise Substitutions
in the area of	near
on a local basis	locally
at a later point in time at a later date at a later time	later
along the lines of similar to	like
in the meantime	meanwhile
in the proximity of	near
at this present time at this point in time at this present point in time	now
in very few cases	seldom
in the very near future	soon
as a result for this reason	therefore
with a view to	to
until such time as	until
as soon as at which time during the period of time during the course of during the time that until such date	when, during
as to whether the question as to whether	whether
in connection with	with

Use Action Verbs, Not Noun Phrases Made Out of Verbs

Sentences filled with abstract noun phrases created from verbs project an image of impersonality. Changing nouns back to verbs will personalize the tone of your sentences. It will clarify your meaning, since many readers find nominalizations difficult to understand.

Wordy

I made an analysis of year-to-year raw materials price variations. (10 words)

Concise
I analyzed year-to-year raw material price variations.
(7 words, a 30% reduction)

Wordy
The subcommittee *made the suggestion* that the full com-
mittee *give consideration* to the bill the League of
Women Voters submitted. (20 words)

Concise
The subcommittee *suggested* that the full committee *consider* the bill the League of Women Voters submitted.
(16 words, a 25% reduction)

On Your Own Fill in the concise version of each nominalized
phrase below.

Nominalized	Concise
make an analysis of	analyze
make approval of	approve
make a decision to	decide
take an action to	act
make an application	apply
give approval to	approve
be in a position to	will
give consideration to	
is corrective of	
bring to an end	
make a decision to	
draw an inference that	
make cognizant of	
make the suggestion that	

Use Short Action-Oriented, Easily Understood Words

Sentences containing action-oriented, easily understood words
project an image of leadership, of someone who communicates clearly to colleagues in order to get things done.

Sentences containing long, unfamiliar, and unpronounceable
words communicate an image of technical narrowness, of someone
who knows a great deal about a small part of the world, but who
has difficulty communicating to nonspecialists.

Exercise   Write the simpler substitute from column B next to its complicated equivalent in column A. This exercise illustrates how often we use a longer word when a shorter, simpler one would do.

A-1	B-1
implement	find out
viable alternative	aware
interface	schedule
output	total
input	name, title
suboptimal	speed up
caveat	carry out
designation	word of caution
effectuate	less than ideal
expedite	accomplish
time frame	facts, data
cognizant of	discuss, meet
aggregate	workable solution
ascertain	results

A-2	B-2
envisage	help
enumerate	start
facilitate	count
finalize	finish
inaugurate	use
institute	sum up
initial	tendency
predisposition	first
recapitualte	begin
utilization	see

In addition, reinforce a dynamic image by selecting dynamic phrases. For example, "I sought out the information" is more dynamic than "I looked for it." Similarly, "this analyzes 1993 profit trends" sounds more dynamic than "this reports 1993 profit trends."

SUMMARY

How credible you are to readers often depends as much on how you write as what you write. Your writing style affects readers' perceptions of you as an individual; your position and rank and the reputation of the department you represent; the power that you hold; elements of your social personality; and impressions of your intelligence, objectivity, reliability, and dynamism. Good writing decisions build images of crediblity just as poor decisions undermine them.

The table on pages 158–159 lists some of the most important dimensions of credibility and shows how the writing decisions discussed throughout this book can build and undermine each.

Exercises   Revise the sentences below.

1. We feel extremely privileged to have received your letter of 9 April 1993. As per your request, under separate cover, enclosed therein, is the bibliography on accounts payable you requested.

2. We are proud to announce that Miss Debby Bryzinski, a hardworking young secretary, is the first nonexempt employee to be elected chairman of the Quality Improvement Committee.

3. I am convinced the investigation will uncover evidence demonstrating beyond a shadow of a doubt that the charges of sexism, racism, and ageism are totally without basis!

4. Sales were up 6%; however, profits were up 10%.

5. The requirement of a foreign language has been completely eliminated by the Curriculum Committee.

6. At this point in time, we have yet to give consideration to the designation of a name for the football stadium that has been proposed by the city council.

Suggested Revisions
1. We have sent, under separate cover, the bibliography you requested on accounts payable.

2. The Quality Improvement Committee elected Deborah Brysinski to lead its meetings.

3. I am confident the investigation will document our department's excellent civil rights record.

4. Sales were up 6%, up 12% vs. year ago. Profits were up 10%, up 28% vs. year ago.

5. The Curriculum Committee eliminated the foreign language requirement.

6. We have not yet considered a name for the proposed football stadium.

Building Credibility Through the Effective Use of Language

Dimensions of Credibility	Ways of Building Image	Ways of Undermining Credibility
expertise	■ be precise ■ use numbers ■ use empirical language ■ show technical concurrence	■ use vague terminology ■ use indecisive language
strategic/analytic insight	■ align doc with company objectives ■ show ownership of information ■ highlight reward/risk ratio and comparative advantages ■ show lessons learned from experience ■ provide logical and persuasive argumentation ■ demonstrate perspective	■ absence of higher-level objective ■ uninterpreted facts ■ absence of risk recognition ■ absence of historical awareness
goodwill	■ show concurrence with ideas ■ appeal to achievement motives ■ relate to continual improvement theme ■ credit others in organization ■ show history of working well with others ■ use appropriate multicultural language ■ use "we" language ■ send timely communication	■ absence of concurrence, ■ pursuit of personal, not company objectives ■ absence of alignment with company goals ■ absence of sharing credit ■ insensitive language ■ excessive "I" language ■ sending info later than promised

Building Credibility Through the Effective Use of Language (continued)

Dimensions of Credibility	Ways of Building Image	Ways of Undermining Credibility
dynamism	■ short memos, paragraphs, sentences, and words; ■ active construction, action words ■ high-level of ownership ■ positive positioning ■ "can do" language ■ use of pro-active language to position ideas in positive light ■ solid, workable action plans with account-ability and timeliness	■ long memos, paragraphs, sentences, words ■ passive constructions ■ passive and negative words ■ low level of ownership ■ "can't do" language ■ vague action plans that lack accountability and timetables
power	■ mention rank, title, place in hierarchy ■ have powerful figure write a cover letter, concur with, or cosign your document ■ highlight previous successes	■ use indecisive language ■ show no concurrences ■ suggest you have little influence over issues discussed
clear communication	■ use highlighting effectively ■ write scannable, skimmable docs ■ organize deductively	■ absence or poor use of highlighting ■ write nonscannable-nonskimmmable docs ■ organize inductively

CHAPTER 10

Edit to Avoid Litigation

T he "litigation explosion" has had a serious impact on business communications. Consider these facts:

Careless words as much as actual business practices have become decisive factors in legal cases, influencing both the decision to bring a case, and the ultimate decision on the merits of the case. Companies must be careful about what they say about themselves as well as about competitors. They must even be careful about what others say about them.

Internal thought processes are subject to discovery. That means that lawyers may subpoena documents to establish company thinking and motives regarding the issue being litigated. The text of documents, as well as comments written in the margins, may be used as evidence.

Some readers may not be your intended readers. Documents, including memos transmitted electronically, may be read by numerous people, holding differing, possibly hostile, frames of reference.

In short, business writing has an uncertain lifespan and may create liabilities for your organization.

This chapter discusses how to write to avoid antitrust, product safety, and employee litigation.

WRITING TO AVOID ANTITRUST LITIGATION

Companies with leading shares in markets often become targets of antitrust suits. Of particular relevance to writers is that their words can be used against their companies. In fact, when intent to monopolize is the key criterion, careless use of words may be the central element in the prosecution's case. Therefore, business writers must select words carefully, avoiding language that suggests market-dominating behavior.

Use Words Carefully

Avoid words in the following categories, as they are most likely to be used against your company in antitrust suits. They may indicate an intent to use unfair practices to dominate a market.

- **Guilt complex words,** such as *Destroy after reading, Confidential, Please destroy, For your eyes only,* and *No copies.* Documents so marked are likely to be the first documents opposing lawyers subpoena.

- **Power, intent, and market share words,** such as *leverage, foreclose, dominate,* and *preempt.* A sentence such as "our objective is to become the market leader in this area, with a share of 55% or more of all items we market" indicates an intent to dominate a market.

- **Bragging words,** such as "we have a lock on this market; no one who values quality and service will buy from anybody else."

- **Overselling words,** such as "this price is for you alone."

- **Overcompetitive words,** such as "Let's give him a strong dose of his own medicine." "Let's cut ABC off at the knees." "This signal on price will surely send our competitors a message about our intent to retain a leading market share."

  Be sure your company is described as competing *vigorously*, not *aggressively*.

- **Undercompetitive words,** such as "Margins were low due to competition, which we expect to be remedied next year."

- **Disparagement,** nonobjective evaluations of competitors' goods and services. You must not be quoted as saying your company can "exploit" its competitor's weaknesses.

- **Loose talk about competitors,** anything that suggests collusion, such as "We have matched their price." Instead, you should "meet" their price.

Focus on Business Benefits

Articulate recommended actions in terms of their benefits to the company, wholesalers, retailers, and end users. These include building volume, delivering better products and value to consumers, communicating benefits clearly, and understanding consumer needs more effectively. This is the proper focus of your company's efforts.

Do not position actions in terms of how they will damage competition. Use language that suggests a positive attitude toward customers and consumers; eliminate passages or words which suggest negligence or market dominating behavior on the part of your company.

Proper vs. Improper Positioning of Ideas

Proper Positioning

- Our jointly devised partnership with BigMart will help our company grow share, give BigMart the inventory control it requires, and save consumers money.

- This new product is projected to generate 500 cases of incremental volume.

Improper Positioning

- Our jointly devised partnership with BigMart will virtually cut our main competitors out of this market. They simply do not have the resources to match our offer to BigMart, given their current financial distress.

- This new product will blow our competition right out of the water!

WRITING TO AVOID PRODUCT SAFETY AND RELATED LITIGATION

Companies are responsible for their safety practices with regard to their products, facilities, equipment, and services. So that your writing does not expose your company to product safety and related suits, use precise descriptions and avoid speculation.

Describe Events Precisely

Imprecise descriptions can lead to serious consequences. For example, an engineer's report stated that an automatic transmission "jumped out of park" when he meant that on "two or three occasions out of ten thousand, a transmission slipped into an intermediate position between park and reverse." This statement played an important part in a prosecutor's product negligence case.

Avoid Speculation, Unless it Is Clearly Labelled as Such

In one case, a scientist wrote a memo speculating on the possible areas of medical attack by the plaintiffs, without clearly labeling the ideas as speculation. In the court case, the opposing attorneys used the memo to attempt to demonstrate the company had concrete knowledge of a number of ways its product was medically unsound. In this case, the writer would have protected his company had he written: "In response to your request concerning possible areas of legal attack on our product, here are the kinds of speculative issues that have been raised previously; none has validity, as I show below."

Speculative vs. Empirically Precise Description

Speculation
```
The tank holding thorium is over 30 years old and proba-
bly leaks like a sieve.
```

Precise Description
```
The tank holding thorium was purchased in 1958 so a
potential for leakage should be investigated, and if
confirmed, appropriate remedial actions taken.
```

Avoid Sensational Language

It can later be used against you. For example, avoid writing something like this:

```
"If the tank does leak, it will result in major contami-
nation of the aquifier for the entire Miami Valley."
```

Instead phrase your position passively and in terms of what the company should do:

```
"Spill protection measures for the thorium tank are
being investigated and evaluated."
```

If You Raise a Problem, Solve the Problem

Make sure the record shows that when you have identified an issue, you have taken steps to address it. For example, instead of writing:

"We need to address this potential leakage problem immediately."

Write:

"To address the potential for leakage, I will call in a consultant within the month to recommend methods for improved spill control."

WRITING TO AVOID EMPLOYEE LITIGATION

Employment law has expanded to encompass a number of issues including defamation, invasion of privacy, discrimination, and unlawful discharge. Therefore, follow the guidelines below in writing about people in your organization.

Be Cautious in What You Write in Letters of Recommendation or in Employment Offers

Employees have sued former employers for libel and slander based on evaluative statements made in letters to prospective employers and for promises to applicants not kept once employment had begun. Some legal experts suggest communicating only indisputable facts in letters of recommendation, such as dates of employment and positions held. Anything suggested orally during an employment interview should be documented in writing so there are no misunderstandings which could later be used in a wrongful discharge case.

Document Disciplinary Interviews, as Well as Terminations Documentation is important because you cannot be sure the supervisor who initiated the disciplinary action will still be employed at the time of a court hearing.

Be Sure Disciplinary Interview Write-Ups Are Complete
They should include the following:

- **A precise statement of the reason for the disciplinary interview,** such as "Your time card indicates that you arrived at work at 9:50 on Monday, one hour and twenty minutes past the starting time for work, and you stated you did not call in to indicate that you would be late or when you would arrive."

- **A statement of the company policy,** such as "I showed Mr. Jones the statement he signed upon employment that company policy requires timely arrival each day of employment on or before 8:30 am. Mr. Jones said he remembers signing that statement and understands the policy is important for the efficient operation of the company."

- **An indication the employee being disciplined had an opportunity to explain why the behavior occurred,** such as "Mr. Jones explained that his alarm clock failed to go off and he did not think to call in his rush to get to work as soon as possible. He said he would purchase a second alarm clock as a backup so this situation could be avoided in the future."

- **A statement indicating what disciplinary action is being taken and what future disciplinary action may be taken if there are future violations,** such as "I explained to Mr. Jones that since this is his second violation in two weeks, a formal letter of discipline will be put in his personnel evaluation file and will be considered during his performance review. I also explained that a third violation of the starting time within the next four months may result in a disciplinary hearing, one which may lead to dismissal."

- **Termination letters should indicate that the action taken is consistent with other actions in similar situations and that the employee was aware such behavior could lead to the termination of employment,** such as "A guard found three company-owned socket wrenches concealed in Mr. Jones' overcoat as he was leaving the workplace. Two coworkers testified at the dismissal hearing that they saw Mr. Jones hide the wrenches in his coat during his afternoon break.

  Mr. Jones signed a statement upon employment indicating that any employee found leaving the premises in possession of company equipment would be subject to immediate dismissal."

Use Objective Language

Evaluate work behaviors, not unobservable factors, such as attitude. In particular, substitute objective, factual descriptions, preferably with reference to measurable company standards, for subjective comments, such as those based on age, gender, race, religion, place of national origin or disability. Protected classes of employees can sue if they have evidence a company has violated their civil rights.

For example, a company lost an unlawful discharge suit on the basis of the testimony of a coworker who said that the unit manager told her the dismissed employee was "too old to effectively handle the lunch hour rush of business." The company would have had a far stronger legal defense had the unit manager said "Mr. Sanchez did not meet bank standards for the number of transactions completed per hour. He completed an average of 16 transactions per hour, 33% fewer than the minimum bank standard of 24 transactions per hour."

Write Candid Performance Evaluations

Often when fired employees sue companies for unlawful discharge, they produce on their behalf years of excellent employee evaluations—evaluations that look little different than those of employees who were not discharged.

Be sure evaluations include discussions of where employees are not meeting expectations for their positions. If you feel uncomfortable identifying flaws in an employee's performance, you are better off not conducting formal appraisals at all.

For example, avoid ambiguous communication, such as "Mr. Jones has the opportunity to further build productive relationships with customer contacts" which, while diplomatic, does not convey precisely the behavior desired. A preferred statement would be "Several of Mr. Jones' clients have asked that he be more responsive to their needs for the size and timing of shipments. Mr. Jones has agreed to listen more carefully and respectfully to his clients, including those with smaller orders, in order to strengthen his customer relations skills."

Be Sure That Policies Written in a Company Manual Are Followed in Actual Company Practice

Seemingly benign statements in a policy manual may be interpreted in court to be part of a binding contract between the company and employees. For example, if an employee manual promises the company will listen to both sides of a dispute, this policy must be followed consistently—with terminations taking place only after a fair hearing of both sides to the dispute.

Add Disclaimers to Company Manuals

Typical disclaimer statements include "This manual does not constitute an employment contract and the company has the right to change it at any time" or "This manual does not affect the company's right to terminate the employment of any employee, for any reason, at any time, nor does it in any way interfere with the right of employees to terminate their employment with the company." Check with legal counsel for the precise wording most appropriate for each state in which your organization operates.

SUMMARY

Good writing is so clear it is not only capable of being understood, it is incapable of being used against you and your company in litigation. When editing documents, ask yourself these questions:

- Does my message suggest an intent to dominate or a disregard for safety concerns?
- Does it suggest unfulfilled promises to employees or unfair treatment of them?

If so, carefully revise your document, so it is free of potentially incriminating statements.

Given the serious consequences of lawsuits, when in doubt, consult your company's legal advisors—especially when discussing patent issues, mergers and acquisitions, and plans to defend against competitive activity. Do not draw legal conclusions, paraphrase legal advice, or speculate about your company's legal position on issues. Your comments may restrict your company's future ability to defend itself. In short, keep in mind how your comments may be used against you and your company every time you write a message.

Exercise Evaluate the following passages; then revise them to improve their legal defensibility.

- We are aggressively leveraging our dominant advertising budget to preempt the impact of the entry of ABC's new product; this will surely send a message of our serious intent to the rest of the market.
- We hired Fred Jones because he exhibited greater maturity and emotional stability than either Debbie Gregory or Juwan Jefferson, two, hardworking, up-and-coming managers.

How did you do?
Alternatives might read as follows:

- We are increasing our advertising budget in response to the heavy advertising supporting ABC's new product.
- We hired Frederick Jones because his education and work experience best met the criteria the company established for this position.

CHAPTER 11

Revise Your Memos and Those of Your Coworkers

Good writing is continually checked and changed to make sure that it proves an argument logically, is well-adapted to readers, and projects positive images of the author, the author's department and the company. Once you've initially edited your document for logic, adaptation, and style, appearance, and legal liability, put it aside; then come back for at least one additional review. For important documents, you may do a series of reviews. In fact, a study at a major consumer products company revealed its marketing department memos are, on average, revised seven times. Company folklore asserts that one was revised over 50 times—all to ensure that the written word accurately reflected the department's best thinking.

This chapter first discusses how to do a final review of your own documents as well as those of others in your organization. It describes the criteria for evaluating a rough draft, provides guidelines for effective revisions, demonstrates a method for proofreading, and concludes by indicating how to tactfully revise the work of your peers and direct reports.

REVISE FOR CLARITY, COHERENCE, AND FOCUS

To revise effectively, you need a clear set of criteria by which to judge your text. All your documents should meet the first of the following three criteria ; your complex documents should meet the other two as well.

Easy to Read and Understand

Good writing is immediately comprehensible to readers. Specifically, it meets five needs.

- **Immediate clarification of the relevance of the document to the readers' concerns.** Readers should immediately find answers to three questions : What is this about? Why has it been sent to me? What do you expect me to do in response to it?
- **Scannability.** Readers should be able to scan a document and then read it through once completely and be confident that they have an accurate understanding of its purpose, logic, data, and indicated action.
- **Easy retrievability.** Readers should be able to find relevant topics and data through scanning, without having to read the entire document.
- **Clear graphics.** Readers should immediately understand the significance of data in tables and graphs.
- **Conciseness.** Readers should read only what they need to know, not everything that you as a writer know. Memos should be 1–4 pages in almost all cases.

Logically Coherent

Your job includes more than just recording data; you must show the reader what data mean, what conclusions should be drawn, what action is indicated. To do this, you should demonstrate a clear understanding of the relationship of your topic to the strategic requirements of your department, division, and overall organization. Good memos are charactized by:

- **Logical argumentation,** where readers perceive clear, consistent, and convincing relationships among Objectives, Evaluation, Reasons, Data and Actions.

- **Persuasive positioning,** including a rationale that answers five key reader questions: worth doing, feasible, cost effective, manageable risks, and on target with the company strategy in this situation.

Strategically Focused

Memos should show an awareness of the principles that are at the heart of the company's past success and a knowledge of how to apply those principles successfully in both the short and the long term. Specifically, memos should reflect:

- **Customer and consumer focus,** a perspective that shows a clear understanding of customer and consumer requirements.
- **Consistency,** an intent that is consistent over time, a set of core strategies that the Company has successfully followed.

HOW TO REVISE MEMOS, LETTERS, AND REPORTS

Once you have a clear idea of the criteria by which you are evaluating your documents, you are ready to begin reviewing them. The following guidelines will help you do a complete, yet efficient, review of your documents.

- **Prepare a neatly typed rough draft with ample white space for comments and changes.**
- **Put aside what you have written for a period of time.** Then come back to it, reading it as if you were its primary and secondary audience.
- **Use a plan for reviewing which follows closely the way your readers will be reading your document:** skim it; scan it; read it word for word. When reading word for word, do three separate readings: for logic and flow; for style; and for correctness.

   Each of these steps requires a different type of editorial focus:

- When you skim, you get a sense of the reader's first impression of your document.
- When you scan, you see if your document is clearly outlined for readers.

- Reading for logic and flow requires a clear focus on the connectivity of your argument.
- Reading for style requires you to be particularly sensitive to audience adaptation; and
- Good proofreading requires a strong attention to spelling, punctuation, numbers, and word usage.

Below are suggestions concerning what to look for in each step.

I. Skim Through the Entire Document to Determine if It Is Inviting to Read

Cosmetics

1. Are pages visually appealing? Does structure jump out at you? Is the subject line easy to find? Are the typeface and size of type appropriate? Is there sufficient space around headings? Are margins wide enough? Do page breaks interrupt the flow of the document? Are visual aids readable and attractive? Is the document printed on high-quality bond paper? Is it free of erasures and inserts? Is it centered on the page? Is it folded into equal thirds so it looks attractive when opened?

Length

2. Is length appropriate for the nature, purpose, and reader expectations of this document?

II. Scan the Memo to Evaluate Purpose, Design, and Logic

Purpose

3. Does the subject line clearly indicate the What? Would it be appropriate to modify it to also indicate the Why of the document?

4. Does the first verb of the first sentence tell the reader whether the intent of the document is to discover, to report, to analyze, to evaluate, or to recommend?

Design

5. Does the opening paragraph accurately predict the rest of the memo? Does it clearly summarize the content of the document? Are key reader questions anticipated and concisely answered?

6. Is the organization of the rest of the document clear? Is highlighting used to reveal hierarchies of information? Does it reveal an organized sequence of ideas that make sense on their own, when scanned? Do headings and subheadings serve as a

table of contents of the document, making it easy for readers to retrieve information from the memo or report? Does highlighted material accurately predict the information that follows it? Is an appropriate amount of space devoted to each section?

7. Are paragraphs 8 lines or more? If so, can they logically be broken into shorter paragraphs? If not, are they organized clearly in a What, Why, Details sequence?

8. Does each visual aid serve a purpose? Does it contain enough information to stand on its own? Could complex text be simplified with additional visual aids? Do the text and related visual aids contain clear cross-references? Is each visual aid properly located for its size and content? Are appendices clearly labelled?

Logic

9. In complex memos, is underlining used to outline the logic of the document? Do the toplines make sense in the sequence in which they are presented? Is the body of the document organized logically—using an appropriate logical pattern, such as by chronology, order of importance, component, comparison contrast, or an umbrella point followed by specific subpoints? Are the toplines phrased in parallel structure?

III. Read the Memo Word-For-Word to Test the Adequacy of Evidence and Logical Progression

Progression

10. Is there good forward movement—nothing that directs your eyes back or ahead? Is a pattern followed in the placement of ideas? Are more important ideas placed ahead of less important ones? When information, such as objectives, methods, and results, are discussed more than once, do the discussions precisely parallel one another with no inconsistencies?

Does each paragraph start with a topic sentence, including the What and sometimes the Why? If the Why is not part of topic sentence, does it immediately follow? Does every sentence in each paragraph help explain or clarify the topic sentence? Are sentences in paragaphs presented in a logical order?

Are transitions accurate? Used between and within paragraphs to show connections between ideas? Are transitions used in toplines to show connections between major points?

Do follow-up actions logically follow from the objectives and analysis that precede them? Do they pass the Therefore test?

Evidence

11. Is each claim immediately documented by proof? Can you apply the Based On test? Is direct proof presented first, followed by qualifiers?

    Is evidence compelling? Recent? Accurate? Relevant? Unbiased? Is it appropriate to meet the needs of readers?

    Has information been interpreted well? Are trends identified? The proper base period used? Nontypical variations explained? Sources identified?

    Do graphs use scales that position results realistically?

IV. Read the Memo Word-For-Word to Check for Reader Analysis and Economy.

Tone

12. When you read the memo out loud, do the words sound natural? Appropriate for your readers? Is the language assertive? Positive? Respectful? Nondogmatic? Well-adapted to a multicultural audience? Are appropriate personal pronouns used?

Sentence Structure

13. Are sentences short, 16–25 words? Can long sentences be broken into shorter ones? Is the Subject-Verb-Object kernel kept together?

Diction

14. Do sentences contain strong nouns and verbs? Are the words of the memo genuinely familiar to readers? Is your vocabulary precise? Can you substitute facts for adjectives and other vague expressions?

Economy

15. Can you cross out words which add length but not meaning? Do visual aids contain unnecessary data?

V. Proofread for Correctness

16. ■ Proofread everything, including titles, subtitles, words, punctuation, capitalizations, indented items, and numbers. In particular, make sure all names are spelled correctly and that the address is correct, even if it means calling to check.

- Concentrate on each word for correct spelling. Check for omitted words and for words a spellchecker will not catch, such as the word *they* when you intended *the*.
- Examine numbers and totals. Recheck calculations and look for misplaced commas and decimal points.
- Make sure all quotation marks, brackets, dashes, and parentheses come in pairs.
- Double-check all highlighted material. Readers are most likely to find mistakes here because highlighted material typically is read more than once.
- Keep a list of repeated errors. See if you find a pattern which will help you proofread future documents more effectively.
- Let someone else read the manuscript. This will give you a second pair of eyes through which to proofread your manuscript.

COACH OTHERS TO WRITE MORE EFFECTIVELY

Once you've gained skill at revising your own work, you can work to help others in your organization write more effectively.

Guidelines for Reviewing the Work of Coworkers

Below are five suggestions to guide such revisions.

- **If someone asks you to evaluate a memo, letter, or report, find out exactly what's expected of you.** Is it simple evaluation (good, fair, poor)? Is it minor editing and proofreading? Is it a major evaluation and revision?
- **If you are expected to do a fairly complete revision, follow these steps.** First, find the main point. Is it clear and easily identified? Second, see if you can outline the argument. Third, look at the evidence. Does it support the main point? Is there enough of it? Too much? Fourth, look at the style and mechanics of the memo. Is the style appropriate for the intended readers? Is the memo neat? Error-free?
- **Use a light pencil if you decide to write on the manuscript.** Comment by using action verbs, such as Clarify, Expand, Revise for Fluency, and Omit, not harsh nouns and adjectives like

awkard, meaning?, logic?, and the infamous X through an entire passage.

- **Talk to the author about the document.** Do not simply return it with written comments without giving the author an opportunity to ask you to explain what you wrote and why you wrote it.

GUIDELINES FOR REVIEWING THE WRITING OF DIRECT REPORTS

If you are working to improve the writing of colleagues who report to you, following the guidelines below will help you help them write more effectively.

- **Let direct reports read and evaluate documents you regard as well written, including some of your own.** This approach has two advantages: (1) direct reports can use your documents as models and (2) they will be more responsive to your evaluations of their documents if you allow them to evaluate yours.

- **If you receive a poor memo, work to improve clarity of purpose and structure of argument before commenting on style or mechanics.** Ask for an outline in which the purpose, key findings, and action steps are highlighted. Then discuss how to use that outline to write a clear concise document. Compare the before and after documents and point out why the after is superior from the reader's point of view.

- **Once you are satisfied with the clarity and logic of a document, identify where the author could improve the style and mechanics of the document.** Then ask for a final draft.

- **Recognize and reward solid improvement, including written or oral public praise of good writing.**

- **Let direct reports see the response others have had to their documents.** Show both positive and negative responses.

- **Rewrite documents direct reports have written only in extreme circumstances.** It consumes your time, does not teach the direct report to write more effectively, and may damage your relationship with the author if objections are raised to the changes you made.

SUMMARY

In short, to revise a document, review the criteria for good writing, follow good overall revision practices by having an uninterrupted and organized atmosphere during the revision process, follow a step-by-step approach to revision which mirrors how readers will read your document, and revise the work of others tactfully and sensitively.

Exercise

1. Use the steps outlined in this chapter to revise a memo, letter, or report you have written.
2. Take a paper a manager or teacher has returned to you and translate all comments into action verbs which indicate what changes would improve the paper. How does this change the tone and tenor of the remarks?

PART IV

SPEAK WITH POWER

CHAPTER 12

Prepare the Presentation

Good oral communications are central to a manager's ability to succeed on the job. During a routine week, a manager is likely to place and receive messages on the phone, engage in problem solving discussions, conduct group and face-to-face meetings, and deliver formal presentations both inside and outside the organization. Therefore, oral communications must be as well-planned and organized as written communications.

We use oral communication because of its immediacy—the ability to get decision makers to commit to a specific course of action during a meeting or subsequent to a presentation. To promote action, effective presenters involve their listeners—both showing the relevance of what they have said to listener concerns, and also allowing listeners to influence them. That is, good speakers are adaptive; they have the ability to recognize how to adjust goals and action plans to the knowledge, experience, ideas, needs, and resources of their listeners.

Given their dynamic nature, face-to-face oral communications often are more complex to execute well than written communications. With an immediate audience, a speaker must generate confidence through effective content and delivery, as well as excellent responses to questions and answers. As a result, while the advice in the chapters on writing skills applies as well to planning oral communications, effective speakers need additional preparation in the areas of content and delivery.

This chapter addresses preparing the content of the presentation and Chapter 13 discusses delivering the presentation.

In planning and organizing the content of an oral presentation, take four steps: (1) analyze the speaking situation; (2) organize the presentation; (3) plan the use of visual aids; and (4) prepare for questions and objections.

ANALYZE THE SPEAKING SITUATION

Before you speak, analyze the speaking situation. Start by filling out a planning sheet like the one suggested in Chapter 1 for memos and reports. Then take five additional steps:

- Determine the type of presentation you are making
- Define an overall presentation objective and four quantitative standards for measuring whether you have achieved those objectives
- Plan an oral communications strategy
- Determine whether the audience will be friendly, apathetic, neutral, or hostile
- Analyze the speaking context.

Determine the Type of Presentation You Plan to Make

Determining the type of presentation you are making is important because the criteria for being successful in each differs dramatically. Most presentations can be divided into one of three categories: *Tell*, such as information and analysis reports; *Sell*, such as proposals for change; and *Collaborate*, such as small group discussions. Depending on the nature of the presentation you are making, you should prepare to meet the criteria for each type of presentation.

Informational and Analytic Presentations For an informational or analytic communication, you should:

- Stress clarity in your presentation, with a major focus on clear organization, clear argument, and frequent reviews of key points.
- Reinforce in listeners' minds the validity of your data, the accuracy of your causal analysis and of the inferences you have drawn from data, as well as the propriety of any next steps.
- Establish your credibility and competence as an expert on the issue you are discussing.

Persuasive Presentations In presenting a proposal, you need high audience involvement, since your objective is to persuade. In your preparation focus your efforts to include developing ways of:

- Getting your audience's immediate attention
- Demonstrating a clear need for a change or an excellent opportunity for improving performance and demonstrating how your recommendation will address these needs or take advantage of these opportunities
- Precisely defining for listeners what you want them to do to implement the recommendation
- Establishing your credibility as a source of perceptive interpretations of data on this topic.

Collaborative Communications In collaborative communications, you are seeking assistance from the audience, generally in a group setting. In preparing these presentations focus on clarifying:

- The objectives of the discussion, the key topics to be discussed, and the amount of time to be devoted to each topic
- Ways of encouraging open and honest discussion of issues
- Ways of reaching consensus on issues, especially those of acceptance and implementation.

Set Objectives

Once you have established whether you are delivering a *Tell, Sell,* or *Collaborative* presentation, set specific objectives for the particular audience you will be addressing.

As Peter Honey points out in *Face to Face,* effective communicators do not speak simply to "get their two cents worth in"; they speak to achieve specific objectives. Objectives are forecasts about events you want to see exist in the future. In the presentations you give or meetings you attend, you should set specific objectives about what the presentation should achieve.

Specifically, you should translate your objectives into four observable and measurable standards, the "quality control" standards of quantity, quality, acceptance, and time.

They are:

1. The amount of work to be done
2. The quality of work to be done

3. The behavior of those involved in achieving the objectives

4. The deadlines and intermediate deadlines needed for achieving the objectives.

Defining your objectives in this way generates three significant advantages.

1. **It clarifies what you have to do to realize your goals.** That is, it encourages you to see the relationship between how you communicate during the meeting and what you achieved. Moreover, it allows you to spot and curb irrelevant behavior on your part and motivates you to plan your behavior so that it is in line with achieving your objectives.

2. **It makes it easier to prepare for meetings,** helping you understand what you need to do before the meeting, during the meeting, and after the meeting to achieve your objectives. In particular, it helps you communicate to others what you want.

3. **It makes it easier to compare actual outcomes of meetings with your objectives.**

Below are three examples of objectives, one for each type of presentation.

Report Presentation

As a result of hearing my presentation, warehouse workers will effectively implement the new procedures for receiving packages.

I shall be successful if:

- Listeners remember all four changes in procedure.

- Listeners are able to explain to me how they will implement these changes effectively in their own areas of responsibility.

- Listeners agree the changes will be beneficial and are able to clarify the rationale for the changes to anyone who requests it.

- This presentation, including questions and answers, takes less than one hour, and the new procedures are implemented within one day of the presentation.

Persuasive Presentation

As a result of hearing my presentation, my listeners will agree to purchase fire insurance to protect our computers.

I shall be successful if:

- The group agrees to purchase computer insurance.
- The group agrees to purchase policies which meet the appropriate criteria for price, coverage, and copayments.
- The group agrees on the nature of the problem and says they are glad I called it to their attention.
- The meeting lasts less than one hour, and the insurance is purchased within 30 days.

Collaborative Communication

As a result of hearing my presentation, the training committee will develop a program of courses which will precisely meet the need of managers in the Finance Division.

I shall be successful if:

- The group returns with a complete list of training courses.
- The group clearly relates these courses to the problems they are to address.
- The group comes to a clear consensus on which courses we should offer to what people, at what times, within what budget.
- The meeting takes less than two hours and the training itself begins within six weeks.

On Your Own   Write out objectives and four standards of success for a presentation you plan to make.

Determine Whether Your Audience Will Be Favorable, Neutral, or Hostile

Unlike written communications—where your audience can quickly scan your document, shuttling back and forth throughout the document to determine your position—you, as speaker, control the order in which you introduce information, including your position.

Favorable Audience   If you are reporting information to a favorable audience, use a deductive pattern, similar to the one used in writing memos and reports. You might also be able to shorten your message given that your listeners are already likely to agree to your position.

Neutral Audience If you are reporting information to listeners who are neutral or indifferent to your analysis, use a deductive method, with a strategy of selecting and organizing information to stimulate interest. You may do this by either highlighting the seriousness of a problem that has arisen, or by showing the connection between your discussion and important goals the organization is committed to achieving.

Hostile Audience If you are reporting information to a hostile audience, use an inductive order. Some psychological studies indicate that listeners are more likely to accept an argument if they accept the first things they hear. Therefore, in discussing a topic with an audience hostile to your thesis, one option is to argue from least controversial point to the most controversial point.

Your objective is to establish credibility early on that will carry over into the more controversial aspects of your presentation, leading listeners to take a more favorable view of your thesis than they would have before regarding you as a highly credible source.

Of course, you may be asked questions early in the presentation which will force you to reveal your position earlier than you planned.

Develop an Oral Communication Planning Strategy

Once you have determined your objectives and analyzed your audience, practice "mental rehearsal" and develop an oral communications strategy, one which allows you to visualize the entire process of the presentation from beginning to end. Below are examples of two oral communication planning schedules, the first for a single persuasive presentation to an audience that knows little about the topic and the second, a presentation plan that covers a sequence of meetings with friendly listeners in preparation for a persuasive presentation to a hostile audience.

Writing out these schedules will help you make a plan that gives you sufficient time to be prepared at each stage of preparation. It also gives direction to your information search, defines a series of objectives that have to be met on the way to the ultimate objective, helps you define what you have to do to adapt your message to your listeners, and helps you prepare for questions and objections, as well as for a fall back position, if your original position is rejected.

Oral Communication Planning Schedule

Ultimate objective
To convince all of our construction site managers to
call on internal auditing to help them develop controls
to prevent fraud, theft, and other kinds of loss on the
construction site.

Steps needed to assure this end result

1. Build an
effective
argument

I shall gather the evidence I need to
develop a sound position. In particular, I need to make sure my facts are
accurate, reflect on the meaning of
these facts in terms of my experience,
check with my contacts within the
organization to see if any thing is
happening or has happened which will
affect what I am planning to say, and
find out how similar problems have
been approached in the past.

2. Plan on how
to adapt this
information
to the target
audience

To develop my position further, I will
also use creative approaches such as
brainstorming, mental rehearsal, and
displayed thinking to make sure that
I have covered all the key issues.

I shall test my ideas with others. In
particular, I will solicit additional
ideas and data, pay particular attention to negatives, and try to get
promises of support and cooperation
for implementing my ideas if they are
approved.

I shall find out as much as I can about
my listeners. I shall try to develop my
presentation in such a way that it not
only meets my needs, but also helps my
listeners see how it will solve problems they have experienced.

I shall also adapt my presentation
planning to the situation in which I
will be finding myself. I will take
into account what has been considered
effective in the past in similar situations.

I shall write out my presentation
objective and test it against four
criteria: (1) the critical reasons why
internal controls are needed; (2) the
cost-benefits of such controls to

construction managers; (3) the importance of getting aid from internal auditing in planning such controls; and (4) the appropriateness of what I have to say in terms of length, content, language, and visual aids to the speaking situation.

3. Organize my presentation

I will select an appropriate sequence in which to organize my presentation, using a deductive order if I expect agreement with my thesis and an inductive order if I believe my thesis will be received negatively.

I shall organize my presentation by time modules, allowing no more than 20% of my time to be spent on the introduction, no more than 10% on the conclusion, and no more time spent on each main point than is proportionate to its importance to the speech.

4. Refining the presentation

I shall plan the use of visual aids for the presentation. Then I will refine the use of my language of my presentation. Finally, I will draw up a list of possible questions, criticisms, and objections and write down answers to them.

5. Rehearsing

I shall practice my entire presentation out loud, preferably before an audience. I shall practice the parts that give me difficulty until I say them smoothly. I will also practice giving answers to questions I am sure I will receive.

6. Giving the presentation

I will do an effective job of convincing construction managers that internal auditing should be part of their construction site planning. I must be sure I am clear as to what I want the group to do, am well-organized in my presentation, and am well-prepared for the kinds of questions I am likely to be asked. In particular, I need to remember to keep my objectives in mind when answering questions

7. Follow-up

If I get agreement, I have to be sure to follow-up effectively so that the implementation conforms to my expectations.

Group Communication Planning Schedule

Ultimate objective
To convince the health and beauty care brand team to agree to a modification of the current accounting mechanisms so that the additional costs of special packs on warehousing, handling, freight, and distribution are accounted for accurately.

Steps needed to assure this end result

1. Define the problem	I need to meet with coworkers in finance & accounting to estimate the significance of the problem.
2. Gather information	I need a second meeting during which my coworkers discuss their findings concerning the precise costs of pre-packs for individual health and beauty care products.
3. Plan on how to adapt this information to the target audience	I need a third meeting in which we discuss what strategy we should adopt to convince the other members of the Health and Beauty Care brand team to agree to our recommended changes. In particular, we need to define the relative cost-benefits of these accounting changes to our target listeners. That is, we need to determine how we can show these managers that our changes will allow them to achieve their objectives more effectively.
4. Make the presentation	I need to do an effective job of getting the brand team to agree to my recommendations. I must be sure I am clear as to what I want the group to do, am well-organized in my presentation, and am well-prepared for the kinds of questions, criticisms, and objections I know I am going to receive. I need to develop a fall-back position in case it becomes apparent that my argument will not carry the day.
5. Follow-up	If I get agreement, I have to be sure to follow-up effectively so that the implementation conforms to our expectations.

On Your Own   Write out a planning schedule for a presentation you plan to make.

Planning for Each Step   After writing out an overall planning schedule, plan for each step. An example is illustrated below.

Planning the First Step

I. **Objective for the first group meeting: to run the meeting in such a way that my colleagues have been encouraged to brainstorm for ideas on how we can more effectively report the costs of special packs.**

I will have achieved my objective if:

- Each team member has contributed at least three ideas on what topics should be explored in trying to establish the significance of the problem.
- We agree on what data should be gathered and have developed assignments for each of the group members to complete.
- At least one-third of those attending the meeting comment that they thought the meeting was productive.
- The meeting is completed in less than two hours.

II. **Improving the environment to make sure my objective for the meeting is met.**

- I will give everyone advance notice of what is expected of them.
- I will send the members relevant data to stimulate their thinking on this topic.
- I will start the meeting by going over its purpose and agenda and by setting time limits for each part of the meeting.
- I will indicate that the first part of the meeting will cover brainstorming and will encourage the group to react positively to all ideas suggested during that part of the meeting.
- I shall encourage the group to set up criteria on how to evaluate whether ideas should be accepted as good ones.
- I shall make up a list of all ideas generated in the brainstorming session and have the group apply the criteria they established to them. Then we will select the best ideas for further discussion.
- I shall make sure that everyone is clear on what has been agreed upon and what they are expected to do between now and the next meeting.

Analyze the Speaking Context

The final step in planning an oral presentation is analyzing the speaking context. This will help you determine the length, formality, and tone of your presentation.

Examine key contextual variables, including the size of the audience, the size of the room, the nature of the seating, and the timing of the presentation.

For example, generally, the larger the audience the more formal the presentation. The larger the room, the more likely it is that you will need a microphone and speakers. The size of the room and audience also affects the kinds of visual aids you can use.

If the seats are uncomfortable, or if there are a number of speakers, consider making shorter remarks.

Similarly, people react differently to you according to the time of day you speak. Avoid speaking so that your remarks cut into break periods, lunch periods, or quitting time. Almost invariably attention will wane as your speaking impinges on those periods. Likewise, after dinner addresses typically should be lighter and more concise than addresses given during business hours.

Planning an oral presentation is similar to planning a written message. You should determine exactly how you want listeners to respond to your message and develop objectives that will help you determine your relative success during the presentation. Your planning should include adapting your message carefully to your listeners' needs and expectations as well as to the speech context.

Once you have completed planning your message, you are ready for the next step: organizing the presentation.

ORGANIZE YOUR PRESENTATION

After analyzing the speaking situation, plan, organize, and write the content of your presentation according to the writing guidelines presented earlier. Limit the number of main points from two to five. Order them logically, taking into account the needs and expectations of your listeners. Use explicit transitions. Summarize at the end of each point. Introduce each new point explicitly with statements such as "the second reason to support . . ." or "the third major component of this point."

In addition, (1) organize your presentation into time blocks and (2) develop effective openings and closings.

Organize by Time Blocks

Whereas a written presentation is limited by the number of allowable pages, oral presentations are limited by the amount of time allotted to them. To help you determine how much information to provide and where to provide it, make an oral presentations outline in which you organize information by time blocks.

Organizing by time blocks is an effective editing device. It ensures that each point will receive adequate attention and also reminds you of the importance of making good transitions and summaries.

The models which follow on pages 192 and 193 give guidelines for Tell, Sell, and Collaborative presentations.

Develop Effective Openings and Closings

Many speakers spend more time preparing and rehearsing their introductions than they do on any other part of their presentations. They do this for two critical reasons: (1) the introduction is usually the best remembered part of the presentation and (2) the introduction shapes listeners' expectations of what will follow in the remainder of the presentation, while the conclusion crystallizes the key elements of the message you want listeners to take away with them.

Develop an Opening The opening is a place to establish four important objectives: to establish competence, credibility, and goodwill, and to gain listener attention.

A graphic follows that shows you how to foster audience confidence in your competence, credibility, and goodwill.

Techniques for Demonstrating Competence, Credibility, and Goodwill

Competence:
- Explain why you are qualified to speak, including your experience, research and training.
- Indicate you have thoroughly researched topic; build up impressiveness of sources of information or care in its selection and development.
- Refrain from making references to your inadequacies.
- Be sure pronunciations and grammar are correct.

Credibility:
- Claim to have looked at both sides of the issue.
- Stress relationship of your discussion to shared lasting values.
- Stress your views have been consistent over time.
- Stress common ground with listeners.

Goodwill:
- Refer to reason audience has gathered.
- Maintain you are pleased to be speaking.
- Pay audience a sincere compliment.

Oral Presentations Outline
(Possible format for a 6–9 minute TELL or SELL presentation)

	TELL	SELL	WORDS	TIME
Opening	Gains immediate attention in a way that directly relates to the thesis of the presentation.		100–190	45–90 sec.
Topic statement (What)	Points listeners in the general direction the presentation is headed.		25–50	10–25 sec.
Thesis statement (Why)	Specifically adapts your presentation objective to your audience.		25–50	10–25 sec.
Preview	States main points in order in which they will be presented.	Establishes the need for change or identifies an opportunity which will build the business.	25–100	10–45 sec.
Background	States facts and events which stimulated you to decide to explore this issue.		50–160	25–75 sec.
Body	Provides information for understanding and/or "how-to" lessons.	Appeals to audience for agreement and action based on benefits to listeners and company.	500–800	3–4 min.
Connectives	Provides explicit internal summaries and transitions to help your listeners see the relationship between your key points and your thesis.			
Initial conclusion	Restates main points.	Restates benefits. Appeals for action.	100–160	45–75 sec.
Response to questions and answers	Remains in line with your presentation objectives.		as appropriate	
Final closing	Restates main points.	Restates benefits. Appeals for action.	100–160	45–75 sec.

Oral Presentations Outline
(Possible format for a 60 minute COLLABORATIVE presentation)

		TIME
Opening	Thank everyone for attending	10 sec.
Topic statement	Point listeners in general direction group meeting will be headed.	25-50 sec.
Thesis statement	Specifically adapt your presentation objective to your audience.	25-50 sec.
Preview	Establish main discussion areas, forecast the order in which items will be discussed, set time limits for discussion of each item.	1-2 min.
Background	State key facts and events which stimulated you to ask this group to explore this topic.	25-75 sec.
Body	For each topic, allot a set amount of time for brainstorming, the uncritical discussion of ideas.	According to number of points discussed and their relative importance.
	For each topic, devote the second half of the discussion to debate and argumentation on the relative merits of the ideas generated in the brain-storming session.	
Connectives	Define areas of agreement, move discussion along, bring out comments of reticent participants, make sure time limits are adhered to, keep discussion relevant to presentation objectives, make sure debate is full and open—continually relate what is said back to reason for convening the meeting.	
Conclusion	Define areas of consensus, responsibilities, and expectations of the actions of group members in carrying out the agreements.	1-5 min.

Gain Attention with an Interesting and Relevant Opening   An excellent introduction captures the listener's attention and focuses it on the topic under discussion. It can excite audience interest by suggesting that the rest of the presentation will be as interesting and carefully prepared as the opening.

Below are listed a number of ways you can get attention in an oral presentation.

- **Pertinent quotations:** *Newsweek* reports that breaches of corporate security have been occurring with alarming frequency over the past three years.

- **Rhetorical question:** How much would you estimate ABC spends on employee health care each year?

- **Humor:** (best used with listeners with whom you are on familiar terms)

    The Foreign Corrupt Practices Act has been called the "Internal Auditor's Guaranteed Employment Act."

    It has been said that "an auditor is a person who comes in after a massacre and bayonets the wounded."

- **Personal anecdote:** I recently met a businessman who told me he decided to purchase a large block of ABC stock after eating a handful of Chippies. He commented, "Any company that could figure out how to get potato chips organized has to be well-run from top to bottom."

- **Using an analogy:** Mr. Minnetti, our vice president of manufacturing, recently encouraged us to kill alligators—to kill those time wasters which prevent us from giving our full attention to really top priority matters. I am here today to propose we kill one such alligator that eats up a significant amount of our time in the air foils division every month.

- **Being positive:** (especially effective when listeners have heard a lot of disappointing news) "I've got some good news to report!"

- **Using an excellent example:** Recently, a construction worker fell through a manhole at one of our construction sites. No warning sign had been posted by the contractor doing the job. The man broke his arm and his collarbone. We thought he would be covered by Workmen's Compensation Insurance. But the injuries were not because our contractor did not carry the proper coverage. The injured party's lawyer sued ABC. We had to take up the valuable time of our lawyers and of our managers, many of whom had to be flown back to Los Angeles for the trial. ABC was found guilty of contributory negligence and had to pay a $50,000 judgment. All of this loss of time, effort, and money could have been avoided if only the purchasing agent checked to make sure the contractor to whom we awarded the job carried the proper insurance.

- **Use of a Visual Aid:** How many of you would bet me a dollar on the flip of this coin? A 50-50 proposition. Now, how many of you would bet me a million dollars? Yet that is precisely what ABC is doing now in its currency hedging operations. And our success in estimating whether the dollar would rise or fall against international currencies has, so far, been no better than our success in this room at predicting whether this coin has come up heads or tails.

Avoid the weak introduction. Examine the following introductions. They are examples of commonly used, but generally ineffective, introductions. They often suggest to listeners that the remainder of the presentation will be as unimaginative as its opening.

- **A repetition of the assignment:** I have been asked to address you on the topic of toxic waste regulations.
- **A colorless statement of intent:** In this presentation I want to talk to you about energy use at the Michigan plant.
- **An unsupported claim of interest:** Health insurance is an important topic to discuss. I have long thought about what it costs to protect people from the high personal bills extensive hospitalization can run up. I am really happy to have this opportunity to discuss a topic of such vital interest to us all.
- **Apologies:** I really do not know how to begin discussing the issue of currency hedging. I am only on my first assignment here at ABC and have had little experience with the subject matter, but since I have been asked to make this presentation, here goes my best shot.
- **A dictionary definition unrelated to your thesis:** One definition for insurance in my pocket dictionary is "Protection from loss." This is a very broad definition. I want to talk about the importance of reducing ABC's Workmen's Compensation Insurance costs.

Orienting Functions of the Introduction
Beyond getting attention, introductions also serve orienting functions, introducing the subject and your attitude toward it, and previewing the structure of the presentation.

Following are some examples of orienting materials that are frequently used in introductions.

- **Introduce the subject and your position regarding it.** Answer the what and the why questions.

  Poor Introduction: "I think something should be done about our excess manufacturing capacity in the private label vitamin market."

  Better Introduction: "I am here to ask your support for entering the private label vitamin market. This plan will generate over $4 million in pretax profit and will even out our production runs. In addition, it will not require any additional permanent personnel and will not compete with our name brand products. This option has been explored completely within our department and we believe it has great merit. I shall expand upon these reasons in the body of the presentation. A. Dennis, C. Herbold, and B. Tan concur with this proposal."

- **Preview the structure of the body of the presentation.** Indicate to readers what will come next and the order in which it will come. This will suggest to listeners that you will present a carefully prepared, well-organized presentation. In a persuasive presentation, state the key benefits of your proposal here in easy-to-remember terms. For example, you might use forecasts similar to the following:

  - "We shall first discuss the need for increased security at ABC and then consider three solutions which address the most important dimensions of the problem."

  - "As this meeting is scheduled for one hour, I think we should spend about 15 minutes discussing the office functions which could most profitably be automated, 30 examining the relative cost-benefits of the various solutions that are proposed, and 15 developing criteria for both selecting the right equipment and for developing a schedule of implementation. In addition, we should take a few minutes to plan the agenda for the next meeting and to discuss our individual assignments with regard to that agenda. When we reconvene we can get right down to the business of deciding which proposals to advance immediately and which to propose farther on down the road."

  - "I am going to discuss three problems that have been spawned by the vastly increased purchases of

```
PC's at ABC. These are the problems of abuse,
misuse, and nonuse."
```

- "The proposal I am asking you to approve is simple,
  cost-effective, and a stimulus to improved manufacturing productivity."

Develop an Effective Conclusion   The conclusion is usually the second most remembered part of a presentation. Therefore,
you need to give extra time and attention to its preparation. At a
minimum, an effective conclusion reviews the benefits of your proposal and requests a commitment from listeners that will fulfill
your objective. In it, you should tell listeners in explicit terms how
you want them to act. When explicit action is not called for, it is
extremely important to wrap things up for listeners, to remind them
of the basic points made in the presentation, and to restate the
presenter's overall position.

The following are some examples of techniques you can use in
writing effective conclusions, ones which end on a note of finality.

Examples of Effective Conclusions

- **Quotation:** Consistent with Howard Jones' dictum that
  "in the long run all costs are variable," we have
  found that when we award contracts on the basis of
  total delivered cost, plants' "fixed costs" do go
  down, sometimes dramatically. Thus, I urge you to
  follow the successful example of our health and beauty care division and use the total-delivered cost
  concept in making sourcing decisions for all our
  divisions. This change is easy to understand and
  implement, and will lead to more plant efficiency,
  lower costs, and higher profits for the company.

- **Personal Anecdote:** When I was playing basketball at a
  small Indiana school, we lost a critical game in the
  state playoffs because in the final minute of the
  game we stopped playing as a team. Each of us played
  as if the others were not on the floor. And we lost
  sight of our objective—to be a winning team.

  On that day 35 years ago, I learned a very important
  lesson about business. Your competition does not beat
  you nearly as much as you beat yourself. You beat
  yourself when you fail to look at the whole picture
  and do not coordinate your activities with those of
  others in the organization. Thus, for the good of the
  entire company, we have to make sure that all of our

divisions cooperate with one another and make decisions based on what is best for the company—even if
it means sacrificing some of your division's current
objectives. For if ABC is to win in the marketplace,
it must do so as a team—with all of us pushing in the
same direction toward common goals.

- **Analogy:** My high school football coach was fond of
saying that three things can happen to a forward
pass, and only one of them—a pass completion—is good.
Similarly, four things can happen when your office
purchases a personal computer, and only one—the proper use of the micro—benefits ABC. Nonuse, abuse, and
misuse of PC's do not build ABC's business. So I urge
all of you to audit the uses of your current PC's and
make sure they are being efficently used only for
legitimate company purposes.

- **Referring Back to the Introduction:** Thus, as part of the
campaign to kill the alligators that eat up our time,
we urge you to authorize the elimination of monthly
plant reports.

- **An Estimate of the Significance of the Conclusions Reached:**
Legal action and public education will not in themselves stop rumors about the ABC trademark. Yet as
injunctions are obeyed, lawsuits won, and the public
informed, baseless rumors about it will become more
difficult and less profitable to perpetrate.

- **A Forewarning or Warning Based on the Facts of the Situation:**
Unless something is done to halt the proliferation of
"hackers" invading corporate computer programs, the
advent of costly and highly inconvenient security
measures is inevitable.

- **Suggestion for Remedial Action:** If auditors would take the
time to really inspect the plants they are auditing—
talking with the technicians and supervisors about
the manufacturing processes of the plant, and then
even discuss these topics with the line workers themselves, they would be taking an essential step toward
improving the reliability of our auditing procedures.

Avoid the Weak Conclusion   Examine the following conclusions; they are examples of cliches masquerading as conclusions.
They fail to deliver a good summary of the presentation and suggest the speaker did not take adequate time to prepare the presentation.

- **The Platitude:** Every person here should think seriously about the problem of safety in the workplace.

- **The Silver Lining:** Although high energy use is a serious and costly problem, much is being done about it.

- **The Cure-All:** If all of us would just practice good safety habits, then we would not have any accidents in our plants.

- **The Conclusion Which Weakens the Point of the Presentation:** Of course, there is little we can do to change human nature, so all solutions in response to safety in the workplace are likely to be ineffective.

Since listeners have their highest levels of recall at the beginning and the end of a presentation, time spent perfecting openings and closings is time well spent. Your opening should gain attention, build your credibility, state your thesis, and forecast the development of your presentation. Your closing should summarize your thesis and end on a note of finality.

PLAN THE USE OF VISUAL AIDS

Once you have finished composing your presentation, take time to prepare visual aids carefully, an important aid to oral presentations. This section discusses the benefits of visual aids, their uses, the most frequently used visual aids, the information to display on them and guidelines of their use.

Benefits of Visual Aids

Studies have shown that visual aids can:

- Reduce the length of business meetings by 28%
- Increase the amount of information retained after three days by 55%
- Make presentations more interactive
- Enhance the perception of the presenter as more professional, believable, and persuasive.

Uses of Visual Aids

Visual aids are typically used to meet the following three objectives:

- To emphasize or reinforce key points by supplementing oral text with a visual complement
- To prove key points by proving supplemental details difficult to cover orally and
- To orient the audience by clarifying the structure of the presentation.

The information to include to achieve each purpose is described in the graphic below.

What Information to Display on Visual Aids

Purpose of the Visual	What to Include
Orientation	Information to orient listeners to thesis and organization of presentation
	"Maps" of the structure of the presentation
	Attention getters, such as quotations
Emphasis	What you most want the audience to remember. Use key words and phrases instead of complete sentences:
	- Presentation objectives
	- Next Steps
	- Recommendation
	- Benefits
	- Critical supporting data
	- Conclusions
	- Key Learnings
Proof	Easily understood representation of support information:
	- Examples
	- Graphs
	- Pie charts
	- Simple tables
	- Maps
	- Flow charts
	- Calculations

Types of Prepared Visual Aids

The most frequently used visual aids in addressing groups of 50 or less are flip charts, overhead transparencies, handouts, and samples and other physical props.

Guidelines for Flip Charts Flip charts are valuable because they are simple, inexpensive, portable, and easy to prepare. Flip charts are best for less formal presentations to audiences of 5 to 20 people. No member of the audience should be more than 25 feet from the flip charts.

Design of Flip Charts
To design effective flip charts:

- Write in large, clear letters and numbers.
- Limit each chart to no more than 6 lines of text and a total of 15 words or numbers.
- Use color to emphasize key information. Color has the most impact when used sparingly.

How to Use Flip Charts
When using flip charts, follow three steps:

- Leave at least one blank sheet after each sheet on which you write.
- Tape each printed sheet to its blank backer sheet by making a "tape tab" near a bottom corner. Put the tab on the side where you plan to stand during the presentation.
- Turn a blank page when you want the audience to focus exclusively on your oral text. Make a tab for this blank page.

Guidelines for Overhead Transparencies Overhead transparencies are highly popular visual aids to use because they are economical, portable, and easy to prepare. Below are guidelines for their use. Overheads can be used for moderately formal presentations to audiences of five to several hundred. Be sure the on-screen image is large enough for the most distant members of the audience to see.

Design of Overheads
To design effective overheads:

- Use large letters and numbers, including both upper and lower case letters. Sans serif typeface is preferred.

- Limit each overhead to no more than 8 lines of text and a total of 25 words or numbers. Many will have far less.
- Use the top two-thirds of the transparency to keep all text on the screen at once.
- Use color to emphasize key information. Color has most impact when used sparingly.
- Mount the transparencies on cardboard frames. Write key words on the frame for references during the presentation.

Use of Overheads
To use overheads well:

- Test the projector for focus and alignment before your audience arrives.
- When it is time for your first overhead, turn on the projector with the transparency already in place.
- Ideally, use a pointer on the screen to lead the audience to a specific location. If you must point at the projector, use a pen or pointer instead of your finger.
- Turn off the projector when you want the audience to focus exclusively on your oral text.

Guidelines for Handouts   Handouts are best for presentations of four or fewer people. With larger groups, handouts can be unacceptably disruptive. If you must use handouts with substantially larger groups, hand them out after the presentation is finished.

Design of Handouts
To design handouts effectively:

- Type them. Handprinted handouts are acceptable only in highly informal situations.
- Use no more than 20 lines of text, fewer if each line contains several words or numbers.
- Photocopy handouts on different color paper for easy reference if their appearance is similar.

How to Use Handouts
- Hand out one sheet at a time to keep audience's attention focussed where you want it.
- Ask the audience to set aside a handout when you have finished with it.
- Pass out highly complex handouts only after you have finished a presentation.

Guidelines for Samples and Other Physical Props Use physical props, such as samples and models, when it is significantly easier to demonstrate something than describe it. Given that physical props can be highly disruptive, be sure the point you are making is important enough to risk the possible disruption.

Design of Physical Props
The prop should accurately demonstrate the point you are trying to make without bringing up other irrelevant issues.

How to Use Physical Props
To use physical props well, provide enough to go around. At a minimum, there should be one copy of each prop for each three people in the audience.

After passing out a prop, give the audience time to examine it before resuming the presentation.

If you don't have enough copies of the prop, hold it up, tell the audience what it is, and invite them to inspect it after the presentation.

General Guidelines for Using Visual Aids In summary, visual aids can be an impressive and important part of your presentation. When using visual aids, be sure to follow these guidelines:

- Observe how visual aids are used by others in your company, especially your superiors.
- Practice your presentation using your visual aids.
- Be prepared to go ahead with the presentation even if you can't use the visual aids you've planned. The slide projector may not work; there may be no chalk for the blackboard. Be prepared to adjust to these contingencies.
- Keep visual aids simple. Use phrases or short sentences to reinforce or outline main points.
- Make sure visual aids are directly related to the presentation.
- Design visual aids that are attractive and interesting to look at. They should be neat and professional looking.
- Choose the right type of visual aid to suit the presentation.
- Make sure your entire audience can see your visual aid.
- Introduce each visual aid orally before revealing it. After revealing it, wait a few seconds before discussing it. This will allow your audience to have time to see the entire visual aid.
- Try to average at least 90–120 seconds between visual aids to maintain a smooth flow and avoid choppiness.

- Keep your audience's focus where you want it. When you want the audience to focus completely on what you are saying, do not display any visual aids.

PREPARE FOR QUESTIONS AND OBJECTIONS

Once you've prepared your entire presentation, anticipate questions and objections.

This section develops a two-fold approach to help you answer questions and objections effectively. It first addresses why people ask questions and raise objections. Then it shows you how to prepare for questions and how to answer them effectively.

Following the audience analysis steps suggested in Chapters 1 and 8 will help you determine what areas of your discussion may raise questions. Listeners may ask you to clarify a train of logic, add background information, or provide additional facts.

Beyond determining what issues may need further clarification, pay close attention to potential objections—since it is your ability to respond to objections effectively that may determine whether you preserve the positive impressions you may have made in your presentation to that point.

Why People Object to Ideas

As a first step, examine reasons why people typically object to ideas.

- **Lack of money, time, authority, or support for your proposal.** All of these objections are serious stoppers. If you propose to show the comparative advantages of switching from a "quality control" system of manufacturing to a "total quality" assurance program at a time when budgets are tight, schedules look difficult to meet, higher level approvals are needed, or managers express satisfaction with the current system, you are likely to hear substantial objections to your proposal.

- **A conflict between accepting what you want listeners to do and what listeners have already publicly committed to.** Barry Staw, an expert in the psychology of commitment, has demonstrated that managers rarely reverse course on a public commitment because they believe to do so will undermine their image of leadership. For example, the leadership of the 1992 Democratic convention refused Governor Carey's request to address the convention because his pro-life views clashed with the pro-choice values of the party's platform.

- **A discrepancy between information you are presenting and information listeners have heard from other sources.** For example, if you assert that a proposed land purchase will appreciate significantly over time and listeners have read a report that concludes that real estate increases in that area will not keep pace with inflation, your listeners may question both your statistic on the land purchase, other facts you present, and the inferences you have drawn from them.

- **A conflict with an assumption about the nature of a problem.** If you assume that objectives are not being met because of a lack of employee effort, whereas listeners believe the problem lies in developing clear objectives, obtaining the proper tools, and giving adequate rewards for the work provided, it is likely you will be asked to address these additional issues by questioners.

- **Hidden reasons listeners may have for opposing your position.** In many ways these are the most difficult to deal with because listeners often will not reveal their true objections, but state other "rational" difficulties as a way of masking these less rational objections. Below are some examples of how listener's may really perceive the impact of a proposal.

Hidden Reasons for Opposing a Position

Your Plan	Listeners' Perception of It
My plan will save money.	Your plan will reduce the control my department has over this matter.
	Your plan will add to the amount of work I shall have to do.
We need more staff in data processing to deal with the increased demands on our time.	You are an empire builder.
My plan will put all accountants on the same floor in the same building and thereby improve communication among them.	I like the people I am working with now. I do not want to move.
	I do not want to lose the status of having an office with a view.
	I do not want to be that close to my bosses' offices.
	Your plan means that I have to fight downtown traffic and pay for parking.

Plan for Questions and Objections

To deal with questions and objections, plan for them. Specifically, while planning the content of your message, take the following steps:

- Write down questions and objections that you believe you will be asked. Use the Journalist's Seven Questions, as well as the previous list of objections, to help you generate this information.

- List all the problems your approach will solve and all the opportunities your idea will create. These two lists will help you demonstrate the further benefits of your position when answering questions.

- List trade-offs that will result from the implementation of your idea. This will allow you to admit disadvantages while demonstrating significant offsetting advantages.

- Mentally rehearse your answers to each question, using the appropriate responding techniques in the sections that follow.

- Define a fall-back position in case it becomes apparent during the presentation that you are not going to get everything you hoped for.

Responding to Questions Effectively

When you are asked a question, respond in the following ways:

- **Be courteous to your entire audience.** Thoughtfully listen to each question. Establish eye contact with the questioner, and let the questioner finish before you begin your answer. If your answer is fairly long, address the entire group before your answer is over, and not simply the questioner.

- **Ask for clarification of vague questions.** This will assure you that you are answering the actual question on the questioner's mind. Answering the wrong question may get you into unnecessary hot water.

    Question: Please evaluate the impact of your proposal on the human beings who are going to be most directly impacted by it.

    Response: *Are you asking how I believe the office environment will be affected by the replacement of typewriters with word processors?*

Question: No, what I am really asking is if we are going to pay for the higher costs of the equipment by letting go of one of the clerical staff.

Response: *Our analysis indicates that all full-time clerical staff will be retained after the purchase. In fact, we project the purchases will pay out in less than one year due to the higher productivity of the word processors and the corresponding reduction in temporary payroll costs from contract labor.*

- **Answer questions directly.** Most often it is best to view your answers as mini-memos organized in What, Why, Details format. The direct response will allow listeners to immediately perceive the answer to their questions, as well as provide the rationale and evidence behind your position.

  By contrast, an indirect response will delay the time it takes listeners to perceive the answer to the question, may leave out important links in the "logic train" or omit critical data, and may raise additional questions.

Question: How and why were members of the Quality Assurance Task Force selected?

Indirect response: *I am glad you asked that excellent question. It is certainly one that deserves addressing and it is something that all of us struggled with for a long time. We had one suggestion that the department heads should simply select committee members, others advocated departmental elections, and others thought anyone who wanted to be on the committee should be allowed to join. The issues of experience and commitment were key. In the end, we decided that each department would elect one member to serve on the committee.*

Direct: response: *The department heads agreed that each department should elect one member to serve on the task force. The two key criteria for selection were experience and commitment. All members of the task force have a minimum six months experience working with their departments. They also have agreed to attend all task force meetings and to prepare both oral and written summaries of how the objectives, goals, strategies, and action plans recommended by the task force affect their departments.*

- **Keep answers in line with your presentation objectives.** That is, argue on your own grounds, not those of your questioner. Often you will find it valuable to state a common objective both you and your listener agree upon, and then show how your proposal will effectively help your organization meet that goal.

Question: You have no idea how tired we get of auditors standing over our shoulders seeing whether we are doing our jobs according to some outdated manual.

Answer: *Our goal, like yours, is to build the business in the most effective ways possible. Our audits insure that projects adhere to the proposed schedule in terms of time, cost, and achievement—while simultaneously making sure that safety standards are met. In fact, when the Jefferson plant was built, audit controls were built into the plans for the plant, and as a result, the plant came in under budget, on time, with no accidents, and with few changes required from the original plan. The cooperation we suggest can lead to a similar win-win solution for the plant you will be building as well.*

- **Agree with a critic's right to an opinion. Then respond to the objection. End with additional benefits of your proposal.**

Question: If we buy this apple orchard now, we may lose our shirts, as the XYZ report predicts only 1–2% annual increases in the value of the property you propose we buy.

Response: *Of course, the report you cite concerns me also. It is based on trends for the entire county, which will probably experience an overall decline in population during the next decade. The basis for our 7% annual increase projection is that the specific area we propose to buy is experiencing the kind of rapid population growth that historically leads to rapid property value acceleration. If prices do go up by 7%, and we believe our projection to be conservative, we will double our investment in 10 years.*

Additionally, our main objective in purchasing this apple orchard is that it will give us the kind of product testing laboratory we believe is essential for producing an apple sauce which meets our company's exacting quality standards. And the laboratory we will construct on the property's north end will put us in close proximity to a large concentration of the type of professionals we want to recruit to staff the laboratory.

- **Use *Yes, and* rather than *Yes, but* responses.** The word *and* typically suggests a cooperative response whereas *but* and similar negative phrases suggest strong disagreement. In addition, a *Yes, and* approach more clearly tells listeners that you share their concerns, even if you are not always in agreement with their methods for achieving goals. As a result, *Yes and* responses are more likely to be accepted than *Yes but* responses.

Question:	Your proposal that we hire an additional staff member violates our productivity guidelines.
Ineffective Answer:	*Yes, but sales are more important to top management than productivity, and our proposal will clearly increase sales.*
More Effective:	*As our analysis indicates, the additional staffing would would allow us to meet our annual sales projection, upper management's top priority for our department. To address your concern, we are now exploring cost savings so we can also meet the productivity standard and accomplish our sales goals, once the new staff member comes on board.*

- **If listeners object because they have already committed to an alternative analysis or solution, position your answer to help you achieve some of your objectives; or alternatively, show the listener how agreeing with you would not require a public change in the previously made commitment.**

Objection:	After exhaustive analysis, we have already agreed to hire a statistician to fill the only authorized line rather than another laboratory analyst.
Answer:	*The objective in hiring that statistician is to check out the validity and reliability of the tests we are currently conducting. Given that one technician already devotes about 20 hours a week to that task now, when the statistician comes on board, I suggest we shift responsibilities so more hours are devoted to reducing the backlog of tests we have been assigned to complete.*
Answer:	*If we hire someone who can do both statistical analysis and laboratory analysis, we can fill the statistician's slot while meeting the need to reduce the backlog of tests we have been assigned to complete.*

Learn to Deal with Special Situations

In addition to answering objections, every speaker confronts special situations which require appropriate adaptions. A number of these situations and appropriate responses are detailed below.

- **How to handle the persistent questioner and the dominator**

Do's	Don'ts
<ul><li>Direct your remarks to the entire group.</li><li>Give support to those in group who support your ideas.</li><li>Allow others to build on your ideas as long as their comments are consistent with your objectives.</li></ul>	<ul><li>Take these questioners on one-on-one.</li><li>Appear to be defensive or obstructive.</li><li>Lapse into sullen silence.</li></ul>

Example

Question: You have not addressed the issue. Training people to use this equipment will take a lot of valuable time.

Answer: Yes initially. And an added benefit of this training is that it will reduce time spent on typing requests by at least 20%, thereby saving time in the long run.

Question: Don't you think that initial training time is a big problem?

Answer: I sense that you think it could. I would be interested in hearing your thinking on this matter, *or*

Answer: I wonder how others in the group feel about this topic, *or*

Answer: I sense that you have already decided that some of my ideas are not workable, so I would like a chance to discuss them some more.

- **How to handle the devil's advocate.** Pretend difficulty staters are inviting you to build on their comments.

    Answer: "So you are saying that if I can show my proposal will not be unduly costly, then you'll support its implementation."
    or

Put the difficulty stater in a proposing mode while you assume a responding mode, a complete reversal of roles.

> Answer: "Specifically what do you propose we do to solve this problem that is advantageous to what we in the finance department have proposed?"

- **How to handle a stall.** Be persistent in pursuing your objectives.

> Question: I'll have to talk to Gibson Edwards about this.

> Answer: Fine, can we bring him to this meeting right now, or talk about it with him immediately afterwards?

> Question: Let me get back to you about it.

> Answer: Fine. I'll summarize my points in a memo and have it in your hands by the end of the day. Now when can we get together on this?

> Question: I have to think about this.

> Answer: Of course, is there something causing you to hesitate about going along with what I have said?

- **How to handle rambling questions.** Rephrase the question in succinct form. Then answer it briefly.

- **How to answer a question which is a multiple question.** Answer that part of the question which best fits your objectives.

- **How to handle an irrelevant question.** Confirm that you understand the question and answer it briefly. If the questioner persists, either say that it is "beyond the scope of this presentation" and offer to discuss the topic after the meeting—or if the questioner is a high-ranking company official, continue to answer the questions!

- **How to handle skepticism.** Expand on your argument. Restate all the benefits.

> Question: We failed the last time we tried to enter the generic aspirin market.

> Answer: *Yes, that is correct. And we have learned a great deal from that experience and are confident that we will not repeat the mistakes we made then. For example . . . In addition, we have found the circumstances today are quite different than they were then . . . In short, we anticipate a successful entry into this market with a pretax profit of $4 million annually from our entry into it.*

> Question: I believe if we entered this market our competitors would lower their prices to retain market share.

Answer: *That is an important consideration—one we have carefully investigated. Our analysis revealed, for example, that
when Company Z introduced Product X on the market last
March, none of the existing brands lowered their prices.
And we expect the same reaction to our new generic product. Our initial evidence shows that it will capture 15
percent of the market, generate $4 million in pretax profit,
and solve one of the problems we have faced in manufacturing—overcapacity for some of our plants almost all of
the time.*

Question: Manufacturing people should stay out of marketing
decisions.

Answer: *Let me review the excellent research into the market we
have done before putting forth this proposal. . . In sum,
our research indicates ABC can add substantially to its
profits with this strategy.*

- **How to handle indifference.** Listeners become indifferent to your
  argument when you include information that is relevant to your
  needs but not to theirs. Thus, when listeners are indifferent you
  must expand on your explanation of benefits to make them relevant to the listeners' needs or you must add new benefits of
  more relevance to the basic concerns of your listeners.

SUMMARY

Preparing the content of an oral presentation requires substantially
more work than writing a memo or report. As this chapter illustrates, in addition to composing the presentation, you have to analyze the speaking situation; organize your material by time blocks,
with a particular focus on preparing an excellent introduction and
conclusion; develop appropriate visual aids; and prepare for questions and objections.

Once you are comfortable with its content, work on delivering
your presentation.

Exercise Prepare an oral presentation of your own using the
steps outlined in this chapter.

CHAPTER 13

Deliver the Presentation

A presentation begins as soon as the audience focuses on you as the speaker; it ends only after the audience directs its attention to another topic and speaker. So you must deliver your remarks effectively from the moment an audience focusses on you until they move onto another topic and speaker.

This chapter discusses key elements of the physical delivery of a presentation. It first shows you how to relax physically and prepare mentally for a presentation; it then discusses vocal and visual effectiveness, and ends with steps on how to prepare for a presentation.

HOW TO RELAX

Many people tremble at the thought of delivering a public speech, primarily because of the tension associated with doing poorly while at the center of public attention. In the *Book of Lists*, giving a public speech was listed as the thing more people feared most, including cancer.

Basically, people feel tension as a result of negative anticipation, the personal embarrassment and possible subsequent negative consequences of speaking in a monotone, forgetting what you wanted to say, being unable to answer questions, and so on. In short, tension issues from a belief that the potential negatives from giving a presentation far outweigh the potential rewards for success.

Fortunately, you can learn not to be tense, or at least to prevent listeners from realizing you are tense. A number of professionals have dealt with these issues and have developed approaches that you can use to deal with them successfully. Although the mind and body function as a unit, it is possible that you can be relaxed mentally and not physically, or vice versa. Research indicates that mental relaxation promotes physical relaxation, just as physical relaxation promotes mental relaxation. The following discussion will show you how to relax physically and how to prepare mentally for a presentation.

Relaxing Yourself Physically

The first step in dealing with tension is to know how physically different it feels to be tense than it does to be relaxed. Tension is blocked energy—holding in energy, instead of letting it out. Do the following two simple exercises, one a breathing exercise, the other an isometric exercise. These allow you to feel the physical differences between tension and relaxation, while also showing you how to put your body in a relaxed state.

1. **Take a deep breath and hold it in for a count of 20.** Focus on the feeling of tension. Exhale slowly. Concentrate on the feeling of relaxation. Notice how tension built when you held your breath and diminished when you released it.

   Use a similar technique, the alternating breathing technique, to relax your entire body. Find a quiet place where there are no distractions. As you do these breathing exercises, keep your mind comfortably focused on the sound of air being breathed in and out. Sit in a hard backed chair and assume a posture in which your back is gently touching the back of the chair; keep your head comfortably raised atop your backbone. Do not let it slump forward.

   Close your eyes; then take a full breath from your diaphragm. When you have filled your lungs, exhale slowly and fully. Concentrate alternately on the feelings of tension and relaxation. Repeat for 5 to 10 minutes. Note how you feel progressively more relaxed each time you exhale.

Tense your hands into tight fists and hold them that way for a count of 20. Release your fists and extend your fingers slowly. Again notice how tension built the longer you held in energy and how tension faded when you let the energy flow out of your body.

2. **Now use similar isometrics to progressively relax your entire body.** Start from the legs and work your way up to your head. First tense all of your leg muscles and hold them for a count of ten; then release them. Do the same thing with your arms, abdominal muscles, chest, shoulders and neck. Finally, tense your face by opening your mouth as wide as you can while closing your eyes as tightly as possible. Repeat the tensing and relaxing exercises for those body areas that remain tense.

Relaxing Yourself Mentally

Mentally prepare yourself for a presentation. Realize that events do not make you nervous; your beliefs about events do. Follow the guidelines below in preparing for a presentation.

Do Positive Self-Talk

Do	Don't
View the situation as an opportunity to share your insights with others.	Blame the situation. "I never do well under the pressure of giving a public speech."
Think in positive terms such as *confident, impressive, prepared,* and *poised.* Replace negative words such as *terrible* with neutral ones such as *unfortunate.*	Think in catastrophic terms such as *terrible, awful,* and *horrible.*
View yourself as an evolving human being. "I may have mumbled in the past, but I am really going to improve on that score in my next presentation."	Give yourself an unflattering label. "I will always be a mumbler."
Be goal oriented. "If I get agreement to my proposal, I will know I have made an effective presentation."	Set up unrealistic goals. "If I make one mistake, it will be a disaster."

Reduce Your Fear of Audience Reproach by Redefining Your Image of Your Listeners   Laughter is a potent antidote to tension. Use it to reduce your fear of audiences by redefining your image of them in a humorous way. FDR countered stage fright by imagining that all the people in his audience had holes in their socks. Winston Churchill went even further, imagining that his listeners were sitting in their underwear. Try their techniques and you may find your tension melting away as you smile at your thoughts of the altered appearance of your listeners.

Practice Autogenic Training   Autogenic training is a combination of mental and physical relaxation techniques. This training is predicated on the idea that you can cause your body to relax by making mental associations with feelings associated with the onset of sleep. To practice autogenic training, take the following steps, spending two to three minutes on each one.

- Close your eyes.
- Concentrate on breathing slowly and deeply.
- Tell yourself that your limbs are very heavy; feel the heaviness of your limbs.
- Tell yourself that your limbs are very warm; feel this warmth.
- Tell your heart to beat slowly and rhythmically.

Relax the Speech Center   Beyond these exercises, work on relaxing in both a standing and a seated position. This will help you succeed in stand-up, group, and one-on-one situations.

Relax in a Standing Position
- Stand at attention, with weight evenly distributed on both feet. Put your shoulders back. Fully extend your fingers.
- Take a breath from your diaphragm. As you do, imagine your back is a broomstick and your head is a beachball balanced on top of it. Strive for a feeling of perfect balance. Exhale. Let all of your muscles relax as you exhale.
- Roll your shoulders in circles. Then gently swing your neck from side to side, your ears nearly touching your shoulder. Roll your neck in half circles, nearly touching your chin to your shoulder.
- If your neck continues to feel tense, do the following exercises:
  —Let your head slowly fall forward until your chin almost touches your chest, exhaling as you lower your head. Close your

eyes. Slowly raise your head, inhaling as you do. Exhale fully. Repeat until your neck and head feel relaxed.

—Open your mouth fully, letting your jaw drop. Let your tongue hang limply over your lip. Inhale and exhale slowly, without pausing. You should begin to feel so relaxed you will be drowsy.

Relax in a Seated Position   Now do these same exercises in a seated position. Sit in "double *L's*" posture, with your legs forming an *L* perpendicular at the knees, while your torso forms an *L* perpendicular to your hips and bottom. Doing these exercises while seated will help you adjust to being relaxed while speaking at a group meeting.

In short, by understanding the mental and physical dimensions of tension and by practicing time-tested techniques of stress reduction, you can teach yourself to relax when making a presentation.

ACHIEVING VOCAL EFFECTIVENESS

Once you have mastered breathing and relaxation, you can work to improve your voice and delivery. To get the most benefit out of the exercises that follow, it is important to record yourself doing each one.

Practice Effective Breath Control

Breath control is required for effective voice production. You should already be able to breathe from the diaphragm with the previous exercises. Now learn to regulate your breath.

Practice saying the alphabet one letter at a time, pronouncing each syllable strongly and clearly, taking a breath from your diaphragm before each letter. Notice how your breath allows you to articulate clearly.

Next practice saying a series of letters, such as *ABCDE* with a single breath. To retain vocal emphasis as you practice longer and longer series of letters, take small breaths rather than a single long breath to sustain speech, much as opera singers do to sustain an aria. Work up to saying the alphabet from *A* to *Z* without stopping. Take a small gulp of air if you begin to run out of breath. This exercise demonstrates that you can create adequate breath to maintain volume and create vocal emphasis at any time during a presentation.

Emphasize Words Effectively

Vocal variety requires emphasizing key words in a message. To achieve a sense of emphasis, read and tape record well-known passages. Vary the way you emphasize words and observe how their meaning changes. Here are some examples:

- We have not yet begun to fight!
- Damn the torpedos! Full speed ahead.
- Go ahead. Make my day.
- Give me liberty or give me death.
- I have come here not to praise Caesar, but to bury him.
- To be or not to be, that is the question.
- These are the best of times; these are the worst of times.
- I love you with the breadth and depth of my soul.

Speak at a Rate Listeners Can Easily Understand

Research indicates that when you speak too fast, you undermine listeners' confidence that they have understood your meaning. A fast rate may also indicate a lack of attention to the audience and its needs. Conversely, a too slow rate may connote a lack of mental acuity on your part. Therefore, tape yourself reading a 300 word passage. See how many words you speak per minute. You are speaking at a rate easy to understand if you speak between 125–250 words per minute. If you are speaking above or below that rate, practice reading the passage aloud until your rates falls into the 125–250 word limit.

You might also find it useful to imitate the rate—and the emphasis—of a favorite national newscaster, an expert trained to speak to be understood immediately.

Pronounce Words So They Are Easily Understood

Mumbling will undermine an image of competence. So your words are easily understood:

- Speak in fluent phrases, not in words; sound vowels fully.
- Give key concepts the greatest emphasis.
- If you hear yourself mumbling, the best cure is to slow down and pronounce words one syllable at a time. Practice saying poly-

syllabic words such as *beautiful, library, government, Saturday, lily livered, stationery, regenerative, et cetera, prognosticate,* and *metaphorical.*

Attain Vocal Variety

Tape record yourself reading aloud from a newspaper. Do you vary the pitch, pacing, and emphasis according to the sense of the document. Is there life, color, and melody in your voice?

If not, you may find practicing the following exercise will help you achieve excellent vocal variety. After doing these 12 examples, with lots of energy and emotion, deliver passages from your own presentations with equal vigor. You will find an excellent carry-over.

SPEAKING EMPHASIS EXERCISE

Politician to crowd: "... and I promise that if I am elected in November, I will work to reduce taxes, reduce crime, reduce unemployment, and reduce inflation."

Irate parent to kids: "I want to know which one of you kids put the Barbie clothes in the toilet! How many times have I told you that you ABSOLUTELY CANNOT PUT THINGS DOWN THE TOILET! Do you have any idea how much a plumber makes per hour?"

Basketball coach to team: "Okay now we've got just one chance left. They're ahead by four points with one minute left on the clock. We gotta foul them and pray they miss the shot. Then we gotta get the rebound and score and hope we can make up the other basket before they score again or we run out of time. Let's go!"

Preacher to congregation: "... if you do not repent, then you will not be saved! You will be damned to eternal separation from God! Time is running out! Judgment is at hand! Confess your sins. Turn your back on the sinful ways of the devil. The time is now!"

Circus barker to crowd: "Step right up ladies and gentlemen and see the amazing Barzinis. They will thrill you with their death-defying, high-wire acrobatics, 200 feet about the ground, without a net."

Elated new parent to friend: "A girl! We just had a girl! After three boys, we've finally got a daughter! This is the happiest day of my life! Here, have a cigar!"

(continued)

Irate spouse to spouse: "What?! You did what?! What do you mean you bought a new car?! How could you even think of spending that kind of money without consulting me? We don't even need a new car! I can't believe you did this!"

Elated lottery winner to spouse: "5 - 1 - 24 - 19 - 8 - 30! Those are my numbers! I won! I won the Lotto! 5 million dollars! We're millionaires! Wait a minute . . . Did I get those numbers right? 5 - 1 - 24 . . . "

Irate doctor to expectant mother: "Mrs. Jones, you've gained eight pounds since last month! That's twice as much as I wanted you to gain! You're just going to have to exert your willpower now and keep the weight gain down to no more that one pound per month for the rest of your pregnancy!"

Teacher to class: "I'm ashamed to say that every single one of you flunked the exam! Not one of you studied! Now we're going to have another exam over the same material one week from today, and if you fail it, you fail for this semester!"

Lawyer to jury: "We intend to prove beyond a shadow of a doubt that the defendant, John E. Jones, on the night of December 4, 1983, did willfully break and enter into the home of Henry Higgins, did assault Mr. Higgins with a deadly weapon, and did steal from his property $37,000 worth of rare coins."

Speak Authoritatively

Much of your credibility as a speaker depends upon how authoritatively you speak. This is especially true for listeners who have had little other exposure to you. Three factors—pitch, inflection, and verbal fillers—all directly influence your ability to speak with authority.

Develop a Low-Pitched Voice Research indicates that men and women with lower pitched voices tend to be perceived as more credible than their counterparts with higher pitched voices. If you have a high-pitched voice, practice the exercise below. It shows you how to speak in a lower range.

- Sit in a chair.
- Lean over until your head is nearly between your knees. Say "COOO" very deeply.

- Raise your body and take a deep breath and say "COOO" again. The deep breath you will have taken will come from the diaphragm.

- As you unbend, keep drawing breath from the same place in your abdomen. That will help you find a good place from which to pitch your voice.

- Discontinue this exercise if it puts a strain on your voice.

End Sentences and Questions with a Downward Inflection

A downward inflection indicates you mean business; an upward inflection suggests that you are asking for listener approval.

Notice how much more authoritative these sentences sound when inflected downwardly.

Upward Inflection:	Downward Inflection:
■ What time should I be there?	■ What time should I be there?
■ How often will this seminar be held?	■ How often will this seminar be held?
■ What has the task force decided?	■ What has the task force decided?

Eliminate Verbal Fillers and Speech "Tics"

Verbal fillers include *um, uh, you know, like, okay,* and other such speech tics. These image killers make you appear indecisive and lacking in knowledge or confidence. Two techniques will help you eliminate such phrases from your speaking.

- **Eliminate fillers through practice.** Most speakers use fillers at places they might ordinarily take a small breath or where they might otherwise pause. To overcome this problem, practice a portion of a presentation out loud. When you say *um* or *uh* or *okay,* stop your practice and start the sentence over. You will feel an urge to repeat the filler. Resist it.

  After enough practice, you find yourself sensing when you are approaching a vocalized pause, and you will simply pause silently rather than use a filler.

- **Substitute good phrases for fillers.** For example, instead of *um* or *uh,* say "My understanding is" or "I see" or "Let me think". Instead of *like, you know* say "a good comparison would be."

Speech tics also include phrases that you as an individual may use habitually. For example, two opponents for the presidency in 1968 earned the following nicknames because of the constant repetition of a single phrase: Richard "I want to make this perfectly clear" Nixon and Hubert "I believe" Humphrey. The exercise recommended for generic fillers also works for this type of problem.

REHEARSING AND EVALUATING YOUR PRESENTATION

An audience reacts not only to what it hears, but also to what it sees. Once you can read through your planned presentation comfortably, it is time to actually practice it out loud. This critical step must be taken so you can hear and see yourself speak much the way your listeners will. Practicing will help you increase your confidence and poise, help your fluency, expose gaps in your memory as well as in your reasoning, and will make you comfortable in working with your visual aids.

Rehearse Your Presentation

- **Familiarize yourself with your material.** Don't memorize it. Confidence comes from a thorough understanding of your topic and your presentation objective.

- **Put your presentation on no more than two note cards.** Write key words on the cards, such as names, statistics, and words which will remind you of key ideas. Avoid using regular-sized paper, which is awkward to hold.

- **Practice the presentation out loud from beginning to end, with visual aids.** Do not stop when you make a mistake. After two or three rehearsals, practice only those sections which give you the most trouble.

EVALUATE YOUR PRESENTATION

To best evaluate your effectiveness, view a videotape of a practice presentation. As you view the tape, ask the following questions:

- **Do you have a confident approach to the podium?** Do you:

   —show enthusiasm when you rise and walk to the podium?

   —stand in front of the audience with a sense of control?

   —survey audience members and engage their attention?

   —briefly review your introduction in your mind?

   —start talking in a clear and audible tone?

- **Are your facial gestures effective?** Does your facial expression appear to be positive toward listeners: warm, enthusiastic, alive, and confident? Or does it communicate negatives, look tense, uninterested, condescending, or sour?

- **Is eye contact effective?** Have you looked into the eyes of each person in the room, lingering longest with decision makers and the friendliest faces in the room? Have you looked into one person's eyes at a time to establish your interest, rather than scanning the room or focusing on a place above the heads of listeners?

- **Are your bodily gestures effective?** Good gesturing can reinforce key points of meaning and emphasis in presentations and also can help relieve stress by allowing you to release energy. The kind and amount of gestures you use should be governed by the size of your audience and the nature of your communication.

   Typically you will use fewer and smaller gestures with small audiences, when you are sitting down, and when the presentation is being taped for rebroadcasting. In these case, gestures similar to those used in a conversation are most appropriate.

   Numerous and fuller gestures are appropriate when you are addressing a large audience in a stand-up presentation. Full gestures, such as fully extending your arm to make a point or to highlight a point on a chart, make the speaker a more arresting stimulus to observe. Likewise, walking forward or backward typically reinforces an action image; whereas pacing sideways reinforces an image of indecision and lack of interest in listeners.

   The key to effective gesturing is planning and rehearsing. Good speakers often move as they begin and end key points. They typically move their arms to signal an important point. They know when to pick up and use props, and when to move to use visual aids.

   After reviewing your tape, repractice any sections where you believe gestures are needed and drop or change those which appear to be distracting or awkwardly completed.

- **Is your vocal delivery effective?**
  Do you:

  —Speak loudly enough to be clearly heard by all listeners?

  —Emphasize words to best communicate the meaning of your message?

  —Speak at a rate listeners can easily understand?

  —Pronounce words clearly?

  —Speak authoritatively? at an easy-to-comprehend rate?

  —Speak without using verbal tics, such as *um* and *OK*?

GET READY FOR YOUR PRESENTATION

Once you've rehearsed your presentation, take steps that will help you relax so you can be as effective in person as you were in practice.

- Dress in comfortable clothing that you believe is appropriate for the situation in which you will be making your presentation.

- Practice relaxation exercises at home.

- Maintain a posture of energetic relaxation on the way to your presentation. Practice exhaling deeply to help you remain calm.

- In your office, do isometric exercises, especially with those muscle groups in which you feel tension.

- Relax your mind. Talk to yourself in positive terms.

- Before you begin speaking, stand or sit in a "double *L's*" posture.

- Take your time walking to the podium. Keep your head up.

- When you get to the podium, take as much time as you need before beginning. Settle into a comfortable posture. Gain eye contact with your audience.

- Set yourself at psychological ease by pretending that all your listeners have holes in their socks (as FDR did) or that all your listeners are dressed in their underwear (as Winston Churchill did).

- As you speak, direct your comments and eye contact at the most influential people in the audience and at people who are responding most positively to what you are saying.

SUMMARY

The ability to deliver a presentation effectively is a key to being perceived as a leader—as the success of American political and religious leaders such as John Kennedy, Ronald Reagan, Martin Luther King, Billy Graham, Barbara Jordan, and Bill Clinton attests. Speakers who display confidence through an effective delivery inspire confidence in their ideas; those who deliver presentations poorly suggest they lack the confidence, commitment, and authority to effectively lead others.

Fortunately, good delivery is a learned skill. By practicing the exercises covered in this chapter, including mental and physical relaxation, developing an authoritative and interesting vocal delivery, and practicing and evaluating vocal quality and physical movement, you can markedly improve your delivery, before both small and large audiences, and as a result, build the confidence of others in your leadership abilities.

PART V

USE MODELS
OF EFFECTIVELY
WRITTEN DOCUMENTS

14 Selected Model Documents

CHAPTER 14

Selected Model Documents

This section contains a wide variety of model letters, memos, and reports. They represent typical documents written in a variety of functional areas, including engineering, manufacturing and science; finance and accounting; sales and advertising; and human resource management.

To use this section as a "good book" in writing your own messages, find the model that best reflects your writing objectives. Then compose a first draft imitating the structure and style of that model. I suggest you photocopy this section on three-hole paper and insert the models into it. Then when one of your own or one of your colleagues' documents receives praise, add it to this collection as a way of compiling a "good book" tailored to the needs of your department.

WRITING BUSINESS LETTERS

Many business letters, such as letters of request, letters in response to requests, letters of complaint, letters in response to complaints, and letters summarizing meetings, follow a similar format.

1. *Orientation to key issues*: The opening sentence or paragraph should explain the purpose of your letter, discussing the What, the Why, and often the When of your document.

2. *Analysis and data supporting the message objective:* Provide analysis and data the reader needs to know to understand your purpose. This can include details of a purchase, data concerning an order that has been shipped, the details of a complaint, the steps being taken in response to a complaint, and the topics covered at a meeting.

Additional analysis and data: Provide supplementary analysis and information, when appropriate, you believe to be valuable to the reader.

3. *Follow-up:* Indicate, as appropriate, follow-up steps, including a telephone number. Close with a complimentary closing, such as "Sincerely yours," and a signature block.

Model #1: Letter of Request

In a letter of request, state what you are requesting in the opening sentence. When appropriate, give enough background to explain why you are making the request. If your request is detailed, use highlighting to make it easy for the reader to comply. For example, in the following letter, the items ordered are organized in a row and column format, with headings identifying number and type of items ordered, their color, unit cost, and total cost. It also specifies a preferred carrier and requests that shipping charges be added to the total of the purchase order.

Dear _____:

Please send me the following supplies, using purchase order #33A. As we are now running short of nearly all of these items in our office, make sure they arrive no later than August 13. Our preferred carrier is ABC Delivery.

#	Description	Color	Unit Cost	Total
4 reams	20lb. bond paper	white	$15.00	$ 60.00
3 reams	20lb. bond paper	#3 beige	20.00	60.00
8 boxes	500 ct. ABC letterhead envelopes	white	30.00	240.00
			Total	$360.00

As you have in the past, please add shipping charges to the purchase order.

Thank you for your prompt reply to this order. We enjoy doing business with you. If you have any questions, please call me at 555–1111.

Model #2: Letter of Complaint

In a letter of complaint your objective should be to achieve an appropriate response to your complaint. To that end, write in a rational, objective tone, one that clearly indicates what you want done in response to your complaint, why this is a reasonable response, as well as the facts that validate your complaint. In short,

Orientation:	▪ Indicate exactly what you want done in response to your complaint.
	▪ Indicate why this is a reasonable request.
Analysis/Details:	▪ Provide the details that support your request.
Follow-up:	▪ Close with an expression of your confidence that your request will be honored.

Dear _____:

I am writing to request reimbursement of $25.00 for the damage your wallpaper hangers caused to my hall carpet. This amount covers the expense I incurred to clean the damage done to my hall carpet.

Copies of the invoices of my purchase and of my payment for the carpet repair, as well as photographs of the damaged carpet, are attached.

Here are the details of what has occurred to date.

1. I contracted with Modern Interiors to paper my upstairs hallway. The paper was hung on March 15, 1993.

2. The installers spilled wet paste on the carpet; subsequently, the carpet became hard and stiff and the hallway smelled of wallpaper paste.

3. The workers also smoked in the house and left cigarette butts in the toilet, as well as ashes on the hall carpet, as I reported to you in my last letter, dated March 16.

4. In order to get my house ready for a party on March 18, I hired Sparkle Cleaners to clean and deodorize the soiled carpet in the hallway. They completed the cleaning on March 17, at a cost of $25.00.

Please call me at 555–1111 should you want to discuss this matter in more detail. At the time of my purchase, Ed Smith, assistant sales manager, assured me that your company stands behind its work, so I am confident that you will reimburse me as soon as possible.

Model #3: Letter Resolving a Complaint

In resolving a complaint, focus specifically on maintaining the good-will of the customer as well as creating a positive image of your organization. Avoid using negative words or phrases that may offend your reader or create a negative image of your organization. Such words include *complaint* and *allege*, which suggest you do not believe the customer, and phrases such as "every right to be disappointed," "hope you have not lost confidence in us," and "an unaccountable error in our quality program" which suggest the customer might be justified in dealing with competitors in the future.

Orientation:
Analysis/Data:
- Accept the complaint at face value.
- Say what you are going to do about it.
- When appropriate, offer a compensatory benefit.

Follow-up:
- Ask for continued business.
- Thank customer for helping you improve your business.

Dear _____:

Thank you for your fax of October 3 in which you note you received only 80% of the ABC minibags you had ordered. Ms. Ellen O'Neal, Customer Service Manager, has looked into the matter. She found that, due to a shortage of supply at the Atlanta Distribution Center, we shipped you 80% of your order last week—with the remaining 20% to be delivered to your warehouse on or before October 10.

In the future we will notify you by phone or by fax of any short shipments and will continue making note of that fact at the bottom of the invoice.

To show that we stand behind our products and services, we are discounting the October 10 shipment by 2%. And, given the success of our long-standing partnership, we are confident you will continue to purchase ABC products.

Thank you for helping us in our quest to continually improve our service to our customers. We appreciate your comments and your business.

Model #4: Letter of Response

In a letter responding to a request, work to achieve two objectives: to indicate you are complying with the client's request and to create goodwill with the client.

Orientation:
- Open by complimenting the reader.
- Indicate you are responding to the reader's request.

Analysis/Data:
- If you are responding to multiple requests, use headings to subdivide the information.

Follow-up:
- Close by indicating you appreciate the positive business relationship you have with the reader.

Dear _____:

I enjoyed meeting with you to learn more about your business. ABC has a long history of success with companies like yours, and we are confident Mass Merchandisers will profit by including our products in its merchandising mix.

Below I have provided the information you requested about our products, broker coverage, and ABC's relationship with Millbrook Distributors.

Product Information. I have attached a list of ABC products which have proven appeal to upscale consumers. Under separate cover I have sent samples of our full line of products.

You will also be receiving pictures of our holiday collection by mid-March. We are excited by the prospect of including ABC novelties in your 1994 Christmas catalog.

Broker Coverage. As you suggested, to ensure the success of our line, we will introduce our products through brokers who have proven track records of providing full and effective coverage.

In fact, as soon as I receive the list of names you will be sending, I will

- complete the contracts and set up meetings in San Francisco at the Exclusive Novelties Show; and
- see Mr. Dierbergen while I am in St. Louis to get additional insights into the names and types of accounts we will be serving.

Millbrook Distributors. I have looked into ABC's relationship to Millbrook Distributors, as you requested. It has been highly successful. Millbrook has distributed ABC products for the past seven years, with consistent increases in the volume of products purchased from us.

Once again, I thank you for the opportunity to discuss being part of your upscale product mix. ABC looks forward to a long and mutually profitable association with Mass Merchandisers. And I look forward to speaking with you in the near future.

Model #5: Letter Summarizing the Results of a Meeting

When summarizing the results of a meeting, remember that your reader does not want to know all the details of your trip or of the meeting. What the reader wants is an answer to these questions: what issues were discussed at the meeting? What was decided? What steps do we take next?

Orientation:	■ Open with a clear statement of the What and the Why of your message.
	■ Forecast the development of the rest of the letter.
Analysis/Data:	■ Use headings to indicate the topics discussed.
	■ Organize paragraphs deductively, beginning with the decision made, followed by the reasons for the decisions, and, when appropriate, the data supporting each decision.
Follow-up:	■ Indicate next steps.

Dear _____ :

I met with the management of Sterling Silver, Inc., today to discuss the three major recommendations we recently made in our annual audit. We came to a compromise agreement on staff reductions, made some progress on the issue of severance pay, and disagreed on the need for cutting medical benefits.

Staff Reductions
Sterling's management agreed to cut the factory staff by a percentage equal to the drop in sales. They also agreed to cut administrative staff by eight people, four fewer than we recommended. They want to judge the effect of the smaller cut before considering a larger one.

Severance Pay
Sterling's management will decide on a compromise severance package awarding workers two weeks' pay per year of service. They agreed that the proposal by Mr. Moore, the vice-president of human resources, of paying one month's payment for each year's service would be too costly. Likewise, they concluded that our proposal of one week's pay per year of service was inadequate compensation.

Medical Benefits
Sterling's management rejected our recommendation that each covered employee pay the first $400 of medical claims annually before the company's health insurance program would begin payment. We had estimated a savings of $13,500 through such a program. Sterling agreed to investigate other ways of stabilizing the annual cost of medical insurance premiums for future years, including eliminating the subsidy of prescription drugs.

After I return to headquarters on Friday, I'll schedule a meeting to discuss revised proposals we can make on medical benefits. I will put them before Sterling's management at our next meeting, on August 4th.

Model #6: Letter of Application

In writing a letter of application, your key task is to prove that you deserve an interview because you are the best qualified applicant for the position. To prove this point, you must demonstrate that your education, experience, and personal qualities precisely meet the criteria stated in the advertisement. Before you write this letter, make a two-columned list. In the right-hand column, list all of the stated criteria for the position; in the left-hand column, write down specific personal details which correspond to each of the criteria. Then use this information in the application letter to prove that you deserve an interview, because you are so clearly qualified for the position.

Orientation:	■ State that you are applying for the advertised position, using the exact title of the job as well as how you found out about the position.
	■ Assert that there is a good fit between the qualities needed to fill the job and your education, experience, and personal qualities.
Analysis/Data:	■ Put your strongest qualification first. Be specific, proving your case with both persuasive reasoning and hard facts.
	■ Develop your other qualifications, again using empirical data to support your claims.
Follow-up:	■ Request an interview. Indicate when you will be available and how you can best be reached.
	■ End on a positive note.

Dear _____:

I am writing to apply for the position of sales manager at Baxley Laboratories, advertised recently in *Sales Quarterly*. Your advertisement calls for an "energetic, self-starter" with previous sales and management experience, and a college degree. I am well-qualified for this position, meeting all criteria.

Experience

As the attached resume demonstrates, I have excellent experience both as a manager and as a sales representative. I am presently employed by Fine Furniture as a sales administrator, reporting directly to the vice president for sales. Fine Furniture is the leading furniture manufacturer in the United States. In my current position, I supervise a staff that conducts showroom and plant visitations, oversees the creation of new sales territories, and monitors the progress of many sales initiatives.

Prior to my promotion to sales administrator, I was a highly successful sales representative. In my five years in that position, I increased sales in my territory by an average of 30% annually, added more new customers during 1986–1991 than any other representative, and was three times named "Sales Representative of the Year."

Education

I have completed both BSBA (1985) and MBA (1992) degrees from Xavier University during nights and weekends, while holding down full-time positions. I maintained better than a 3.5 average in both degree programs, a testament to my intellectual and time management skills.

Energy

I am also highly energetic. In addition to the above accomplishments, I have served three terms as a city councilman and headed up the most successful United Way campaign in my division's history.

I am very interested in the sales management position at Baxley Laboratories and would welcome the opportunity to discuss the position more fully. Please call me at 555–1111 to arrange an interview.

Model #7: Resume

An effective resume demonstrates that you have the education, work experience, and personal characteristics necessary to meet the criteria for a position for which you have applied. It should show a clear relationship between your experience and education and the job objective you have listed; stress your accomplishments; be one or two pages long; and be neatly typed, error-free, and designed to be easily scanned.

Orientation:
- Put your name, address, and telephone number first on the resume. This tells the reader who you are and how to get in touch with you.
- Next write either a reasonably specific, employer-oriented objective, or a personal summary that describes what kinds of contributions you can make to an organization.
- Provide data in the remainder of the resume that supports the claims made in this section.

Analysis/Data:
- Use headings to separate the major categories of your resume, including education, work experience, and personal interests.
- Use design techniques to make it easy for readers to find out this information: a complete sequence of dates for your work experience as well as your education; the sequence of positions you have held; and the sequence of companies for which you have worked.
- Position facts positively.
  —Use action verbs to describe your work. For example, you'll project a more active image of yourself if you say you "successfully managed inventories in the warehouse as well as the store floor" than if you say you were "responsible for managing warehouse and store floor inventories."
  —Include accomplishments, such as paying for 100% of tuition through grants and part-time work; making the Dean's List; being nominated for a customer service award; receiving a most valuable player award; being elected president of a community organization; and receiving promotions.

Follow-up:
- If you have room, close the resume with a follow-up statement that "references are available upon request."

HOWARD JONES
100 Clenay Drive
Cincinnati, Ohio 45205
(555) 745–2025

OBJECTIVE: Position as a managment trainee in a people-oriented organization where excellent customer relations are desired.

EDUCATION: Xavier University, Cincinnati, Ohio; College of Business Administration, B.S.B.A. Management.
To graduate December, 1988 with high honors.
- Major GPA 4.0, overall 3.73; Dean's List all semesters.
- Admitted with distinction, recipient of Trustee Scholarship (4 year) awarded for academic achievement.
- Financed education through academic scholarships, part-time employment and student loans.
- Fall 1987 achieved a 3.83 GPA (eighteen hours) while working ten to twenty hours weekly.
- Experience in BASIC computer language.

6/86-5/87   La Sorbonne—Universite de Paris, Paris, France
- Financed in part through the Fredin Memorial Scholarship given by Xavier University.
- Read, write, and speak French proficiently.
- Discovered the value and pleasure of travel.

WORK EXPERIENCE:

12/87 to
present
Associate—Tender Sender at **Lazarus**, Cincinnati, Ohio.
- Completed customer requests quickly and professionally.
- Assumed new responsibility to accurately record data.
- Identified as a "good worker" and "very personable."
- Implemented new techniques in serving customers more quickly and with improved quality.
- Achieved and maintained sales averages above expected levels.
- Entrusted to handle entire department alone.

6/87 to
present
Message Center Operator—**DuBois Chemicals**, Cincinnati, Ohio.
- Assisted disgruntled clients in an effective manner while maintaining an amiable, business-like attitude.
- Promoted after probation period with a 6.25% raise.

Summers
1983–1985
Swim Coach/Instructor, Lifeguard, Pool Maintenance—**Delhi Swim Club**, Cincinnati, Ohio.
- Promoted in three years from head lifeguard to assistant swim team coach and swim lessons instructor.
- Coached approximately 50 children through two seasons of competition, leading the team from fourteenth place to a seventh place finish in league championships.

ACTIVITIES:
- Coached several St. Francis Parish Soccer teams.
- Member of St. Francis Singers and St. Francis Church Choir.
- Member of Xavier University Scholar's Program and Marketing Club.

INTERESTS: Enjoy singing, swimming, and coaching.

Marcus Riley
3030 Autumn Way Court
Cincinnati, Ohio 45238
Home: (555) 530–9871
Work: (555) 767–1168

SUMMARY OF QUALIFICATIONS

- Goal-oriented, enthusiastic individual looking for challenge.
- 14 years experience in the chemical industry.
- Liberal Arts Degree from Xavier University in December 1993.
- Associate Degree in Business Management from Miami University.
- Strong industrial marketing, sales and research background.

EXPERIENCE

1991 to 1992   DUBOIS USA—DIV. OF DIVERSEY CORP., Cincinnati, Ohio
Manufacturing Specialist
- Coordinated marketing activities for Dubois' large account development program.
- Conducted customer audits and plant surveys; submitted numerous proposals resulting in new and additional business.
- Developed and presented complete training program for selling industrial lubrication.
- Monitored progress and promoted new products from research.
- Promoted to project manager for new target areas in steel mills and printing, July 1992.
- Fostered growth in lubrication product lines with development and introduction of new specialized equipment.

1990 to 1991   DUBOIS USA—DIV. OF DIVERSEY CORP., Cincinnati, Ohio
Product Manager
- Managed a line of 25 industrial greases.
- Promoted and provided support for a full line of industrial lubricants.
- Introduced five new greases into the industrial market which had a positive impact on the sales and growth of the lubrication line for DuBois.

1990   DUBOIS CHEMICAL—DIV. OF CHEMED CORP., Cincinnati, Ohio
Applications Engineer
- Monitored and performed troubleshooting functions for new and existing customers in the plant pretreatment area.
- Assisted in technical service and training functions in DuBois' research facility.

(continued)

1989 to   DUBOIS CHEMICALS—DIV. OF CHEMED CORP., Columbus, Ohio
  1990   **Industrial Sales Representative**
           ▪ Sold and serviced a full line of industrial specialty chemicals to
           central Ohio region.
           ▪ Sold and serviced over 50 major industrial accounts with no lost
           accounts and positive increases in every sales quarter.
           ▪ Opened several new accounts that are still active DuBois
           accounts today.

1987 to   DUBOIS CHEMICALS—DIV. OF CHEMED CORP., Cincinnati, Ohio
  1989   **Chemist**
           ▪ Maintained and improved lubricant testing service and support
           for 800 sales representatives and a product line of 50 specialty
           lubricants.
           ▪ Participated in many sales support activities.
           ▪ Formulated synthetic chain lubricants and heat transfer oils for
           the industrial marketplace.

1979 to   DUBOIS CHEMICALS—DIV. OF W. R. GRACE, Cincinnati, Ohio
  1987   **Various titles and positions**
           ▪ Held a variety of positions in the research center for DuBois.
           Steadily progressed in responsibility with each position while
           attending night school at Miami University.

EDUCATION

> **Xavier University, Cincinnati Ohio**
> BLA—Bachelor of Liberal Arts, December 1993
> Major: Liberal Arts
> Minor: Marketing
> GPA: 3.46
> Dean's List
>
> **Miami University, Oxford and Hamilton Campuses**
> AAB Associate of Applied Business, May 1986
> Major: Management of Business Technology
> GPA: 3.20

COMPUTER SKILLS

> Proficient in the following software packages:
>
> Word Perfect, Lotus 123, Microsoft Works, Microsoft Excel, DBase 3+
> Reflex, Show Partner, Harvard Graphics, First Publisher.

REFERENCES

> Available upon request.

Model #8: Thank You Letter

In the thank you letter, you have two objectives: to express your gratitude and to promote your business objective, whether to help advance a job application, provide additional sales, or strengthen a positive working relationship. When writing thank you letters, provide specific information that reinforces your purpose. For example, in a follow-up to a job interview, point out a new fact about yourself that proves you have a quality the interviewer mentioned was crucial for the position; in a letter to a customer, summarize what you perceive as the mutual benefits of your partnership; in attempting to cement a good working relationship, be specific in identifying exactly what you find to be rewarding about your relationship.

Orientation: ■ Say thank you.

Analysis/Data: ■ Provide specific data that contributes to your purpose in writing the thank you letter.

Follow-up: ■ Express gratitude; when appropriate, indicate you are willing to take extra steps to further strengthen your positive relationship.

Dear _____:

Thank you for the time you took out of your busy schedule to interview me. During the interview you indicated you were looking for a director of nursing who could skillfully initiate a strong cost control program while maintaining a high level of esprit de corps among fellow workers.

I am such a person, having already achieved these twin goals while employed at St. Vincent's Hospital in Indianapolis. During my tenure there, I effectively reduced total compensation costs for both pharmaceutical and registry nursing staff while maintaining the highest level of retention and lowest level of turnover in the hospital. Part of my success is attributable to an effective cross-training program I initiated.

As we discussed, I am challenged by the opportunity to help you establish a "business mentality" in the nursing area to help contribute to General's fiscal viability while also assuring that the care you deliver meets the highest standards.

I am confident that General Hospital will benefit from my leadership skills.

I will call on February 4 to discuss your decision, unless I hear from you sooner.

Model #9: Management Letter

In the management letter, your objective is to state a series of recommendations, politely and in a language and format easily understood by your readers. Two examples of management reports follow. The first, focused on a single topic, uses a series of toplines to allow readers to quickly scan the logic of the argument. The second, a report covering a variety of issues, uses headings to help readers easily locate topics of interest.

Orientation:	▪ The opening should clearly orient readers to the key dimensions of the report, including answers to the what, why, and when questions. In long reports you should also forecast the development of the report in the opening.
Analysis/Data:	▪ The body should use headings, lists, indentation, and, when appropriate, numbered, underlined sentences to subdivide topics and indicate the support provided for each recommendation. When using an outline form, check carefully to make sure your lists are all in parallel structure.
Follow up:	▪ Close with a statement of goodwill and an offer to address any questions or concerns about your report.

Subject: <u>BUSINESS IMPLICATIONS OF THE AGE</u>
<u>DISCRIMINATION IN EMPLOYMENT ACT</u>

Dear _____ :

This report explains the amendments Congress enacted to the federal Age Discrimination in Employment Act (ADEA). As a result of ADEA, companies are now required to meet clear criteria in both benefit and early retirement decisions.

Given that many employers are currently (a) attempting to hold down the escalating costs of medical, disability, and retirement benefits and (b) contemplating downsizing their workforces, it is important to be aware of the business implications of these amendments.

IMPLICATIONS FOR BENEFIT DECISIONS

1. <u>Companies must make benefits available equally to older and younger employees</u>.

   The government made this rule to forbid age discrimination in employment benefits. As a result:
   - Retirement eligibility cannot be a basis for denying either severance pay or disability benefits.
   - Medical coverage must be the same for all members of the group.

2. <u>Companies are allowed to make two significant exceptions to these rules</u>.
   - The present value of retiree medical coverage and the value of pension "bridge" benefits may be used to offset severance payments in some circumstances.
   - Age-related differences in benefits may be justified if they can be demonstrated to be based on sound actuarial principles.

IMPLICATIONS FOR EARLY RETIREMENT

3. <u>Early retirement systems are legal only if companies can prove the decision to retire is voluntary</u>.

   The following factors may prove voluntariness.
   - The amount of time given employees to consider the decision.
   - Whether the information provided on benefits available under the option was accurate and complete.
   - Whether threats, intimidation, or coercion accompanied the offer.

(continued)

4. <u>The new law restricts the employer's ability to secure a waiver from employees of any future age discrimination claims</u>.
To be considered voluntary, waivers must now:
- be written so they are easily understood;
- not waive later-arising claims or rights;
- refer to the ADEA act by name;
- include a severance benefit of value to which the employee is not otherwise entitled;
- advise the employee to consult a lawyer, prior to executing the waiver;
- give 21–45 days to consider the waiver;
- include a provision that the waiver can be revoked within seven days of its execution.

5. <u>These requirements may cause some companies to not seek releases and not provide severance pay</u>.

Companies might take such action to avoid possible future age discrimination lawsuits. Ironically, this may make separation for some employees far more traumatic than it would if the previous rules for waivers were still in effect.

Should you want more information on how this act applies to your company, please telephone me at 555-0000, and I will be pleased to make an appointment to discuss it with you in person.

We will continue to update you on this and other issues.

Dear _____:

The following is the report you requested analyzing your company's internal controls and accounting systems for the year ended December 31, 1985.

The report is divided into two parts. Part One lists a series of recommendations in the areas of internal control, fixed assets, cash management, life insurance, and computer usage, which, we believe, when implemented, will make your already good accounting systems even better. Part Two is a profit analysis.

RECOMMENDATIONS

INTERNAL CONTROLS
1. Paperwork controls:
   - Use prenumbered receipts to improve control over cash received and to reduce the possibility of omitted sales or collections.
   - Prenumber purchase orders to reduce the likelihood of double payment of purchases.
   - Use voucher numbers on bank reconciliations to speed up the reconciliation process.
   - Prepare written purchase requisitions for equipment and send a copy to the receiving department to ensure that the correct items are received.
2. Collections:
   Improve collections (and cash flow) by sending monthly statements to customers with outstanding balances over 60 days.
3. Petty Cash:
   - Assign one person to be solely responsible for the petty cash fund.
   - Prohibit employees from cashing payroll checks at the company. This will reduce the funding needed in petty cash and could also improve controls over payroll.
4. Fire and Theft:
   - Store stock certificates and securities offsite to protect against fire or theft.
   - Make backup copies of software and store them offsite to protect against fire and theft.

FIXED ASSETS
1. Capitalize all fixed assets over a certain amount and expense items under that amount.
2. For the machine remake kits which were capitalized, maintain each kit as a separate item, but reference it to the piece of equipment with which it is associated (for example, machine number 000-A).

(continued)

CASH MANAGEMENT
1. Reduce your cash balance by investing additional cash in short-term securities which earn market interest rates.
2. Deposit cigarette money daily both to earn additional interest and to reduce the risk of theft.
3. Make voluntary payments to the Ohio Bureau of Employment Services. Had you contributed $191 in determining your 1986 contribution rate, it would have resulted in Ohio unemployment tax savings amounting to at least $425.

LIFE INSURANCE
Update one of your life insurance policies so that Allman is listed as the beneficiary, not Bennett.

COMPUTERIZATION
Use your IBM PC-XT to help you complete more business functions. Its applications (some of which require enhancements) include the following:
- a fixed asset depreciation and maintenance program
- a budgeting program
- a financial projection program
- an investment tracking program
- a word processing program.

PROFIT ANALYSIS

The profitability of the company improved largely because of the following three items:

1. Gross profit increased because sales increased at a much higher rate than did the cost of sales.
2. In 1985 the company recognized a gain on the sale of securities. It also showed a lower loss on the sale of its fixed assets as a result of faster depreciation methods implemented in 1983.
3. Supplies expense was reduced substantially because during the audit it was determined that the kits that had been previously expensed should be capitalized.

Should you want to discuss further any of the items contained in this report, please let us know. We will be happy to answer any questions, and we can help you implement any of the recommendations.

Congratulations on a successful year, a success which we believe you can extend into 1986 and beyond. We thank you and your employees for the helpful and professional attitude exhibited during the audit, and we look forward to a continuing and rewarding relationship in the future.

Model #10: The Letter Proposal

The objective of a letter proposal is to persuade a person or organization to purchase a product or service. Given that most proposals are submitted in a competitive environment, they must convince readers that your organization can do a better and more cost-effective job of satisfying the client's needs than can the competition. Thus, the focus of the proposal must be on meeting client needs.

Letter Proposal Outline

1. **Opening paragraph(s)**
   The opening paragraph should contain both a goodwill statement and a benefit statement including:
   - A positive first sentence that expresses goodwill toward the client
   - A statement expressing confidence in your company's ability to meet the client's needs
   - A forecast of the contents of the proposal.

2. **Results paragraph(s)**
   The results paragraph should expand on exactly what needs your service will fulfill, with a clear focus on the benefits to the client.

3. **Fees paragraph**
   The fees paragraph should be as concise as possible, and near the end of the document. To expend significant space on fees or to put a discussion of fees up front would suggest more interest in being paid than in meeting client needs.

4. **Mutual Responsibilities paragraph(s)**
   The mutual responsibilities paragraph provides additional details to your proposal, including when you plan to initiate and complete the work, the people to call with questions, guarantees of confidentiality, potential risks, and possible alternatives to the proposal.

   This paragraph also spells out the client's responsibilities if the proposal is accepted.

5. **Action Steps**
   The action steps paragraph suggests next steps, such as a time and place to discuss the proposal further. It also expresses confidence that acceptance of this proposal will continue (or initiate) what has been (or will be) a mutually profitable association.

Dear _____ :

We enjoyed talking with you last week and learning about the public accounting needs of Fred Smith Automobile. Littlejohn & Cohen specializes in serving Tri-State automobile dealerships. In fact, the 45 dealerships which currently employ us are testimony to the fact that we provide excellent accounting services—at highly competitive fees.

The proposal below describes the results we will achieve, our estimated fees, and the mutual responsibilities for the engagement.

RESULTS

We will provide Fred Smith Automobile with:
- year-end audit and tax reporting,
- year-end LIFO reporting, and
- management advisory services, as requested.

Audit and Tax Reporting

We will examine your financial statements in accordance with generally accepted auditing standards for the period ending December 31, 1990, and subsequently report to the board of directors of Fred Smith Automobile.

In addition, we will prepare all federal, state, and city corporate income tax returns for the year ended December 31, 1990.

In relation to the above returns, we would examine any assessment notices relative to those returns, and we would advise on income tax matters generally.

LIFO Reporting

LIFO can be performed on all new vehicles and on parts inventories. All necessary computations will be based on our cost information obtained from the company's secretary/treasurer.

(continued)

Management Advisory Services

At your request, we will provide management advisory services. We have successfully provided such assistance to dealerships in the following areas:

1. Parts inventory operational audit and evaluation.
2. Periodic accounting operational audits above and beyond the normal audit work.
3. Acquisitions or dispositions of dealerships.
4. Personal financial planning.
5. Qualified retirement plan design and administration.
6. Any other management advisory services that you would request.

FEES

Our fees for these services will be no more than $5,500 for audit and tax reporting services, $1,500 for the new vehicle LIFO work, $300 for the parts inventory LIFO work. Management advisory services are billed at the hourly rate of the individuals performing the work. We match the experience of the individuals with the experience needed on a particular job so that you receive the best available expertise at an appropriate cost. Our hourly rates range from $35 per hour to $200 per hour.

MUTUAL RESPONSIBILITIES

We propose to begin this work in early March so that our reports will be ready for the March 25 meeting of your board of directors.

Benjamin Cohen will be responsible for managing all the work proposed and he and his staff will report directly to you. All of our findings will be kept in the strictest confidence.

To help keep your costs to a minimum, our proposal assumes that you make available to us prior to the beginning of field work copies of the following:

- all agreements and organizational documents;
- a listing of all equipment, along with vendor invoices;
- details of all unwritten agreements and loans;
- schedules of any income receivable as of December 31, 1990;
- schedules of all expenses payable as of December 31, 1990.

We will be in touch with you in the next week to arrange a time when we can discuss this proposal with you and answer any questions that you may have. We look forward to working with you.

WRITING MEMOS AND REPORTS

When writing to colleagues within your company, use formats which make it easy for readers to immediately understand your meaning, easily retrieve information from your document, and clearly perceive the logic of your argument.

1. Subject line and opening paragraph:
- The subject line should clearly announce the What of your message and the opening paragraph should concisely summarize the document, indicating the What, Why, and When as well as other information needed to predict the remainder of the document.

2. Background:
- When necessary, the background paragraph should include facts that clarify the context in which the document was generated. It should be written in an objective tone.

3. Body:
- The body should use headings, lists, indentation, and, when appropriate, numbered, underlined sentences to subdivide topics and indicate the support provided for each point. Be sure to use parallel constructions when writing in an outline form.

4. Further discussion:
- When appropriate, discuss issues not previously addressed, such as alternative solutions rejected, risks, and constraints.

5. Action steps:
- Indicate what follow-up will or should take place as a response to the memo or report. Typically this section should answer the "Who does What, When, and Why" questions.

Meeting Announcement

Given that many people identify attending meetings as a key waste of their time on the job, take time to write meeting announcements that highlight the significance of the issues to be discussed. Make sure you use highlighting to allow readers to find the time and place of the meeting easily. And inform readers of how you expect them to prepare for the meeting.

Meeting Announcement Outline

1. **Subject line**
   The subject line should announce the topic of the meeting and highlight meeting details, including time and place.

2. **Opening paragraph**
   The opening paragraph should highlight the purpose of the meeting, including:
   - A first sentence that requests readers to attend the meeting
   - A clear statement of the purpose of the meeting
   - When appropriate, a description of guest speakers or guest attendees
   - A description of attachments

3. **Importance of decision paragraph**
   This paragraph should further emphasize why this meeting is significant to those attending.

4. **Actions requested paragraph**
   This paragraph should indicate what participants should do in advance of the meeting to be prepared to participate in it.

Subj: <u>MEETING TO DISCUSS THE PURCHASE OF WILSON
LAPTOP COMPUTERS</u>

> When: October 28
> 3:00–4:00 pm, with Dr. Gooding
> 4:00–5:00 pm, without Dr. Gooding
>
> Where: Conference Room 6

<u>Purpose of the Meeting</u>

Please clear your schedules so you can attend a meeting with Dr. Marsha Gooding, a field representative with Wilson Computers. She will be demonstrating the value of using Wilson Laptops and Wilson Audit Software when conducting field audits at remote sites. Given our agreement to purchase laptops this year, your input into which model laptop and which software to purchase is important to our decision process.

Attached is a copy of the Wilson proposal, as well as descriptions of their products.

<u>Importance of this Decision</u>

We will be spending $50–60,000 for laptops this fiscal year. Once we have agreed on a supplier, we will be committed to using their products for at least three years. So we want to make the right choice! And we need your insight at this meeting.

<u>Actions Requested</u>

1. Please write a concise report summarizing your reaction to the Wilson proposal by 1 October. I will summarize the feedback from all field auditors and distribute it prior to the Wilson meeting. This will allow us all to ask informed questions.
2. If you cannot attend the meeting, let me know who you are sending in your place.

Meeting Summary Report

The purpose of a meeting summary report is to clarify the relationship among the objectives of a meeting, the decisions made at the meeting, and the next steps agreed to by the meeting participants.

Meeting Summary Report Outline

1. **Opening paragraph(s)**
   The opening paragraphs should serve as an orientation to the entire document, including:
   - A first sentence that states the date and purpose of the meeting
   - A clear statement of the objectives of the meeting
   - A list of participants
   - The location of the meeting, when appropriate.

2. **Background**
   Background should provide details clarifying Why the meeting was held.

3. **Decisions**
   The Decisions section summarizes agreements; it should be organized deductively, meeting the following criteria:
   - *Easy to scan summaries of agreements*—a series of numbered, underlined topic sentences which clearly relate each agreement to the objective.
   - *Effectively sequenced toplines*—toplined agreements organized to make sense when scanned.
   - *Logically developed points*—explanations of each topline are organized so their relationship to meeting objectives is clear. The explanations provide both a rationale for the toplined claim and data to support it.

4. **Topics Requiring Additional Discussion**
   The Topics Requiring Further Discussion section highlights topics that require further data or additional discussion before decisions can be made. This section should be organized according to the same principles as the Decisions section.

5. **Indicated Action**
   The Indicated Action section lists the steps the committee has agreed to take. This section should answer the Who does What When questions, and, when appropriate, the objective to which each step contributes.

Subject: <u>WEIGHT REDUCTION TEST MEETING, 1/18/94</u>

This summarizes the results of a meeting on 1/18/94 between the Sweet-Free team and Drs. Morris Black and Laura DuBois regarding the planning of a study on the effectiveness of noncaloric sweeteners as weight reduction agents. The objective of the study is to determine if the substitution of a noncaloric sweetener for sugars in diets leads to weight loss. As detailed below, a variety of decisions were made on how to proceed.

Background
Drs. Black and DuBois represent Mountaintop Laboratories, the research laboratory the SweetFree team previously agreed to hire to advise us on appropriate methods for conducting the tests using state-of-the-art methods. Research indicates that the rat is the best research subject for the test objectives and test methods being used in this study.

Decisions
1. <u>The study will initially use two dozen 3-week old Harvard rats</u>. Mountaintop will use these rats to investigate weight gain using SweetFree artificial sweetener in place of sugar in rat food. The Harvard rats were selected because they best meet the weight and age requirements of the test. The Cambridge rats also meet the minimum requirements for weight and age.

2. <u>The rats will be weaned on a special experimental diet formulated by Oxford Labs</u>. They will need this diet for two weeks because Harvard rats are usually weaned between four and five weeks on a normal rat diet. During the acclimation week, the weaning diet will be reduced by incrementally mixing it with a special diet that will be formulated by Oxford Labs Inc. Past experience indicates the rats will accept such a regimen.

   In response to Dr. Black's observation that the original diet formulated at Oxford Labs lacks the proper amount of protein needed for rapidly growing rats, we are developing, with Anne Smith and others at the laboratory, a higher protein formula. Once we confirm that the diet has the proper amount of protein, we will order a supply of the diet from Oxford Labs.

3. <u>Special skills, supplied externally, will be used to evaluate the rats' weight gain.</u> Brown Laboratories, which has substantial experience in this area, will administer the diet and conduct the tests at our facilities.

   The rats will be divided into two groups, a control group fed a diet with substantial amounts of sugars in it and an experimental group fed the same diet with noncaloric sweeteners substituted for the sugars. A two week test will be used to determine if the substitution of a noncaloric sweetener will lead to weight loss if other dietary factors are held constant.

(continued)

-2-

4. <u>The rats will be housed in white mouse cages</u>.
The animals will be housed in white mouse cages for the duration of the pilot study. The cages will be fitted with special trays to collect the feces and urine.

5. <u>The study can begin no earlier than 6/5/94, the earliest date by which the company can receive an adequate stock of Harvard rats</u>.
Assuming we place the order this week, Budding Laboratory in New Jersey will send the rats on a truck in an environmentally controlled trailer. Other suppliers that we considered either could not guarantee comparable delivery or were located too far away to guarantee the delivery of healthy rats.

Issues Requiring Further Discussion

1. <u>The committee agreed to further discuss housing, following an investigation into the availability and cost of glass metabolism caging large enough to hold the Harvard rat</u>.
Some committee members expressed concern that the rats could not adjust comfortably in cages designed for white mice. D. B. Jones agreed to investigate this issue and bring his findings to the next meeting.

2. <u>The committee also agreed to further discuss the laboratory preparation needed for the tests</u>.
A concern was raised that the group needs to carefully schedule time and space so that concurrent projects would not compete for the same space and manpower resources. J. L. Paretti agreed to gather information on this topic for discussion at a future meeting.

Indicated Action
A document confirming the above protocol will be sent to Drs. Black and DuBois.

Trip Report

The purpose of a trip report is to summarize what you have learned during a visit to a plant or office site, a supplier, a customer, or a convention that will help your organization better meet one or more of its objectives.

Trip Report Outline

1. **Opening paragraph(s):**
   The opening paragraph(s) should contain these items:
   - The location or locations you visited
   - Date(s) of the trip
   - Company objectives met by the trip; these may be included in opening paragraph or in a separate paragraph following the opening paragraph
   - When appropriate, brief evaluation of trip
   - When relevant, others who made the trip.

2. **Background paragraph(s)**
   Background may include the following:
   - Information that clarifies the context of the trip, such as details about why you or others were selected to make the trip
   - Description of event, such as the stated purpose of a convention and the number and types of people attending the convention.

3. **Key Learnings**
   The key learnings section should be organized deductively meeting the following criteria:
   - *Easy to scan summaries of learnings*—a series of numbered and underlined topic sentences which clearly relate your learnings to the objectives stated in the opening.
   - *Effectively sequenced toplines*—toplined learnings are sequenced in a logical order, so they make sense when scanned separately from the text that follows them.
   - *Clear, relevant argumentation*—explanations of the learnings which follow the toplines are organized so that their relationship to division and company goals is clear. The explanations provide both a rationale for the toplined claim and data for it.

4. **Indicated Action**
   The Indicated Action section suggests appropriate next steps. It should suggest one or more steps as follow up to each learning, assigning, where appropriate, the responsibilities and timing for each step.

Subj: <u>KEY LEARNINGS FROM OFFICE TECHNOLOGY CONFERENCE</u>

I have written this report to summarize my learnings from attending the Office Technology Applications Show held in San Antonio on August 2, 1988.

<u>OBJECTIVES</u>

I attended this show to learn if ABC could apply any voice processing technologies to its current communication systems.

<u>BACKGROUND</u>

The Office Technology Applications Show is an annual event sponsored by Office Clearinghouse, the publisher of *Office Update Newsletter*. It brings together people who conceive, develop, create, manufacture, sell, and purchase office technology.

<u>KEY LEARNINGS</u>

1. <u>Voice mail technologies could be applied immediately to our communication system</u>.

   We can use voice mail immediately with our telephone answering machines, and, with some adaptation, use it in conjunction with our electronic mail system. This system could prove to be a major benefit to our international businesses, reducing the communication problems we have faced because of time zone differences.

2. <u>Current voice recognition and speech synthesis technologies are not sufficiently developed to be of immediate value to ABC</u>.

   - <u>Voice recognition</u>: Current products lack (1) speaker independent voice recognition; (2) continuous speech recognition; and (3) large vocabularies. A number of leading computer manufacturers, including ABM, are working to perfect this technology over the next five years.

   - <u>Speech synthesis:</u> The quality of speech synthesis output is poor, both in intelligibility and naturalness. Henri Dupuy, associate professor of speech at Ohio State University, claimed speech synthesis will not be commercially acceptable until the voices sound natural. His evidence indicates office employees have low tolerances for talking and listening to computers that sound like computers.

<u>STEPS</u>

1. I will recommend the formation of a task force to apply voice mail learnings throughout the company.

2. I will continue to read articles and books on improving office technologies and will issue additional key learnings reports to update you on further developments in this area.

Progress Reports

The progress report has two main purposes: to summarize significant events of a period of time and to indicate what you plan to accomplish in the month or months ahead. To meet reader needs, summarize key accomplishments in the opening, use headings and other forms of highlighting in the body to make it easy for readers to find the details about each topic, and in the closing provide a list of actions being undertaken in the current month, or that will be undertaken in the future.

In the three examples of progress reports that follow, the first is a simple monthly report covering a variety of issues under the responsibility of the author. The other two are focused reports, the first reporting bimonthly share results, the second progress on a long-term scientific project.

Monthly Report Outline

1. **Opening Paragraph**
   The opening should summarize the entire document, including a statement indicating what progress has been made.

2. **Analysis/Data**
   This section provides data on the progress made. It should be well-designed, using headings and indentation in simple reports, and toplined, summarizing sentences in more complex reports.

3. **Indicated Action**
   This section spells out for readers what is being done currently toward objectives, as well as what future plans have been made in pursuing these objectives. In highly complex or very long reports, actions steps may be placed immediately after analysis. When this is done, the action steps should be indented from the rest of the text or in some other way presented, so the reader can scan through the action steps alone to get a sense of what the total package of planned actions look like.

Re: <u>MIS Monthly Report for March, 1991</u>   Date: April 9, 1991

We have completed Phase I and started Phase II of the MIS Projects. We also improved the MIS data base in three areas: estimated revenues from uninvoiced shipments; initial lumber business data; and PC data transfer. We ordered a software product to improve retrieval response time.

I. <u>Phase I and Phase II MIS Projects</u>
   A. The Phase I MIS project is complete, and upper management is now using the system.
   B. Phase II of this project, estimated to take six months to complete, has been initiated. This project will emphasize: (1) broadening the data available from the MIS; (2) extending use of the system to additional members of the organization; and (3) working jointly with accounting to study the feasibility of streamlining administrative information flows in the division.

II. <u>Development of MIS Data</u>
   A. <u>Estimated Revenues for Uninvoiced Shipments</u>: Improvements were made to the accuracy of estimated revenues for uninvoiced shipments. Manufacturing costs, which have formerly been stored as monthly unit costs ($/ton), are now stored as both unit cost and total costs. This change permits weighted average costs to be easily calculated (using total cost and total production) over user-selected time periods.
   B. <u>Business Data</u>: An initial set of lumber business data now resides in the MIS. Included are fairly high-level summaries of lumber shipments, prices, sales dollars, production, and inventory status. A standard structure has been recommended for storing Woodlands cost data in the MIS. Accounting is reviewing the feasibility of establishing standard divisional Woodlands operating expenses statements, which would be the source of such data for the MIS.
   C. <u>PC Data Transfer</u>: Work is nearly complete on data upload capability to move automatically data prepared on HP150 personal computers to the MIS data base. This important capability will simplify the acquisition of considerable data which are currently prepared on PC's, including shipment forecasts and pricing P&L data.

(continued)

III. Improved MIS Data Retrieval Response Time
   A. FASTRAN is a new commercial software product which improves the efficiency of programs written in the TRANS-ACT/3000 language, such as the MIS. Tests conducted to date demonstrate MIS data retrieval times to be reduced by a factor of 3 to 4 using FASTRAN.
   B. We now have the FASTRAN package on order, and we expect to install it for use by the MIS by May 1.

Goals for April 1991
- Continue work on Phase II MIS project
- Continue developing lumber business data base
- Complete PC data transfer capability
- Begin installing Fastran software

SUBJECT: <u>DISPOSABLE RAZOR SHARE RESULTS, SEPTEMBER–OCTOBER, 1992</u>

This summarizes September–October, 1992 disposable razor shares, as they compare with previous results in the past year. Overall, ABC's Nielsen Share of 53.4% was up 4.4% versus year ago, but down –.8 points versus previous period.

<u>DISPOSABLE RAZOR CATEGORY SHARE RESULTS</u>
<u>SO '92 AS COMPARED TO PREVIOUS RESULTS</u>

Recent Share Trends

	SO 92	vs. prior 2-mo	vs. prior 6-mo	vs. YAG
1. SmoothSkin	37.8%	–1.2%	+2.7%	+8.2%
2. FreeRazor	20.2%	+3.3%	+12.8%	+20.8%
3. Balance	17.6	–4.5	–10.2	–12.6
4. Ladies Ch	<u>15.6</u>	<u>+0.4</u>	<u>–4.7</u>	<u>–3.8</u>
5. TOTAL ABC	53.4%	–0.8%	–2.1%	+4.4%
6. McQueen	29.1%	+1.1%	+1.6%	–3.7%
7. All Other	<u>17.5</u>	<u>–0.3</u>	<u>+0.5</u>	<u>–0.7</u>
8. TOTAL OTHER	46.6%	+0.8%	2.1%	–4.4%

<u>Total Market Growth in Disposible Razor Market vs. YAG</u>

9. Mkt. Grth	–1.1%	–1.5%	+2.0%	–1.1%

MARKET— <u>In SO'92, the total disposable razor market was down 1.1% versus year ago, largely because of a 1.5% decrease in the target population for the last three months vs. YAG.</u>

Action: The Brands will continue to monitor changes in the market.

SmoothSkin— <u>SmoothSkin share at 37.8 is +8.2 points vs. YAG, but –1.2 points versus previous period, a decline attributable to losses in our nonpromoted business.</u>

The loss versus previous period traces entirely to our nonpromoted business (–4.0) as our Free Razor business was +2.8 behind the convenience pack introduction. The decline in our business stems from a 21¢ pricing disparity versus McQueen since all our promotion/sales support was directed toward our Free Razor promotion.

Action: We are rebuilding our regular business by beginning with a joint sales merchandising strategy and by continuing our focus on merchandising and couponing activity through JFM.

(continued)

Ladies Ch —

Ladies Ch share of 15.6 is +.4 vs. previous period reflecting growth behind a Jumbo Pack introduction, but share is –3.8 points versus YAG because of product and pricing disparities. Ladies Ch 0.8 share point increase versus previous period reflects initial growth behind the 8/25/92 Ladies Ch Jumbo Pack introduction. Despite share progress behind Jumbo Packs, business results remain driven by two factors: (a) basic product inferiority with both SmoothSkin and McQueen, both in regular and Convenience Packs, and (b) Ladies Ch SQ'92 ScanTrack Convenience pricing disadvantage versus McQueen (–$.20/carton) and SmoothSkin (–$.25/carton).

Action: To increase share, the brand is introducing Ladies Ch Convenience and basic sizes on January 5, 1993. To address pricing, the brand is taking the following measures—a 12/1 $2.00 mailed coupon, a 1/12 $2.00 FSCI, and a 3/1 $3.00 cash refund offer to complement the already strong JFM'93 promotion plan.

McQueen —

McQueen share of 29.1 was +1.1 versus previous period, due largely to increased spending levels and couponing. McQueen share is –3.7 versus YAG. This gain versus previous period reflects McQueen increased spending levels (up to $4.00 OI in some districts) resulting in a strong pricing advantage versus Ladies Ch (+$.20/carton) and parity pricing with Ultra SmoothSkin (during their Ultra Convenience Pack introduction). Additionally, targeted couponing behind the accelerated SuperSmooth rollout (in 85% U.S. by 12/31/92) hurt both Ladies Ch and SmoothSkin.

NOV–DEC —
FORECAST

We expect a total ABC share of 52.8, with the SmoothSkin share holding steady at 37.8 and the Ladies Ch share declining to 15.0. Gains in SmoothSkin business will probably be offset by losses in the Ladies Ch business. Similarly, we project a .6 decline in Ladies Ch share because of expected losses in the convenience pack market.

Subj: <u>CLEENUP POLYMER DELIVERY TEST</u>

This report summarizes progress to date in identifying which solvent is optimum for CleenUp window cleaner. This research is part of the polymer delivery subteam's objective of identifying low-cost delivery media for the CleenUP polymers which also meet flow rate and other formula criteria.

Results to date indicate more technical testing of Formula X is needed to determine if it meets the criteria for use in the CleenUp formulation.

<u>Initial Test Results</u>

- <u>Initial tests indicate Formula X produces an easy flow for the window cleaning polymer</u>.

  Test results suggest Formula X fits with CleenUp's system. Product viscosities, feel tests, and shine retention tests were performed on two test formulations, the current CleenUp formula and the All-surface CleenUp formula. Formula X worked well in each.

<u>Tests In Progress</u>

- <u>Additional tests we are now conducting have been designed to create a data base to determine the best use of Formula X in the CleenUp formulations</u>.

Specifically the tests do the following:
  —Measure viscosities on varying levels of polymer in Formula X. This information will be useful for plant scale polymer processing.
  —Submit CleenUp formulations with varying levels of Formula X through the battery of technical tests, such as drying time and surface feel. This information will provide understanding of how much Formula X can be tolerated in a formulation.

<u>Future Tests</u>

- <u>Assuming this approach is successful, the CleenUp team will move ahead on the three key issues listed below</u>.
  —Delivery media for the CleenUp polymer
  —Processing options for the formulation
  —Formulation approaches of the new product

Please call me at 555-4444 if you have any questions.

Procedural Memo

The purpose of a procedural memo is to highlight steps to be taken to fulfill a company objective. Effective procedural memos allow readers to do both "big picture" and "little picture" thinking. Use a chronologically ordered series of numbered and underlined sentences to highlight each discrete step in the process. Then use a list format to clarify the criteria for fulfilling each toplined step.

Procedural Memo Outline

1. **Opening paragraph(s):**
   The opening paragraph(s) should contain these items:
   - An orientation statement, highlighting the What and, when relevant, the Why
   - A statement indicating When the procedures should be started and finished.

2. **Background paragraph(s)***
   Background includes information that clarifies the context of the procedures, such as details as to why these procedures are being implemented and how the decision was made.

3. **Guidelines**
   The guidelines section should be organized deductively meeting the following criteria:
   - *Easy to scan summaries of steps*—a series of numbered and underlined topic sentences which clearly describe a step in the procedure. Each should start with a verb.
   - *Effectively sequenced toplines*—toplined procedures are sequenced in a chronological order, so they make sense when scanned separately from the text that follows them.
   - *Clear, relevant argumentation*—explanations of how to implement each step are organized so that their relationship to the toplined step is clear.

4. **Indicated Action**
   The indicated action section suggests appropriate next steps. Typically in a procedural memo it lists a phone number to call if the reader has further questions about the memo.

Subject: <u>SAFETY PROCEDURES FOR RENTAL VEHICLES</u>

Please follow the inspection procedures below before every one-way and local rental of ABC trucks. These guidelines have been implemented to both protect the company and its franchisees from litigation and to ensure that our customers enjoy a trouble-free rental.

<u>Background</u>
The audit committee devised these guidelines in response to a study which revealed that consumer lawsuits brought against ABC cost the company and its licensees over $20 million annually to litigate. All 3,000 ABC rental agencies will follow these guidelines.

<u>Guidelines</u>
1. <u>Check lights, tires, gauges, and fluids</u>.
   - Circle the truck, checking turn signals, brake lights, and headlights.
   - Be sure tire tread meets the company standard of 1/2" safety depth and tire pressure is at 30 lbs.
   - Lift the hood and check fluids, including engine and transmission oils, as well as coolants and windshield wiper fluids.
   - Make sure the fluid levels agree with the levels shown on the gauges on the inside dashboard.

2. <u>Review truck operating guidelines with customers</u>.

   Some customers are not familiar with the differences between operating a car and a large truck.
   - Carefully explain how to use side mirrors while backing up and while changing lanes.
   - Describe the importance of making sure that all overpasses are higher than the height of the truck.
   - Explain how a driver must make a wider than normal radius when turning because of the length of the truck.

3. <u>Explain the benefits of ABC insurance policies</u>.

   In the rental contract, the customer has two options for insurance. Be sure the customer understands the implications of each choice.
   - By accepting the insurance on the truck for $15 per day, the customer will be fully covered by ABC in case of an accident.
   - By declining the insurance, the customer is fully liable for all costs and damages sustained by the vehicle.

<u>Future improvements</u>

An updated safety guide will be available for distribution to customers on August 31. This guide will contain emergency numbers and a list of safety tips.

I appreciate your cooperation in implementing this program. Please call me at (513) 555–8252 with questions, concerns, or suggestions.

Recommendation Memo

The purpose of a recommendation memo is to request approval to change your organization in some way, such as changing a policy or procedure to save time or improve efficiency, or spending money to purchase equipment or fund an advertising program. Your objective is to show that the change you are proposing is advantageous as compared to the current system and alternative systems.

Recommendation Memo Outline

1. **Opening paragraph(s)**
   The opening paragraph(s) should contain these items:
   - A one sentence statement of exactly What action is being recommended and When it is to be implemented.
   - A statement showing how this effort is aligned with a higher level Company Why.
   - A summary of benefits.
   - A statement of costs, including, when relevant, the payback period and a statement of whether the money is already budgeted.
   - A listing of names of those who concur with your recommendation.

2. **Background paragraph(s)**
   Background may include the following:
   - A concise summary of historical facts that clarify why the memo is being written now.
   - A statement linking the recommendation to previous documents the readers have received on the topic.

3. **Recommendation paragraph(s)***
   The recommendation paragraph(s) should:
   - Expand upon the one sentence description in the opening paragraph, precisely describing What is being proposed, and briefly, How it is to be carried out.
   - Not contain any "why" or benefit statements.

4. **Rationale for Recommendation paragraphs**
   The rationale for the recommendation section should be organized deductively, meeting the following criteria:
   - *Toplined summaries of benefits*—statements summarizing each of the benefits of the proposal compared to the current situation. Each benefit statement should be numbered, underlined, and written in a full sentence. Each should make sense when

read in sequence as well as when the word "because" is inserted between the recommendation and each reason. Include at least two and no more than three reasons.

- *Alignment with opening paragraph:* Each of the benefit statements should be predicted by the benefit summary in the opening paragraph and should be discussed in the same order as stated in the opening paragraph.
- *Effective proof:* Facts and reasons should be positioned and interpreted so that the recommendation makes sense. The argument should show a positive impact upon the business, especially highlighting relationships to department, division, and company goals. The argument should be supported by good evidence, including precedent, past company experience, quantitative and qualitative proof, as well as "this makes sense" reasoning.

5. **Details/Discussion***
   Discuss in this section issues not previously discussed, such as:
   - *Implementation details,* an expansion on how it will be accomplished, including, where relevant, timing, quantities, costs, personnel, and any other basic assumptions that should be kept in mind.
   - *Constraints,* a discussion of the risks from external forces, such as government agencies, trade customers, consumers, and competitors, as well as internal constraints such as budget issues, training, and potential technical problems.
   - *Payback,* when appropriate, a calculation of how long it will take a proposal to pay back its investment.
   - *Alternative solutions rejected,* an outline of alternatives and reasons why they were not chosen.

6. **Indicated Action**
   Orient readers to what they are to do—and when they are to do it—to authorize implementation of the recommended actions.

*These paragraphs not always required. Use a separate recommendation paragraph when you have concluded that your one-sentence description in the opening paragraph inadequately describes exactly the plan you are proposing.

Subject: <u>RECOMMENDATION TO PURCHASE PC'S FOR COST
STUDY GROUP</u>

The Cost Accounting Department requests a $31,000 authorization to purchase four ABM 3000 personal computers and six cost-estimating software packages. Using the PC's will increase our productivity by improving the speed and accuracy of our cost analyses.

We will bring the PC's on-line within three weeks of approval and will begin training within one week of approval. The $1,000 training costs are provided in our current year budget. We estimate a payback period of one year. M. Andersen and S. Rashid concur.

<u>BACKGROUND</u>

Our four cost accountants currently do 800 cost studies per year, all computed on a desktop calculator. A survey we conducted revealed that they spend approximately four hours on each cost study. When changes are made to a cost study, the entire calculation must be refigured; often the new results are not available until the next day.

Our survey also revealed that about 700 of our cost studies used similar formulas and therefore were excellent candidates for computerization.

<u>REASONS FOR RECOMMENDATION</u>

1. <u>We will complete cost studies faster</u>.

Our research indicates we can complete the average cost study in 10–15 minutes on the ABM PC's, compared to a 3–4 hour average doing the analyses manually. In fact, *Modern Machine Newsletter* cites a case in which a machine tool company averaged only 10 minutes per cost analysis after computerization, versus five hours on a calculator. A demonstration by an ABM sales representative confirmed that the ABM PC's can achieve a similar result.

2. <u>We will improve the accuracy of our cost studies</u>.

The PC's promise error-free cost studies because the formulas for each type of cost study will be carefully checked prior to their initial use. From then on, we can be assured the correct formulas will be used each time. A review we conducted of our current system indicated about 8% of our current cost analyses contained mistakes because of an incorrect entry of a formula in the calculation.

(continued)

IMPLEMENTATION

Our maintenance group will install the PC's, with the assistance of ABM's service representative.

The training classes will be taught by Abacus Computer Training, at a cost of $1,000.00. The classes will consist of three one-day sessions, with one half-day devoted to each of the six software packages appropriate to the type of cost studies we conduct.

To make sure we are using the computers correctly, we will complete both manual and computerized cost analyses for one week.

PAYBACK

We estimate a payback period of one year. This figure is based on a savings of 2,100 hours per year, as we conservatively estimate we will save at least three hours on approximately 700 studies per year. As our cost analysts are paid an average of $15.00 per hour, we estimate a $31,500 annual savings.

ACTION STEPS

May we have your immediate approval to purchase the ABM PC's and arrange with Abacus for the computer training?

Plan Description

Plan description reports describe the key elements of a plan of action, such as plan objectives, rationale, obstacles, and implementation steps. It answers questions such as: What objectives is this plan designed to achieve? What strategic assumptions support the plan? How will the plan be implemented?

Two examples of plan descriptions follow, one written in full memo form, the other as a "forwardable outline," a report form preferred at some companies because readers can so easily scan its logic and evidence. When using this outline form in particular, proofread to make sure your lists are in parallel constructions.

Plan Description Outline

1. **Opening paragraph**
   The opening paragraph should serve as a concise summary of the entire document, including a description of the What and the Why(s) of the plan.

2. **Background paragraph***
   The background paragraph provides historical data about why the plan was developed and when it was approved for implementation.

3. **Analysis/Data paragraphs**
   The analysis/data paragraphs should be organized deductively, meeting the following criteria:
   - *Easy to scan descriptions of plan strategy and plan details*—a series of numbered, underlined topic sentences which clearly communicate the logic of the plan and the major steps needed to undertake the plan.
   - *Effective proof*—facts and reasons positioned so the plan makes sense. Each argument should be supported by good logic and evidence.
   - *Effectively sequenced toplines*—toplined analysis organized to make sense when scanned.

4. **Plan Obstacles***
   The plan obstacles paragraphs describe the limitations of the plan, especially in light of limiting variables you have identified.

5. **Next Steps**
   The next section answers the "Who does What and When" questions.

*not always required

Subject: <u>Wake Up SALES PLAN IN CHARLOTTE REGION 21</u>

In response to your request, I have outlined the sales plan for the Charlotte Region 21. Its objective is to reach a 6 share over the next 4–5 months. We are executing this plan to increase reach, trial and share through temporary price reductions, wet-sampling, and a Nascar sponsorship.

This cost-effective, consumer-oriented strategy is designed to offset the distribution, trade dollar, share of voice, and display advantages of Roberta Morrison (RM) and Sunshine. Plan details and obstacles follow.

<u>PLAN DETAILS</u>

1. <u>Deep-cut feature pricing will increase trial and share</u>.

    This program will allow retailers to feature Wake Up at $1.39/2.49, 50–60 cents below competitive prices in January–February. Company experience shows this level of price cut doubles share initially, as current users stock up and competitive brand users buy Wake Up in place of their normal brand.

2. <u>A wet-sampling plan will encourage trial and also reinforce the price reduction strategy</u>.

    Free samples, actively given out at 100 stores over a two-day period in January, will encourage trial by (1) effectively demonstrating the superior taste of Wake Up, (2) directly promoting the purchase of the product, and (3) calling attention to the reduced feature price of Wake Up.

3. <u>An entire season of Nascar sponsorship will help Wake Up reach a target market currently dominated by competitors</u>.

    This sponsorship will cost effectively bring our name in front of a key target market: race car enthusiasts. Research shows this group to be heavy coffee drinkers, with a preference for R & G brands, which currently hold 38% share. Past experience with sponsorships demonstrates their effectiveness in expanding reach and encouraging trial, especially when feature and promotion activity is tied into them directly.

(continued)

PLAN OBSTACLES

Experience shows it takes constant sales and merchandising pressure to gain and hold share in this category. The brands currently holding lead shares have major trade advantages with retail clients. In addition, the relatively limited scope of our District 21 program suggests it will take a relatively longer time to achieve share objectives than it has for programs with wider distribution and trade dollar incentives.

1. We offer fewer total trade dollars and have a smaller share of voice than RM or Sunshine.

   For example, Kroger Roanoke's RM's trade funds are $600M annually, whereas Wake Up's soluble and ground funds are $70M. So although we match our larger competitors on a per case and dollar purchase basis, accounts see us as offering far fewer total dollars.

   Reports from Sales representatives in this area also suggest Wake Up has considerably less share of voice than either RM or Magpie.

2. Wake Up's distribution is less than RM or Sunshine, which limits the effectiveness of Wake Up's promotions, feature, and display.

   Given our test geography, we are not participating in all stores of many accounts, thus precluding us from inclusion in chain-wide promotions.

   In addition, an independent audit of distribution shows us at 95% ACV, not the 70–80% Nielson quotes, indicating that our current display and feature efforts have been less effective than previously believed.

3. The limited product line and reduced trade dollars make it unlikely this event will be as immediately effective as the Uptown rollout in Dallas.

   In the Dallas event an entire line, over 20 SKU's, was introduced, and initial trade spending was three times higher than what we have planned for the Charlotte district.

NEXT STEPS

The sales force is confident it will make this plan work and that Wake Up brands can sustain a "6" share in 4–5 months.

BUILDING RAISIN CANDY MINIPAK BUSINESS

<u>Objective</u>: Build minipak business by reducing out-of-stock by 50% and by improving packaging.

<u>Strategy</u>: Use sales force to implement low-cost strategies in districts with greatest out-of-stocks.

<u>Expected payoff</u>: 25M additional cases per year. This calculation is based on shipments per distribution point.

<u>Analysis</u>:

- <u>Current minipak out-of-stock level up +2% vs. last year represents a major business loss</u>.

  Due to low consumer loyalty, Out-of-Stocks mean lost sales because consumers will purchase another brand rather go to another store.

- <u>High minipak out-of-stock stems from insufficient minipak inventory</u>.

  The trade maintains an average of only 5 days supply of minipak with 1.5 days in reserve. By contrast, the Trade maintains an average of 10 days supply of bar size with 4.1 days supply inventory in reserve.

<u>Raisin Candy Inventory Levels</u>
(Avg. Past 6 Mos.)

	Days supply	Days supply on Shelf	Days supply in Back Room
Bars	10	5.9	4.1
Minipaks	5	3.5	1.5

- <u>Sales reports that minipak current packaging is not clearly enough distinguished from bar packaging</u>.

  Reports from the field indicate that store managers have commented that the similarity of packaging of bar and minipak has led to stocking difficulties.

(continued)

Details of Plan:
The program will concentrate on the 11 districts with an Out-of-Stock level of 10% or greater.

First Stage:
1. Communicate to sales force in the spring promotion package how to achieve low minipak out-of-stocks.
   - Target for increase of on-shelf inventory to 7 days supply.
   - Outline shelving principles that have produced low minipak Out-of-Stocks in several districts (see Exhibit II).
     First choice: 2–3 facings on base shelf next to bars.
     Second choice: 2–3 facings on the shelf right above bars.

2. Differentiate minipak's cardboard case from bar case to make stocking easier.
   - Increase size of THE MINIPAK flag.
   - Use different color inks on bar and minipak cases.
   - Increase size of minipak label.

Second stage:
3. Optimize use of sales time spent on minipak with an aggressive minipak out-of-stock reduction program in next national expansion of a minipak line extension.

Case:
Case change: No cost if done concurrently with 1/90 changeover to laser reading technology.

Next Steps:
1. Incorporate minipak out-of-stock plan in spring promotion package to be released 1/9/90.
2. Work with technical packaging to make case changes.
3. Plan second stage to coincide with introductory effort behind next minipak line extension.

Test Results Report

The purpose of the test results report is to interpret the meaning of test results. It answers the questions: What test was conducted? Why was it conducted? What were the results? What do these results mean? What steps should the company take next?

Test Results Report Outline

1. **Opening paragraph(s)**
   The opening paragraph(s) should serve as a concise summary of the entire document, including:
   - A concise description of the test, including where and when the test was conducted.
   - A concise rationale for the test, including its relationship to Company goals.
   - A one-sentence summary of the test results.
   - A one-sentence description of follow-up steps.

2. **Background and Methods paragraph(s)**
   Background and Methods should be brief, factual, and objective, including:
   - Historical facts that clarify why the data is being collected.
   - A justification of why the researcher believes that methods selected were the right ones given the question the data was gathered to answer.
   - A description of the methods used in carrying out the test.
   - Numbered steps, separated from succeeding steps with white space.

3. **Conclusion**
   The conclusion should be an evaluation of what the test results mean; it should contain an evaluation term, such as *successful, unsuccessful, confirm, do not confirm,* and *inconclusive.* The conclusion should be phrased so that it is consistent with the action steps section.

4. **Findings**
   The findings section should be organized deductively, meeting the following criteria:
   - *Toplined summaries of results*—statements which introduce data, telling readers what each set of data mean. Each summary of findings is numbered, underlined, and written in a full sentence.

- *Effectively sequenced toplines*—each topline should make sense both when scanned and in sequence; each should also logically follow an implied "Because" between the conclusion and each finding.
- *Clear, relevant argumentation*—explanations of data that follow the toplines are organized so that their relationship to the conclusion is clear. The explanations provide both a rationale for the toplined claim and data for it.

4. **Discussion**

Discussion includes issues not previously addressed, such as risks or limitations of measurement instruments.

5. **Indicated Action**

The indicated action section should tell readers what you intend to do in response to your interpretation of the findings and when you intend to do it. It can also highlight what you believe others in the organization should do in response to these findings.

Subject: <u>Analysis of Welcome Wagon Coupon Test</u>

This summarizes research conducted in July 1988 to determine if a Welcome Wagon Coupon (WWC, sample attached) would increase trial of our refrigerator deodorant among consumers who had moved.

In this test, WWC proved to be an effective vehicle both in redemption and in reach. Additional tests are being conducted.

Mr. Sabatelli of Market Research agrees this summary is technically correct and consistent with the findings.

BACKGROUND

The Welcome Wagon program supplements our Appliance Sample program, which packs a box of our deodorant in new refrigerators to generate trial among new owners. This program does not reach consumers who move to residences which already provide a refrigerator, or those who have moved their own refrigerator.

We tested the Welcome Wagon idea in Dayton, Ohio; Jackson, Missouri; and Altavista, Virginia. The coupon distributed was redeemable for a free box of our refrigerator deodorant.

CONCLUSION

We have concluded that the Welcome Wagon coupon is an effective way of reaching new consumers and additional testing should be undertaken.

FINDINGS

1. <u>The Welcome Wagon coupon generated significant increases in trial</u>.

   47% of the specially marked coupons were redeemed, with a high of 55% in Dayton and a low of 35% in Altavista. This compares to a 4% redemption on our average Sunday newspaper coupon.

2. <u>The Welcome Wagon Coupon reached a significant number of movers</u>.

   Coupons were distributed to 4,375 households. This constitutes 35% of the 12,500 estimated moves during April–June in these three cities. This estimate is based on the total number of new residential telephone numbers issued during 1987.

INDICATED ACTION

Given the promising tests results, we are conducting further tests using the WWC in six additional cities over the next three months. If we achieve a comparable success in these cities, we will forward a recommendatoin for a national trial of the WWC.

Subject: RESULTS OF TEST DESIGNED TO REDUCE DUST LEVELS AT THE
            SACRAMENTO PLANT

From: Date: 1/22/92
To: Retention Date: 1/25/93

This memo reports the results of an experimental test conducted at the Sacramento
oat cereal production facility on January 18, 1992. The test was conducted to evaluate the effect of adding water to the cereal recipe on the dust level in the plant.
No differences were found in the trial. Follow-up tests are being conducted. Tower
operation results are attached.

BACKGROUND
The dust level at the Sacramento facility exceeds ABC standards by up to 25% and
represents a potential problem for oat cereal expansion plans. We hypothesized
that using additional moisture in the cereal recipe would prevent a significant
amount of oat dust from entering the plant's atmosphere.

METHODS
- We added 10 gallons of water to the regular recipe in the oat cereal mixer
  and monitored the effect on dust for 2 hours. Prior to this run, we monitored
  the control recipe for 2 hours.
- We collected dust samples every fifteen minutes for evaluation.
- We also collected a drum of the moistened recipe, with an average moisture
  of 22%, and one of our current recipe with an average moisture of 15%.
  These drums will be used for storage stability tests.

CONCLUSION
The test was inconclusive. We need to conduct further tests to reduce undesirable
dust levels in the Sacramento plant.

FINDINGS
1. Both products had comparably high dust levels.
   - At Cenco moistures of 18-26% the dust grades on both products were in
     the range of 7.5–9.0 units, well in excess of our 7.0 standard.
2. Test conditions may have affected the results.
   - We had trouble measuring the effect of the test recipe because the
     operator had difficulty controlling moisture and density throughout the
     production period of both products.

NEXT STEPS
1. We will replicate the test as soon as we determine ways to better control
   moisture and density in the control and experimental recipes.
2. We are placing storage tests to determine the effect of the new recipe on the
   freshness of our baking mixture.
3. We will monitor dust levels with additional levels of moisture to see if that
   will reduce the dust level of the plant.

TOWER OPERATION

	CONTROL PROD.X RANGE	PROD.X RANGE	CONTROL PROD.X AVERAGE	PROD.X AVERAGE
FINISHED PRODUCT RATE (#/HR.)	38–40	40–42	39	41.0
NOZZLE CONFIGURATION TOP/MIDDLE/BOTTOM	2-2-4	2-2-4	2-2-4	2-2-4
HIGH PRESSURE DISCHARGE PSI	880	860–880	880	870
NOZZLE PRESSURE DISCHARGE PSI	900–940	880–960	920	913
TOWER INLET TEMP. °F	685–700	670–700	693	690
TOWER EXHAUST TEMP. °F	165–170	150–180	168	167
BASE-OF-TOWER TEMP. °F	183–200	185–195	192	190
DROP TANK TEMP. °F	172–174	162–174	173	169

Employee Evaluation Reports

Reports which evaluate the performance of coworkers are difficult to write because they are likely to evoke strong reactions from those evaluated. This section provides examples of three evaluation reports, the first, intended to be a positive document, and two intended as negative evaluations, one which summarizes a disciplinary interview and one which is a request for report compliance.

The first, focused on a single subject, uses underlining to allow an easy scan of key points; the last two, which cover a variety of topics, use headings to allow readers to locate information easily.

Positive Performance Evaluation Report   Research tells us that employees are motivated to perform best when given four positive strokes for every one negative stroke. Yet many in American management practice "management by exception," the idea of focusing solely on actions that are below standard. Thus, in writing a balanced appraisal of an employee's performance, focus on praising good performance. Indicate what future positive behaviors should replace substandard past performances.

Positive Performance Evaluation Report Outline

1. **Opening paragraph**
   The opening paragraph should include a goodwill statement, an orientation statement, and an invitation to speak further about the issues raised in the report.

2. **Analysis/Data paragraph**
   The analysis/data paragraphs should topline agreed upon future behaviors, meeting the following criteria:
   - *Toplined summaries of key performance principles*—statements summarizing each of the principles of behavior appropriate in this situation. Each principle should be underlined, numbered, and written in a full sentence. Each should make sense when read in sequence. Cover no more than five principles.
   - *Parallel structure*—each principle should be stated as an action sentence, starting with an action verb.

- *Good reasoning and data*—each toplined summary should be followed by an explanation of why the principle is appropriate in this situation; data should follow rationale, consisting of either an example of how the principle was put into effect to good result, or how a poor result occurred because the principle was not adhered to. Putting negative data in the context of a positive principle focuses the report on desired future behavior, rather than on negative past behavior.

3. **Goodwill closing**
   The closing should express confidence in the reader's ability to successfully implement the toplined standards of performance.

Subject: <u>FIELD TRAINING REVIEW: 5/5/91</u>

I enjoyed accompanying you on sales calls in southwest Fresno. Your success in selling our product is a reflection of your growing enthusiasm, confidence, and professionalism. Below I recap the key steps we agreed should be taken to continuously improve your performance as an ABC representative. Call me if you have any questions or comments about these recommendations.

<u>KEY LEARNINGS</u>

1. <u>Continue to practice excellent fundamental selling skills</u>.

   These skills constitute an excellent platform on which to build future sales successes. I observed that you demonstrated an aptitude to set objectives, make six-step calls, and sell with enthusiasm.

2. <u>Check your performance against selling procedure criteria after each call</u>.

   This procedural review will help you understand what you did correctly in the sales interview as well as where you will be able to improve in the future. The best way to conduct the review is to compare your results to your objectives, following the six-step format we discussed.

3. <u>Focus on selling customer benefits to clients.</u>

   Customers buy from companies that consistently deliver benefits to them. Look at the sales interview from the customer's point-of-view and tailor your presentation to what you have learned are the client's "hot buttons." As we discovered, selling benefits to ABC or to yourself does not produce sales.

4. <u>Improve your preplanning</u>.

   Preplanning will save you time while also making your sales calls more efficient and effective. Organize documentation in advance of each day's calls. I suggest planning against a written checklist to ensure that you have brought your pitch book, point-of-sale information, pictures of display pieces, and all needed surveys in the store on your first trip.

(continued)

5. <u>Continue to hone your skills at answering objections</u>.

Overcoming objections is key to effective selling. You answered objections customers raised well. For example, when a customer objected that promotions were running together, you were able to show that we have a distribution system which will allow deliveries to avoid overlap. And I was particularly pleased when you walked a manager through the store to overcome an objection that the store had too little space for our product. Your plan for stocking our product in existing space was convincing and well executed. Good job!

Helen, congratulations on great strides you are making as a sales rep. I was impressed with your high enthusiasm and professional selling skills. I am confident that by following the guidelines above, you will see even more positive results in the future.

Keep up the hard work! We appreciate your effort.

Disciplinary Memo   When writing up a violation of company policy, write in a highly factual, objective tone. Include a discussion of the specifics of the violation, the company policy, a summary of the discussion, a summary of disciplinary actions, and a statement of confidence that this violation will not reoccur. Avoid including positive statements about other aspects of the employee's performance as they will limit your company's ability to use the report in future disciplinary or termination actions.

Disciplinary Memo Outline

1. **Opening paragraph**
   The opening paragraph should serve as a concise summary of the entire document. It should include the What and Why of the report, as well as a forecast of the development of the rest of the document.

2. **Policy Violations paragraph**
   The policy violations paragraph should discuss the following:
   - The specifics of the violation
   - The company policy violated
   - A justification for the company policy
   - A statement indicating the disciplinee knew the company policy
   - A summary of the disciplinee's explanation as to why the violation occurred
   - A summary of the action plan which will be put into effect to prevent future violations

3. **Disciplinary Actions paragraph**
   The disciplinary actions paragraph should indicate the following:
   - The disciplinary action taken in response to the violation
   - The possible consequences of future similar violations

4. **Goodwill paragraph**
   The goodwill paragraph should indicate confidence that the agreed upon plan will prevent future violations.

Subject: <u>File memo summarizing December 4 meeting with John Doe
to discuss violations of company policies on authorized breaks
from work</u>

To: John Doe   Copies: Personal file
From: Your Name   Date: December 11, 1991

This is to record the issues in our conversation about strictly adhering to
the time limits for morning, lunch, and afternoon breaks. The meeting
discussed the specifics of the violations, the company policy violated, Mr.
Doe's explanation for why the violations occurred, the consequences of
the current and of future violations, and a mutually agreed upon plan of
action to correct the problem.

<u>Policy Violations</u>
Your supervisor reported that you were 5 minutes late returning from
your morning break and 20 minutes late returning from your lunch break
on December 4, 1991. As discussed in the company manual, Section 3.1.1,
and by your supervisor with you during orientation, your morning and
afternoon breaks may not exceed 15 minutes and your lunch breaks may
be no more than 30 minutes. This policy is important to the orderly and
efficient operation of our business, and applies equally to all sales representatives at ABC, unless a specific exemption is authorized.

You explained that you did not wear a watch that day and lost track of
time. You have agreed to wear a watch to work from now on and to
carefully adhere to the time limits on breaks in the future.

<u>Disciplinary Actions</u>
Given that this is the second violation since you began work on October
28, 1991, a formal written reminder has been added to your file. This is in
addition to the oral reminder I gave you on November 22, 1991. The oral
reminder will now be placed in your working file along with the written
reminder. Both will be part of the evidence considered during your performance review and will remain there for one year. They will be removed
at that time if there are no further policy violations.

Additional violations will lead to additional corrective actions, including
the possibility of dismissal.

I am pleased that we took the time to speak about this issue, and I am
confident that you are taking steps to ensure that all future breaks you
take will adhere to company guidelines.

Negative Performance Evaluation Report When writing to a poor performing employee about a number of topics, you may choose to use headings rather than toplined sentences to communicate your meaning. With this procedure each heading introduces a "mini-memo," organized in a What, Why, How format.

Negative Performance Evaluation Report Outline

1. **Opening paragraph**
   The opening paragraph should answer the What, Why, and When questions. It should forecast the development of the rest of the document and indicate the importance of compliance to a positive performance appraisal.

2. **Analysis/Data paragraphs**
   The analysis/data paragraphs should consist of a series of headings. Each heading should be followed by a statement of the performance expected, why it is important, and how to comply.

3. **Follow-up paragraph**
   If necessary, list additional follow-up that is necessary. Express confidence the reader will meet your performance expectations in the immediate future.

Subject: <u>SUPERVISION REPORTING REQUIREMENTS</u>

Please send me by July 31 the following reports: (a) store check forms and supervision letters; (b) letter of direction on promotion activities and objectives for the most recent period; (c) retail coverage action report for all units; (d) display activity action plan; (e) sales career evaluations. They are already past due.

The information in these documents is vital to our division's short, intermediate, and long-term decision making—and, therefore, part of your evaluation as a sales manager includes the completeness, thoughtfulness, and timeliness of these reports.

STORE CHECK FORMS AND SUPERVISION LETTERS

Store check forms, supervision letters, and weekly field recaps are essential to an accurate understanding of the competitive environment.

To review, whenever you are working with a sales person or a unit manager, furnish this office with a copy of a store check form for each store visited, as well as a recap of the supervision. The letter should highlight the outstanding activity of the sales representative or unit manager as well as direction on areas of improvement.

LETTER OF DIRECTION AND OBJECTIVES FOR PROMOTIONAL ACTIVITY

In advance of each promotion period, prepare a memo which indicates to all sales reps and unit managers the direction you expect them to take to achieve total retail sales volume versus objectives. Always copy me on this field memo. This report helps us evaluate whether the activities of all units are in alignment with company sales objectives.

RETAIL COVERAGE REPORT

Send me a report of the steps you are taking to ensure that retail coverage meets our objectives, especially in light of the substandard coverage in some units.

DISPLAY ACTIVITY REPORT

In concert with unit managers, develop a written plan of action for ensuring that stores in your unit meet objectives for display of our products. Currently display activity in all units is well below expectations—in some cases by as much as 50%. Communicating a clear strategy and effective tactics to meet agreed-upon targets is a prerequisite to effective action in the field.

SALES CAREER EVALUATIONS

Send me a report in which you (a) list sales reps whom you believe would be effective sales managers, (b) justify your selections, and (c) describe what special projects you have or will be giving them to test and develop their managerial talents. These reports provide information which is essential in developing good human resource plans.

Call me if you have questions or comments. I look forward to reading these reports in the near future.

APPENDICES

APPENDIX A

Guide to Word Choice, Usage, Punctuation, Spelling and Capitalization

TABLE OF CONTENTS

USAGE

Abbreviations

Abbreviations allow writers to avoid repeating long words and phrases, including titles, names of companies, governmental and private agencies, and countries. Use them in reports as well as in tables and graphs.

1. *Clarify an unfamiliar abbreviation by enclosing its unabbreviated title after its first use.*

   The JIB (Job Incentive Bonus) is offered to all administrative and technical employees who complete 40 or more overtime hours per quarter.

2. *Write standard abbreviations without periods.*

   GE, AT&T, and P&G stock are all traded on the NYSE.

3. *Use Latin abbreviations sparingly.* Most contemporary writers use Latin abbreviations only in lists of works cited. Use English equivalents in memos, letters, and reports.

   For example (not e.g.), Dr. Jonas holds that disintermediation is the prime cause of the failure of American savings and loan institutions; that is (not i.e.), she holds that when short-term interest rates exceeded rates previously charged on long-term loans by 5%, the savings and loan industry suffered unprecedented losses, losses that still plague it today.

4. *Abbreviate units of measurement only when they are used in conjunction with a number.*

   This ruler is scaled in inches and in feet.

   The playing field is 100 yds by 300 yds.

5. *Only use symbol forms of abbreviations in visual aids, such as tables, graphs, and illustrations.*

   Cisneros received 66 percent (not 66%) of the vote.

6. *Use acronyms sparingly.*

   (Unclear) EEOC cited GG&E for failing to comply with PUMP, START, and ECOP guidelines.

   (Clear) The Equal Employment Opportunities Commission cited General Gas and Electric for failing to meet minimum hiring standards for black, female, and handicapped employees.

Agreement

Subject-verb agreement requires that singular verbs be used with singular subjects and that plural verbs be used with plural subjects.

1. *Use verbs that agree with the subject.*

   The <u>list</u> of union demands grows longer by the hour. (The verb <u>grows</u> agrees with the singular *list* not the plural <u>demands</u>, which is not the subject, but part of a prepositional phrase modifying the subject).

   The Systems <u>Analyst</u> along with three assistants <u>determines</u> which computers are compatible with our network and which are incompatible.

2. *Use plural verbs with compound subjects.*

   Hernandez and Tamayaka <u>are</u> the best guard combination in women's college basketball.

   The spelling bee winner and her teacher <u>were</u> honored at the annual Rotary Club awards dinner.

3. *Singular subjects connected by* not only . . . but also, either . . . or, *and* neither . . . nor *require a singular verb.*

   Not only the finished product but also the production process *is* seriously flawed.

   Either J. Smith or L. Hernandez *is* willing to call you with the details of the offer.

   Neither the university nor the faculty advisor *is* responsible for a student's failure to take prerequisite courses in the required order.

4. *When used as subjects, the following words require a singular verb:* anybody, another, a person, each, either, every, everybody, neither, nobody, no one, one, somebody, *and* someone.

   Each offer <u>is</u> contingent upon a lawyer's final approval.

   Nobody <u>is</u> sorry that the import tax was repealed.

5. *Use a singular verb with a collective or compound noun, when the noun emphasizes the unity of a group.*

   A faculty <u>committee</u> *is* meeting to resolve that issue.

   This <u>troupe</u> of travelling minstrels <u>donates</u> half of its proceeds to the Save the Children Fund.

   <u>Every</u> man, woman, and child in the village <u>was</u> required to testify in the case.

Modifiers

Modifiers are words or groups of words that explain, describe, define, or limit other words. Place modifiers so that readers can clearly understand what words are being modified.

1. *Put dependent clauses and prepositional phrases as close as possible to the words they modify.*

   Unclear: Mr. Yastremski stressed the relationship between ABC's profits and the market price for cattle speaking in hushed tones.

   Clear: Speaking in hushed tones, Mr. Yastremski stressed the relationship between ABC's profits and the market price for cattle.

   Unclear: Erika was informed that her training course no longer would be offered by the Personnel Department.

   Clear: The Personnel Department told Erika that ABC had decided to discontinue her training course.

2. *Ensure that opening and closing modifiers are placed close to the noun they modify.*

   Unclear: While operating the CDC machine, the president told the tool and die maker of the need to reduce scrap metal.

   Clear: While the tool and die maker was operating the CDC machine, the president spoke of the need to reduce scrap metal.

3. *Use the word that to clarify your meaning when a modifier's meaning is ambiguous.*

   Unclear: Mr. Forrester said during the pretrial meeting Judge Allen displayed significant bias toward labor unions.

   Clear: Mr. Forrester said during the pretrial meeting <u>that</u> Judge Allen displayed significant bias toward labor unions.

   Clear: Mr. Forrester said <u>that</u> during the pretrial meeting, Judge Allen displayed significant bias toward labor unions.

4. *Put limiting modifiers where they best reinforce your meaning.*

   Note how the placement of the word *only* in the sentences below dramatically changes their meaning.

   <u>Only</u> Johnson wants double time for Sunday work.

   Johnson <u>only</u> wants double time for Sunday work.

   Johnson wants double time <u>only</u> for Sunday work.

Parallelism

Parallelism is a convention that means that ideas of equal importance should be expressed in a similar fashion. This structure meets readers' expectations of symmetry between form and meaning. In practice, parallelism requires that you make sure that two or more parts of speech behaving similarly in a sentence are parallel in construction. Thus, you should use nouns with other nouns, verbs with other verbs of the same tense, and so on.

1. *Maintain parallelism in sentences.*

   Below the first sentence in each pair is *not* in parallel order. Note how each is transformed into parallel construction in the second sentence of each pair.

   NP   Clark's references indicate he is intelligent, dependable, and <u>a loyal team player</u>.

   adjective

   P   Clark's references indicate he is intelligent, dependable, cooperative, and loyal.

   NP   Our report includes an assessment of the management functions of planning, organizing, staffing, and <u>motivation</u> at ABC.

   P   Our report includes an assessment of the management functions of planning, organizing, staffing, and motivating at ABC.

   NP   In writing recommendation reports, describe what you want, why you want it, and <u>the benefits the company will gain from it</u>.

   P   In writing recommendation reports, describe what you want, why you want it, and what benefits you believe will accrue to the company.

   NP   Distribution is responsible for getting the product to our customers and also <u>will handle all returns</u>.

   P   Distribution is responsible for getting the product to our customers and is also responsible for handling returns.

2. *Maintain parallelism in lists.*

   The manual includes the following topics:

Not Parallel	Parallel
▪ Getting Ready	▪ Getting Ready
▪ <u>Content</u>	▪ Developing Content
▪ Making the Parts	▪ Making the Parts
▪ Making the Whole	▪ Making the Whole
▪ Producing the Newsletter	▪ Producing the Newsletter

PUNCTUATION

Apostrophes

Apostrophes have three uses: to indicate that letters have been omitted, to show possession, and to form some plurals.

1. *Use apostrophes to indicate omitted letters in a contraction.*

   It'll take a determined effort to produce world class advertising. (It will take a determined effort. . . .)

   Our '86 results were far better than our current year results. (Our 1986 results. . . .)

   Who's going to volunteer to head United Appeal? (Who is going to volunteer. . . .)

2. *Use apostrophes to show possession.*

   AT&T's WATS line commercial won three awards.

   Employees who work four consecutive Sundays will be awarded an extra week's wages.

3. *Add only an apostrophe to indicate possession in words that already end with an s.*

   Allegis' car rental unit lost money last quarter.

   Joe Thomas' speech was the highlight of the conference.

4. *Use an apostrophe to form plurals of letters, numbers, letters used as words, acronyms, and abbreviations.*

   Watch your *p*'s and *q*'s.

   Our printer is omitting 1's from the dateline.

   Tyson Farms employs eight Ph.D's.

5. *Use* its *and* it's *properly.*

   It's is a contraction for *it is. Its* is the possessive form of *it.*

   It's a cost savings program.

   Its sole benefit is its low cost.

6. *Do not use apostrophes with possessive pronouns.*

   The idea was hers.

   The game was theirs to win or lose.

Colon

Colons add emphasis to writing by indicating that additional information is about to be given about the subject introduced in the opening clause of the sentence.

1. *Use a colon to introduce a list or a series.*

   ABC markets seven products: Pretend, Pork-X, MisO, Daybreak, SoapScreen, Oilaway, and Crunchy Bark.

   The training course covers the following five topics:
   1. Thinking before you write
   2. Outlining your thoughts
   3. Writing the first draft
   4. Editing for logical clarity
   5. Editing for style and tone

2. *Do not use colons between a verb and its complement.*

   Incorrect: ABC's seven products are: Pretend, Pork-X, Misto, Daybreak, SoapScreen, Oilaway, and Crunchy Bark.

   Correct: ABC's seven products are Pretend, Pork-X, Misto, Daybreak, SoapScreen, Oilaway, and Crunchy Bark.

3. *Use a colon to indicate further explanation.*

   The Product X advertising campaign lacks one key ingredient: heart.

   Inside salespeople must meet the following company requirements: a minimum of 80 calls per day, including at least 40 cold calls and at least 20 follow-up calls.

4. *Use a colon to introduce a direct quotation.*

   John Swale, ABC's president, made a startling prediction: "Merger-mania will end in 1993 because of stricter enforcement of anti-trust laws."

5. *Use colons following the salutation in a formal letter.*

   Dear Mr. Takayama:
   To Whom It May Concern:

6. *Use colons between numbers for hours and minutes, between volumes and pages, and between titles and subtitles.*

   The group is leaving for Cincinnati at 2:15 p.m.

   See <u>Thomas' Register,</u> 12:333.

   <u>Interviewing: Principles and Practices</u>

Commas

Commas help clarify the meaning of sentences by separating elements in them. Use them to show how words, phrases, and clauses are grouped in a sentence.

1. *Use commas to separate complete thoughts joined by coordinating conjunctions, such as* and, but, for, nor, so, yet, *and* or. (Use semicolons to separate complete thoughts that are not separated by coordinating conjunctions.)

   Jones holds BSBA and MBA degrees, <u>and</u> he has sixteen years of experience as a production supervisor.

   The economy of the USA generates more jobs than any other, <u>but</u> Japan, Italy, France, and West Germany's economies have much higher rates of annual productivity gains.

2. *Use commas to separate words, phrases or clauses in a series.*

   Managers must submit reports weekly, monthly, quarterly, and annually.

   Jones will make the reservation, Smith will rent the van, and I will pay the bill. (Commas in this sentence separate three independent clauses that are joined by a coordinating conjunction.)

   Our data indicate that writing unsolicited letters, calling unlisted phone numbers, and sending free samples in the mail are ineffective ways to promote our product.

3. *Use commas to set off nonrestrictive clauses.* Nonrestrictive clauses are nonessential descriptive phrases in a sentence. They are usually introduced by clauses beginning with *that, which,* and *who.*

   The field audit report, a document which is updated monthly, indicates two serious areas of concern.

   Dr. Phil Eustis, who wrote an award-winning book on performance appraisal, will speak to the Montgomery Rotary Club in early April.

4. *Do not use commas to set off restrictive clauses.* Restrictive clauses are those which cannot be removed from the sentence without changing its meaning. A simple way to tell a restrictive clause from a nonrestrictive clause is to see if the sentence still makes sense when the clause is removed.

   The field audit report which Tom Jones completed indicates two serious areas of concern.

   Next month's speaker is the man who won the Simmons prize for his book on performance appraisal.

5. *Use a comma to separate a long introductory subordinate clause from the rest of the sentence.*

Although the new package design did not meet our initial pay-out targets, we believe it will improve our sales in the long run.

Given ABC's likely response to a $70.00 bid, we should raise our offer to $75.00 per share.

6. *Use commas to set off introductory verbal phrases and adverbs.*

To show concern, we should donate our surplus peanut butter to the Free Store.

Subsequently, investigation of the claim that our product fades sulfur-dyed fabrics proceeded slowly.

7. *Use commas to separate two or more adjectives that modify a noun equally.*

The computer contains an advanced, powerful disc drive.

- Do not use a comma to separate adjectives if the initial adjective (or adjectives) modifies not only the noun, but also another adjective.

Please send six large party trays to ABC's headquarters by noon on December 22.

8. *Use commas to set off parenthetical information.*

We have written to NASA, the National Aeronautical Space Administration, for complete details on the timing of their next launch.

9. *Use commas to separate items in names, dates and addresses.*

William Bush, Jr., will succeed his father, William Bush, Sr., as president of Union Electronics, Inc.

Professor Robes Robert, Ph.D, teaches organizational behavior and business policy at Texas State University.

Paul Smithson, Esq., signed the contract on March 15, 1987.

XYZ's new address is 100 Oak Street, San Antonio, Texas.

10. *Use commas following the salutation in informal letters.*
Dear Harriet,

- Use colons following the salutation in formal letters.
Dear General Powell:

11. *Use commas following the complimentary closing in letters.*
Sincerely yours,

Respectfully,

Cordially,

12. *Use commas to set off transitional words and expressions.*

Words and phrases such as *for example, however, therefore, nevertheless, consequently, for instance, accordingly, furthermore, indeed, on the contrary, thus, on the other hand, then,* and *nonetheless* logically connect ideas in sentences. They are set off by commas because they do not grammatically link ideas.

The second analysis, on the other hand, did confirm the hypothesis.

Nonetheless, the data indicate this product will pay out in three years.

The takeover seemed inevitable; therefore, Pillsbury's board approved the merger.

- Omit punctuation when words such as *however, indeed, then,* and *thus* modify main thoughts and do not act as transitions.

Thus interpreted, the contract is null and void.

However unjustified the charges appear to be, Mrs. Sinatra will have to stand trial.

13. *Use commas to set off statements which introduce direct quotations.*

Ms. Jablonski then said, "We do not agree with that assessment."

14. *Put commas inside of quotation marks and outside of brackets and parentheses.*

The key phrase of the law, "lessee further agrees and promises to maintain said premises in the same conditions in which he finds them," applies directly to the Abbott case.

Your health plan will reimburse you for up to 50 psychiatric visits. (To be precise, they allow you a maximum of $1,000 per year [$20 per visit], for no more than one year.)

With the help of three ABC account executives (Grant, Pearsoll, and Morgan), we put the mainframe back on-line by midmorning.

Dashes

Dashes are excellent devices for highlighting important information in a sentence. Although they serve purposes similar to those of colons, commas, parentheses, and semicolons, they call greater attention to the material they set off than do other grammatical devices.

Create dashes by typing two hyphens with no spaces before or after them.

1. *Use dashes to give special emphasis to parenthetical comments.*

   Texaco thoroughly underestimated the appeal of Pennzoil's legal position—a mistake that cost them dearly.

2. *Use dashes to set off appositives that contain commas.*

   Mrs. Rice Foods—a conglomerate including ABC Yogurt, Louisiana Gold Orange Juice, Princess Chinese Foods, and Miss Lillian's Lemon Pies—was recently acquired for $2,000,000.

3. *Use dashes to relate introductory and closing thoughts to the rest of the sentence.*

   We made heroic efforts to meet the deadline—yet we failed because of slow shipments from one of our suppliers.

   Toothpaste, diapers, and soap—those everyday products are the heart and soul of XYZ's operations.

4. *Use dashes to introduce a list.*

   Good managers possess five skills—planning, organizing, staffing, motivating, and controlling.

5. *Use dashes to indicate a shift of thought or action.*

   Our customer service department—not our engineers—contributed the key idea that made the new product an instant success.

6. *Avoid overusing the dash.*

   Improper: The rotor valves—damaged beyond repair—arrived Monday morning—just before closing time—in a box—torn and battered.

   Proper: The rotor valves arrived Monday morning, just before closing time. The box in which the valves were packed was torn and battered, and the valves themselves were damaged beyond repair.

Hyphens

Hyphens serve two functions: to form compound words and to divide words at the end of a line. The rules governing hyphens are complex and sometimes apply only under specific circumstances. Below are guidelines for conventional usage.

1. *Hyphenate some, but not all, compound nouns, verbs, and adjectives.* Check a dictionary if you are unsure of how a compound word should be written.

hyphenated compound nouns	*unhyphenated compound nouns*
sister-in-law	bookkeeper
know-how	bus driver

hyphenated compound verbs	*unhyphenated compound verbs*
to double-check	to highlight
to re-edit	to proofread

hyphenated compound adjectives	*unhyphenated compound adjectives*
world-class advertising	worldwide change
part-time employees	crosstown expressway
no-nonsense approach	halfhearted efforts

2. *Hyphenate words using prefixes and suffixes that are complete words by themselves, such as all, self, and elect. Also hyphenate any word using the prefix ex-.*

   all-knowing leader
   self-discipline
   senator-elect
   ex-president

3. *Hyphenate compound numbers from twenty-one to ninety-nine.*

   forty-six
   fifty-three
   seventy-nine

4. *Hyphenate fractions and compound adjectives that start with a number.*

   one-half
   three-eighths
   seventy-three volume encyclopedia
   ten-foot-long boa constrictor

5. *Hyphenate words that must be continued on the next line.*

   Hyphenate words between syllables.

agree-	hyper-	misunder-
ment	ventilate	standing

6. *Do not hyphenate one-syllable words or make a division that leaves only one letter at the end of a line or three syllables at the beginning of a line.*

Improper:	a-	e-	o-	stra-
	part	gress	pen	ight
	read-	comptroll-	remark-	
	y	er	ed	
Proper:	apart	egress	open	straight
	ready	comptroller	remarked	

7. *Avoid divisions which may confuse readers.*

Improper:	front-	of-	anx-
	ier	ten	ious
Proper:	frontier	often	anxious

8. *Divide compound words only between the words that form them.*

Improper:	six-	inter-	time-sav-
	ty-five	est-bearing notes	er
Proper:	sixty-	interest-	time-
	five	bearing notes	saver

9. *Hyphenate words that precede a noun and act together to modify it.*

   the over-the-counter stocks
   the 78-inch-long border

10. *Use a hyphen between a prefix and a capitalized word.*
    un-American
    mid-April
    pre-Columbian
    post-Renaissance
    non-Existentialist

11. *Use a hyphen after a prefix or in a compound word, when without the hyphen, readers might misunderstand your meaning.*

    The new-oil prices are substantially higher than the government-controlled old-oil prices.

    We re-leased (leased again) the building for another year.

Parentheses

Parentheses set off relatively unessential information in sentences. They are also used to enclose letters and numbers within sentences.

1. *Use parentheses to set off parenthetical information.*

   The entire site has been contaminated by radioactive material (thorium, plutonium, uranium tracings).

2. *Use parentheses to enclose references, citations, abbreviations, and acronyms.*

   The data indicate (see Table 1) that Lush with Calcium meets a significant consumer need.

   Research suggests that negative wording makes sentences harder to recall (Miller, 1962; Froman, 1987).

   The USSBA (United States Small Business Administration) has over 50 regional offices throughout the United States.

   FRESH (Fernald Residents for Environmentally Safe Housing) activists picketed the ABC uranium enrichment plant.

3. *Use parentheses around letters and figures that label items in a list within the sentence.*

   The new personal computers have (1) 64K memories; (2) dual disk drives; (3) a printer that transfers 50 characters a second to plain paper; and (4) a keyboard that sends infrared signals to the main box.

4. *Do not overuse parentheses.* Overuse of parentheses suggests the writer is imprecise and immature, one who could not decide what to include and what to omit. Substitute commas for parentheses if you tend to overuse parentheses. Note how the second passage projects a more objective tone than the first passage, which contains four sets of parentheses.

   The test (held in Boston on 1/6/88) was administered to (approximately 22 in total) adolescents (ages 12–16) to determine their response to Lush PC (plus calcium).

   The test, held in Boston on 1/6/88, was administered to 22 subjects, aged twelve through sixteen, to determine their response to Lush plus calcium.

Periods

A period is one of the strongest punctuation marks because it signals a full stop, not a pause, the way commas, parentheses, colons, dashes, and semicolons do. Periods are also used with most abbreviations.

1. *Use periods to end statements, indirect questions, and mild commands.*

Statement:	The FORTRAN project is now underway.
Indirect question:	The committee wants to know how you would react to a request for a larger budget.
Mild command:	Please limit your breaks to fifteen minutes.

2. *Use periods with most abbreviations.*

   Dr. Thomas Clark
   e.g.
   10 a.m.
   Mr. George P. Brown
   p. 7, pp. 6–10

   ▪ NOTE: Some abbreviations no longer require periods, such as names of well-known companies, universities, and government organizations.

Companies:	IBM, GM, P&G, AT&T, NBC
Universities:	UCLA, UNC, NYU, MSU, BYU, UTEP
Government:	NASA, HUD, DOE, FDA

3. *Use periods in numbers that contain decimals.*

   3.1415
   314.15
   1,489.75

Question Marks

1. *Use question marks after direct questions.*

   May we have your permission to proceed?

   - When a sentence asking a question also contains a question at its end, use only one question mark. Place question marks inside of quotation marks, parentheses, or brackets only when they are part of the quotation.

   Incorrect: Why did the Treasurer ask, "How much will this cost?"?

   Incorrect: After the presentation, the Treasurer asked: "How much will this proposal cost"?

   Correct: After the presentation, the Treasurer asked: "How much will this presentation cost?"

   Correct: Why did the Treasurer comment, "Let's look very carefully at what this will cost"?

2. *Use a question mark within parentheses to indicate doubt.*

   The University of Indiana began researching DNA in 1911(?).

   Senator Wilson's office claims it has already conducted an objective (?) investigation in the charges of impropriety.

Quotation Marks

1. *Use quotation marks to enclose direct quotations.* Do not use quotation marks around indirect quotations.

   Correct: The manual states, "Parking with a valid permit only."
   (direct quotation of actual words)

   Correct: The manual states that only vehicles with valid permits will be allowed entrance to the lot.
   (indirect quotation which paraphrases actual words)

   Incorrect: The manual states "that only vehicles with valid permits will be allowed entrance to the lot."
   (puts indirect quotation in quotation marks)

   NOTE: Use indenting of both the left and right margins to enclose quotations exceeding six lines as an alternative to quotation marks. When you indent a quotation, you omit the quotation marks if the passage is one paragraph long. If the quotation is two paragraphs or longer, quotation marks should appear at the beginning and end of the entire quotation and at the beginning of each new paragraph of the quotation.

2. *Use single quotation marks to enclose quotations within quotations.*

   The manual states, "Only vehicles bearing a 'UNCC-1989' sticker will be allowed to park in designated lots."

3. *Use quotation marks to enclose titles of articles and chapters of books.* Use underlining to highlight complete works, such as the titles of books and magazines.

   "Stick to the Knitting" is the best chapter in <u>In Search of Excellence</u>.

   "Language and Corporate Values," by K. Rentz and M. Debs, appears in the Summer 1987 issue of <u>The Journal of Business Communication</u>.

4. *Use quotation marks to indicate a word is being used in a unique or unusual sense.*

   The "corrected" version of the report contained numerous errors of fact and interpretation.

   That's your idea of a "nonpartisan" speech?

5. *Place commas and periods inside of closing quotation marks.*

The authors revised the third chapter, "Organizing for Profit," three times before the publisher accepted it.

The publisher agreed to publish the book once the authors agreed to revise the third chapter, "Organizing for Profit."

6. Place colons and semicolons outside of quotation marks.

File the following information under the heading, "Accrual Accounting":
   a. SBA pamphlet 221, "Accrual Accounting for the Small Service Firm."
   b. "Accrual Accounting," <u>Proceedings of the 1988 Small Business Institute Director's Association Meeting</u>.

The American dollar reads, "Federal Reserve Note"; the Canadian dollar reads, "Bank of Canada."

7. *Place dashes, question marks, and exclamation points inside quotation marks only when they are part of the quotation.*

Ms. Jones said to Mr. Agnelli, "Do you enjoy asking such trivial questions?"

Why did Ms. Jones comment, "This is taking a long time"?

General Bradley said, "Charge!"

Kirstein's single comment—"Nonsense"—quieted the protesting shareholders.

Semicolons

Semicolons serve two main functions: to indicate the end of an independent clause and to separate items in a series.

1. *Use semicolons to separate closely related independent clauses that are not connected by a coordinating conjunction.* (Coordinating conjunctions include *and, but, or, nor, for, so, yet, whereas.*)

   Getting the product to the test market by April was only a secondary consideration; our primary objective was to produce a noticeable improvement in the cleaning power of our detergent.

   John Smith will lead the group in prayer; Helen Goldman will review the minutes of the last meeting; Joaquin Valdez will introduce the guest speaker.

2. *Use semicolons to separate independent clauses separated by a conjunctive adverb.* (Conjunctive adverbs include *however, indeed, nonetheless, on the other hand, hence, therefore, thus.*)

   Management reacted well to the proposed benefit cuts; however, the union leadership summarily rejected them.

   Consumers like sweet foods; therefore, we need to increase the amount of sugar we put in our frozen yogurt bars.

3. *Use semicolons to separate items in a series when the items themselves must be separated by commas.*

   Her itinerary includes Honolulu, Hawaii; Spokane, Washington; Los Angeles, California; and Dallas, Texas.

4. *Do not use a semicolon to introduce a list.*

   Incorrect: Three members of our management made the trip; Barrett, McConkey, and Van Handel.

   Correct: Three members of our management made the trip: Barrett, McConkey, and Van Handel.

Underlining

Underlining is used to give emphasis to typed material. Those with access to sophisticated word processors can often substitute italics or bold face for underlining as a way of highlighting information.

1. *Underline titles of complete works, such as books, periodicals, published speeches, television programs, and newspapers. Also underline the names of ships, trains, airplanes, and spacecraft.*

   <u>Business Week</u> is publishing a special issue on the <u>Voyager II</u> mission.

   The <u>Wall Street Journal</u> contains excellent articles on Texaco's legal battle with Pennzoil.

   At our annual Fourth of July picnic, Carl Noble will narrate <u>The Gettysburg Address</u>.

2. *Underline words used as words.*

   We interpret <u>mutually exclusive</u> to mean you cannot both work for ABC and consult for one of its competitors.

3. *Underline foreign words that are not part of conventional English usage.*

   <u>Tempus edax rerum</u>, "time heals all things," is the theme for this week's homily.

   - NOTE: Do not underline foreign words—such as buffet, sombrero, coup d'etat, or siesta—that have been absorbed into everyday English.

4. *Underline headings, sentences, phrases, and words to create emphasis.*

   We must have the completed manuscript by <u>December 31</u>.

   Turn <u>right</u> at Vine and <u>left</u> at Elm.

SPELLING

Correct spelling is an essential ingredient in all business documents. It aids clarity and reinforces a positive image of the author. On the other hand, misspelled words call attention to themselves, shifting the reader's attention toward mechanics and away from the ideas being expressed.

In addition to slowing down readers, misspelled words also may damage an author's image, suggesting sloppiness, carelessness, and inattention to detail.

The rules below will help you improve your spelling. As a word of caution, English spelling frequently is not logical. About 10 percent of all English words are irregular, meaning they do not follow normal English spelling conventions.

As George Bernard Shaw observed, the word *fish* could as logically be spelled *ghoti*: *gh* as in *rough, o* as in *woman,* and *ti* as in *portion.* Thus, when in doubt, use the spelling program on your word processor as well as a dictionary to check spelling.

1. *Use* i *before* e *except after* c, *or when pronounced* ay *as in* neighbor *or* weigh.

believe	receive	sleigh
relief	deceive	vein

   Exceptions: counterfeit, either, foreign, height, heir, seize, weird

2. *Change a final* y *to* i *before adding an ending, except if the ending is* ing.

activity	+	es	=	activities
city	+	es	=	cities
happy	+	ly	=	happily
rely	+	es	=	relies
rely	+	ing	=	relying
rely	+	able	=	reliable
rely	+	ant	=	reliant
study	+	ing	=	studying

   Exception: When a final y ends a proper name or is preceded by a vowel, retain the y. (Reilly + s = Reillys) (lay + s = lays).

3. *Drop a final* e *before suffixes beginning with a vowel but not before suffixes beginning with a consonant.*

receive	+	ing	=	receiving
desire	+	able	=	desirable

noble	+	ity	=	nobility
grave	+	ly	=	gravely
found	+	ling	=	foundling

Exceptions: argument, dyeing, dying, changeable, noticeable, mileage, ninth, truly, duly.

4. *Double a final consonant by adding an ending to a word if it is preceded by a single vowel. Do not double a final consonant if it is preceded by another consonant or by two vowels.*

hit	+	t	+	ing	=	hitting
rock			+	ing	=	rocking
sail			+	ing	=	sailing
begin	+	n	+	ing	=	beginning
refer	+	r	+	ed	=	referred
attack			+	ing	=	attacking

5. *Adding a prefix to a word does not alter its spelling.*

pre	+	work	=	prework
un	+	able	=	unable
post	+	date	=	postdate

6. *Form plurals with care.*

- Form the plural of most nouns by adding an s.

duck	+	s	=	ducks
bill	+	s	=	bills

- Form the plural of some nouns ending in *f* by changing the ending to *ves*.

wife	to	wives
knife	to	knives

- Add *es* to form the plural of words ending in -*ch*, -*s*, -*sh*, and -*x*.

church	to	churches
mess	to	messes
wish	to	wishes
box	to	boxes

- When two or more main words form a compound noun, make the last word into the plural.

proofreader	to	proofreaders
bookkeeper	to	bookkeepers
salesperson	to	salespersons

- When the first part of a compound word is a noun and the second part is another part of speech, make the first word the plural.

senator-elect	to	senators-elect
sister-in-law	to	sisters-in-law

7. *Check the accuracy of your spelling against the following list of commonly misspelled words.*

abbreviate	biscuit	condescend
absence	boundary	conquer
absolutely	breath	conscience
absurd	breathe	conscientious
accelerate	brilliant	conscious
accidentally	bulletin	consensus
accommodate	buoyant	consistent
accompanying	bureau	contemptible
accomplish	buried	control
according	burying	controlled
accumulate	business	convenient
achievement	busy	cooperate
acquire		courteous
across	cafeteria	criticism
address	calendar	criticize
aggravate	candidate	curriculum
all right	casualties	cylinder
alleviate	category	
allotted	ceiling	defendant
allowed	cemetery	deferred
although	changeable	deficient
altogether	changing	dependent
amateur	characteristic	descendant
ambiguous	chief	desirable
amount	climbed	desperate
analysis	column	dictionary
analyze	commission	disastrous
anxiety	commitment	discipline
apparatus	committed	dissatisfied
argument	committee	dissipate
athletics	comparatively	dominant
authorities	compel	
auxiliary	compelled	efficient
	competent	eighth
bachelor	competition	eligible
barring	complaint	embarrass
beggar	compulsory	eminent
beginning	concede	emphasize
believe	conceivable	employee
beneficial	conceive	equipped
benefitted	condemn	equivalent

especially
eventually
exaggerate
exceed
excel
excellent
excitement
exercise
exhaust
existence

facilitate
fallacy
financier
forfeit
forty
fulfill

government
grammar
guarantee

handicapped
harass
height
hindrance
hundredths
hygiene
hypocrisy

illiterate
illogical
imaginary
imitative
implement
impromptu
incredible
independent
indicted
indispensable
inoculate
intercede
interrupt

invariably
irrelevant
irreverent

laboratory
legitimate
leisure
library
lightning
likable
livelihood
loneliness

maintenance
maneuver
mathematics
medicine
miniature
miscellaneous
mottoes

naive
nickel
ninety
ninth
noticeable

occasionally
occur
occurred
occurrence
officious
omission
omit
omitted
orthodox
outrageous

parallel
parliament
partner
pastime
perceive

perform
perseverance
persuade
physical
plausible
practically
precede
prefer
preference
preferred
primitive
privilege
proceed
professor
pronounce
pronunciation
propaganda
propeller
protein

questionnaire
quiet
quizzes

recede
receipt
receive
refer
reference
referred
regretted
relevant
remittance
reservoir
resistance
rhetoric
rhythm
ridiculous

sacrifice
sacrilegious
salary
schedule

secretary
seize
sensible
separate
siege
sieve
similar
skeptical
sophomore
stationary
stationery
subtle
succeed
supersede
surely
surprise
symmetry
synonymous

temperament
temperature
tenant
thorough
thousandths
tolerance
tournament
transferred
truly
twelfth

unanimous
undoubtedly
unnecessary
usage
useful

vacuum
vengeance
visible

waive
warrant
worrying

CAPITALIZATION

Capitalization serves two main purposes: it signals the beginning of a sentence, and it identifies proper nouns.

1. *Capitalize the first word of every sentence.*

   The inspection revealed that everything is in working order.

   May we have your permission to proceed?

2. *Capitalize proper nouns and common nouns that are an integral part of a proper name. Do not capitalize common nouns when they are used alone or when they are not an integral part of a proper name.*

	Proper noun	**Common noun**
Addresses	Oak Street	a street
	Cincinnati	a city
	Morris County	the county
Names	President Bush	a president
	Jesse Jackson	a leader
Geography	the Middle East	the desert
	China	a country
	Danube River	the river
	the South	southern exposure
	Northwest Territories	northwest of Ohio
Organizations	General Motors	an automobile manufacturer
	U.S. Government	a government
	Sycamore High School	a high school
	the Lions Club	a service organization
	Democratic Party	a democratic government
	Teamsters Union	a union representing truck drivers
Titles	Dr. Dan Geeding	business school dean
	Professor J. Anderson	J. Anderson, professor
	Captain Mark Clark	regimental leader

	Prime Minister Hogg	Q. Hogg, a prime minister
	Ambassador Khalif	O. Khalif, an ambassador
Nationalities	Chinese	china dishes
	Japanese	cameras
	Manilans	manila folders
Branches of	U.S. Army	the army
Government	State Department	state employees

Titles of Books, Chapters, Films, Television Programs, Magazines, and Similar Works	Dorothy Sarnoff's <u>Speech Can Change Your Life</u>
	"The Importance of Pathos in Persuasive Appeals," <u>The Bulletin of the Association for Business Communication</u>
	NBC's <u>The Cosby Show</u>
	<u>Ghandi</u>, winner of the Oscar for Best Picture
	"Psycholinguistics," (a chapter in <u>Document Design: A Review of the Relevant Research</u>)

Note: Be careful not to overcapitalize. In particular, do not capitalize common nouns following proper names. Note how this convention is reflected in the following examples.

Religions	Methodist	minister
	Buddhist	priest
	Islamic	fundamentalist
Months	June	bride
Holidays	Fourth of July	celebration
	Christmas	cards
Events	Battle of Bull Run	casualty
	Vietnam War	veteran
	Renaissance	artist
	Beatles	drummer

DICTION

Choosing the correct word to express your ideas is critical to building credibility in your writing. Review the alphabetical list below. It contains some of the words and phrases which are frequently misused.

About, around.
> Avoid *at about* and *at around.*

Correct: We will leave about one o'clock.
> We will return around two o'clock.

Incorrect: We will leave at about one o'clock.
> We will return at around two o'clock.

Accept, except.
> *Accept*, a verb, means "to receive, to approve, to agree to."
> *Except*, a preposition, means "all but."
> Bush accepted the nomination.
> All, except Mary, received merit raises.

In accordance with.
> This phrase is stiff and now is only commonly used in legal writing. *As* is a good substitute. "As you suggested" vs. "In accordance with your suggestion."

Acknowledge.
> Substitute the less formal "We received your letter of June 1" for the stilted "This is to acknowledge the receipt of your letter of June 1."

Advice, advise.
> *Advice*, a noun, means a suggestion or opinion.
> *Advise*, a verb, means to offer a suggestion or opinion.

Correct: Jones advised Sanchez to reject the advice.

Affect, effect.
> *Affect* is always a verb. It means to act on, influence, or impress.
> *Effect* can be either a noun or a verb. The noun means the result of an action. The verb means to bring about or accomplish.

Correct: Unexpected management resistance did not affect Trump's determination to purchase the company.

The main effect of the proposal is to decrease shareholder equity in the firm.

ABC will effect the changes in three months.

ABC effected the change in three months.

Agree to, agree with.

Agree *to* means to accept.

Agree *with* means to share beliefs. Thus, one agrees to abide by a contract, while one agrees with a person.

Correct: The union's leadership agreed to meet monthly with management to address grievances.

The union's leadership agreed with the idea that grievances should be discussed regularly.

A lot. Use the correct form, *a lot*, not *alot*, which is incorrect.

All ready, already.

All ready, a pronoun plus a verb, is an adjective phrase. It means prepared in all aspects.

Already is an adverb meaning previously or prior to.

Correct: The contract is all ready to sign.

Mr. Francois has already prepared the proposal.

All right. *All right* is correctly written as two words. *Alright* is improper.

Correct: If it is all right with Mr. Owens, I will schedule the meeting for tomorrow morning.

Altogether, all together.

Altogether, an adverb, means completely.

All together, an adjective phrase, means everyone or everything at once.

Correct: Project Unity requires participants to work on problems all together.

Project A is altogether different from Project B.

Allusion, illusion.

Allusion means a reference to.

Illusion means something that misleads one's senses or thinking.

Correct: Brazil's current prosperity is an illusion created by rapid inflation of the money supply and tightly imposed wage-and-price controls.

Her allusion to Shakespeare was a stroke of genius.

Among, between.
> Use *among* to describe the relationship among three or more people or things.
> Use *between* to describe the relationship between two people or things.

Correct: ABC had to choose among Johnson, Smith, and Yee for the new position.
> ABC had to choose between Smith and Yee for the new position.

Amount, number, in the amount of.
> *Amount* refers to quantities that cannot be counted separately.
> *Number* refers to people or things that can be counted. *In the amount of* is wordy and should be replaced with briefer expressions.

Correct: He sold a significant amount of milk.
> He sold a number of gallons of milk.

Wordy: He received a rebate check in the amount of two dollars.
Concise: He received a two dollar rebate check.

And/or.   Avoid using this confusing phrase. Be precise. Use either *and* or *or*.

Appreciate. *Appreciate* is often overused in business writing. It can often be replaced with a briefer phrase.
Wordy: We would appreciate a reply by next week.
Concise: Please reply by next week.

As, like.   Use *as* as a connective between clauses. Use *like* as a preposition.
Correct: Update this system completely as you did with the FASTRON project.
> The documentation project is like the FASTRON project.

Bad, badly. Use *bad* as an adjective, to modify nouns. Use *badly* as an adverb, to modify verbs.
Correct: We received bad news from our Paris office.
> ABC stock performed badly last quarter.

Because, since, being as, being that, seeing as.
> Use *because* to mean the reason that.
> Use *since* to mean from a definite time past until now.

Avoid using *due to the fact that* or *on account of* because they are wordy.

Do not use the substandard forms *being as, being that,* and *seeing as.*

Correct: I stopped in Cleveland because we have two clients there.

Correct: I have not stopped in Cleveland since last February.

Incorrect: I stopped in Cleveland since we have two clients there.
The reason I stopped in Cleveland was because we have two clients there. (Wordy and redundant.)
I stopped in Cleveland being that we have two clients there.

Borrow, loan.

Borrow and *loan* are opposite words. *Borrow* means to take something for temporary use. *Loan* means to give something for temporary use.

Can, may. *Can* indicates ability to do something; *may* indicates permission to do something.

Correct: ABC can complete the order on schedule.
ABC's managers may take up to two weeks' vacation for Christmas.

Center on, center around. Use *center on. Center around* is substandard English.

Correct: Let's center on the most promising alternative.

Close proximity.

Use *proximity*; it means near in place or in time.

Compare to, compare with.

Compare to means to show how people or things are similar.

Compare with has a broader meaning. It means to show how people and things are both alike and dissimilar.

Correct: The travel agent compared a vacation at French Lick Springs to a ride on a merry-go-round.
The historian compared Reagan's speaking style with Jesse Jackson's.

Complement, compliment.

Complement means to complete.

Compliment means to give praise.

Correct: This printer is a perfect complement to our word processors.

Jill Jackson received numerous compliments on the quality of materials printed on our new word processor.

Confer with, confer on.

Confer with means to talk with; *confer on* means to talk about.

Correct: Michelle will confer with Jason about the awards ceremony.

Michelle and Jason conferred on the protocol for the awards ceremony.

Continual, continuous.

Continual means happening repeatedly.

Continuous means happening without stopping.

Correct: Adjusting inventory is a continual process.

Electric power plants run continuously.

Could of, should of, would of.

These forms are all substandard. Use *could have, should have,* and *would have.*

Data.   *Data* is the plural of *datum.* It takes a plural verb.

Correct: The data we gathered are ready for interpretation.

Different from, different than.

Different from is preferable in formal business writing.

Disinterested, uninterested.

Disinterested means objective, detached.

Uninterested means not interested or unconcerned.

Correct: We need to hire disinterested experts to advise us on the oil futures market.

ABC is uninterested in investing in the oil futures market.

Etc.   Omit this abbreviation in formal business writing.

Preferred: New policies must cover all sexual illnesses, including AIDS, herpes, and syphilis.

Not Preferred:

New policies must cover all sexual illnesses, including AIDS, herpes, syphilis, etc.

Farther, further.

Farther indicates physical distance.

Further describes degree, time, or quality.

Correct: ABC's new offices are much farther from downtown than are its old offices.

We will report back after further investigation of the issue.

Fewer, less.

Fewer refers to number.

Less refers to things that cannot be counted.

Correct: Fewer than 20 percent of those polled responded.

We had less response to the last survey than to any of the others.

Imply, infer.

Imply means to suggest something, to hint at something.

Infer means to draw a conclusion.

Correct: The agent implied the house could be purchased for less.

I inferred from the agent's comments that the house could be purchased for less.

Irregardless.

Use *regardless*. *Irregardless* is substandard English.

Its, it's, its'.

Its is the possessive of *it*.

It's is a contraction for *it is*.

Its' is substandard English.

Correct: It's fourteen miles from the airport to the plant.

Each document was sealed in its own folder.

Incorrect: Each document was sealed in its' own folder.

Lay, lie. *Lay* always takes an object. It means to place.

Lie does not take an object. It means to recline or rest.

Correct: Lay each valve on its flat side.

Lie down on the bed.

Lend, loan.

Loan is a noun.

Lend is a verb.

Correct: Star Bank will lend ABC the money it needs for its statewide expansion.

Loose, lose.

> *Loose* is an adjective meaning not tightly bound.
> *Lose* is a verb meaning to miss from one's possession.

Correct: Tom Peters prefers loose controls to tight controls.
American companies will lose their competitive edge if they do not adopt modern cost accounting procedures.

Off of.   Use *off*, a preposition, by itself.
Correct: The shipment fell off the truck and blocked the highway.

Principle, principal.

> *Principle* is an adjective or noun meaning fundamental truth.
> *Principal* is an adjective or noun meaning most important or chief.

Correct: XYZ's success rests on its adherence to the principle of fiscal conservation.
Jackson Salt is a principled chief operating officer.
Mr. Berry was principal of Maple Dale Elementary School.
Robert Klekamp is a principal of Muehling, Klekamp, and Ching.
Outdated equipment is XYZ's principal problem.

Quotation. Use the more formal *quotation*, rather than the informal *quote* in business writing.

Respectfully, respectively.

> *Respectfully* is an adverb meaning to show respect.
> *Respectively* is an adverb meaning in a given order.

Correct: I respectfully accept this honor.
John, Susan, and Keisha are sixteen, twelve, and six years old respectively.

That, which, who.

> Use *that* to refer to people or things.
> Use *which* to refer to things.
> Use *who* to refer to people.

Correct: The company that I prefer is XYZ.
The advertisement which won the award is on display in the lobby.
People who live in glass houses should not throw stones.

Their, there, they're.

> *Their* is a possessive pronoun for *they;* it means belonging to them.
>
> *There*, an adverb, means place or position.
>
> *They're* is a contraction meaning *they are.*

Correct: Their product is far inferior to ours.

> We stored the product in the refrigerator because Mr. Jones recommended we put it there.
>
> They're the only two managers in the personnel department with advanced degrees.

Use.   Use the concise *use* in preference to *utilize* and *utilization.*

Wait for, wait on.

> *Wait for* means to remain in a place in expectation or readiness.
>
> *Wait on* means to attend to someone's needs.

Correct: We should wait for Mr. Smith for at least another ten minutes.

> I waited on Mr. Smith when he ate here last Thursday.

Whose, who's.

> *Whose* is the possessive of *who.*
>
> *Who's* is a contraction of *who is.*

Correct: Whose document is this?

> Who's going to volunteer to manage this year's office party?

APPENDIX B

Formats for Business Letters

CONVENTIONAL ELEMENTS OF LETTERS

Heading: the address of the sender
the date the letter was written

Inside address: the address of the receiver

Salutation: addresses reader

Subject Line: summarizes topic of letter (optional)

Body: content of the letter

Salutation: complimentary closing of letter

Signature block: name and title of letter sender

Full Block Format

All lines begin at the left margin.

[Heading]
<u>Letterhead Address</u>
[skip 2–4 spaces]

Date
[skip 2 to 4 spaces]

[Inside Address]
Company name (underlined and in all caps)
Street or Post Office Address
City, State, and Zip Code
      Attn: Name of Addressee
              Title of Addressee
[skip 2 spaces]

[Subj line: optional, centered, underlined, all caps]
Subj: _____
[skip 2 spaces]

[Salutation]
[skip 2 spaces]

Dear :
[skip 2 spaces]

[Body]
[skip 2 spaces]

[Complimentary Close]
[skip 4 spaces]

Signature
Title

Modified Block Format

The date, the salutation, and the signature block all are placed right of center. Body paragraphs all start at the left margin.

Company Letterhead

[Heading]

<u>Letterhead Address</u>
[skip 2–4 spaces]

Date
[skip 2 to 4 spaces]

[Inside Address]
Company name (underlined and in all caps)
Street or Post Office Address
City, State, and Zip Code
    Attn: Name of Addressee
             Title of Addressee
[skip 2 spaces]

[Subj line: optional, centered, underlined, all caps]
Subj: _____
[skip 2 spaces]

[Salutation]
[skip 2 spaces]

Dear :
[skip 2 spaces]

[Body]
[skip 2 spaces]

[Complimentary Close]
[skip 4 spaces]

Signature
Title

Semiblock Format

The date, salutation, and signature block are all right of center. The first sentence of each paragraph is indented five spaces.

Company Letterhead
[Heading]

<u>Letterhead Address</u>
[skip 2–4 spaces]

Date
[skip 2 to 4 spaces]

[Inside Address]
Company name (underlined and in all caps)
Street or Post Office Address
City, State, and Zip Code
      Attn: Name of Addressee
               Title of Addressee
[skip 2 spaces]

[Subj line: optional, centered, underlined, all caps]
Subj: _____
[skip 2 spaces]

[Salutation]
[skip 2 spaces]

Dear   :
[skip 2 spaces]

[Body] (Indent the first sentence of each paragraph five spaces)
[skip 2 spaces]

[Complimentary Close]
[skip 4 spaces]

Signature
Title

APPENDIX C

Delivering Effective Telephone Messages

1. BRIEFLY OUTLINE YOUR MESSAGE ON PAPER
   a. What you are calling for.
   b. Why your call is important to listener.
   c. How and when you want listener to respond.
   d. The telephone, Fax number, or address to which you want the listener to reply.

2. DELIVER THE MESSAGE EFFECTIVELY
   a. Begin by identifying yourself and your return telephone number, the first two items of information on most telephone message pads.
   b. State what you want the listener to do.
   c. Explain Why it is significant to listener.
   d. Clarify How and When you want the listener to respond.
   e. Repeat your telephone number, as that is the information most frequently misunderstood in a telephone message.
   f. Close with a courteous remark, such as "Thank you for your cooperation. I appreciate it."

APPENDIX D

Writing and Reading Computer-Generated Messages

1. **Write concisely.** You need to compose computer-to-computer messages concisely because of the size of the computer screen and because checking of logic is more difficult on a screen than it is on paper. You will fit 250–300 words on a computer page. That is, readers scrolling a computer message can only see 20–25 lines at a time—and computer lines generally are shorter than lines written by a typewriter.

   Ideally, edit your message to be no more than 25 lines. If your argument requires more space, take it, making sure to use highlighting to make it easy for readers to find objectives, analysis, evidence, and actions. Taking these steps is important because once readers scroll past a passage, it becomes more difficult for them to "shuttle" back and forth to check if the author is arguing consistently or not.

2. **Print out important computer-generated messages.** When reading computer-generated messages, print out those which are (1) important, and (2) longer than one page. This will make it easier for you to check their logical consistency. It will also give you a place on which to jot evaluations of what you have read.

APPENDIX E

Team Writing

1. **Clarify goals and gain commitment to them.**
   - Fill out a planning sheet at a group meeting, focussing on agreement of objectives and audience analysis
   - Decide which tasks will be done by consensus and which by individual team members
   - Decide how to deal with people who do not meet deadlines.
2. **Clarify roles and tasks.**
   - Who will be researching?
   - Who will be drafting?
   - Who will be editing?
   - Who is responsible for which sections?
   - What deadlines need to be met?
3. **Determine writing schedules.**

Decision Makers:	Consult writers before finalizing schedules
Researchers & Authors:	Negotiate realistic schedules; renegotiate as soon as you are aware you probably will not meet a deadline
Editors:	Communicate a schedule for review Inform team of your progress

Include in schedules periodic meetings to share findings and insights; this will help members see relationships of their parts to other parts of the document and will help avoid efforts that overlap.

4. **Generate data and, as a group, analyze what the data mean.** In particular, determine the relationship of the data to goals and objectives.

5. **Devise a matrix outline so the group can agree on objectives, interpretation of findings, and next steps.** Avoid editing for style at this meeting.

6. **Develop a first draft, assigning sections to responsible team members.**

7. **Edit your own work.**
   Do four readings: one for logical flow; one for correctness of data and interpretation; one for style, format, and audience adaptation; and one for correctness.

8. **Ask team members to edit all other sections, following the same steps as in 7.**

9. **Have each team member edit the entire document.** Meet to agree on the final form of the document.

APPENDIX F

Writing for Another's Signature

1. Discuss and clarify objectives of requester in writing the memo or report.
2. Determine requester's relationship to primary reader to help you determine which information to include and what tone to project.
3. Use a format and style which is consistent with that of other memos and reports signed by the requester.
4. Show requester a preliminary draft of the memo or report to make sure you are on the right track.
5. Encourage the requester to revise your final draft.
6. Do not tell others that you have written documents on which someone else's signature appears.

Suggested Further Reading

John J. Clancy, *The Invisible Powers: The Language of Business*, (Boston: Lexington Books, 1989).

Veda R. Charrow, *Clear and Effective Legal Writing*, (Boston: Little Brown & Co, 1986).

Joseph DeVito, *The Elements of Public Speaking*, (New York: Harper & Row, 1990).

Peter Drucker, *Management: Tasks, Responsibilities, Practices*, (New York: Harper & Row, 1974).

Daniel Felker, *Guidelines for Document Designers*, (Washington, DC: American Institutes for Research, 1981).

James Hartley, *Designing Instructional Text*, (London: Kegan Paul, 1985).

Peter Honey, *Face to Face*, (Englewood Cliffs, New Jersey: Prentice Hall, 1976).

Marya Holcombe and Judith K. Stein, *Writing for Decision Makers*, (Belmont, California: Lifetime Learning Publications, 1981).

Richard A. Lanham, *Revising Business Prose*, (New York: Macmillan, 1987).

Mary Munter, *Guide to Managerial Communication*, Englewood Cliffs, New Jersey: Prentice Hall, 1992).

Scott Pancoast and Lance W. White, *The Business Grammar Handbook*, (New York: M. Evans & Co., 1987).

Bruce Robertson, *How to Draw Charts and Diagrams*, (Cincinnati: Northlight Books, 1988).

Ken Roman and Joel Raphaelson, *Writing That Works*, (New York: Harper and Row, 1981).

William Strunk and E.B. White, *Elements of Style*, (New York: Macmillan, 1979).

Sherry Sweetnam, *The Executive Memo* (New York: John Wiley, 1986).

Deborah Tannen, *You Just Don't Understand*, (New York: Ballentine Books, 1990).

Elizabeth Tebeaux, *Design of Business Communication*, (New York: Macmillan, 1990).

Joseph Williams, *Style: Ten Lessons in Clarity and Grace*, (Glenview: Illinois: Scott Foresman, 1981).

INDEX

Communication Skills Training

An organizations's efforts to improve its productivity depend to a large extent upon the ability of its workforce to write and speak clearly and persuasively.

While most readers will find that they have learned a great deal from this book, they may also want to have their learning further reinforced in a workshop tailored to their specific needs—one in which they can ask questions, compare notes with other participants, and receive one-on-one feedback from experts on actual documents they have written and on oral presentations they have prepared and delivered for review on videotape.

To find out more information about the training programs that my colleagues and I have designed to teach the skills described in *POWERCommunication*, direct inquiries to:

CommuniSkills
8749 Apalachee Drive
Cincinnati, OH 45249-2501
Attn: Dr. Thomas Clark
President

or call, (513) 489-0352